Social Security and the Family

Edited by Melissa M. Favreault,
Frank J. Sammartino,
and C. Eugene Steuerle

Social Security and the Family

Addressing Unmet Needs in an Underfunded System

THE URBAN INSTITUTE PRESS
Washington, D.C.

MT

THE URBAN INSTITUTE PRESS
2100 M Street, N.W.
Washington, DC 20037

Library of Congress Cataloging in Publication Data

Social security and the family: addressing unmet needs in an underfunded system / edited by Melissa M. Favreault, Frank J. Sammartino, and C. Eugene Steuerle.
    p. cm.
Includes bibliographical references and index.
    ISBN 0-87766-708-X (pbk. : alk. paper)
1. Social security—United States. 2. Family policy—United States. I. Favreault, Melissa M. II. Sammartino, Frank. III. Steuerle, C. Eugene
    HD7125 .S5959 2001
    368.4'3'00973—dc21

2001008025

Printed in the United States of America

THE URBAN INSTITUTE is a nonprofit policy research and educational organization established in Washington, D.C., in 1968. Its staff investigates the social, economic, and governance problems confronting the nation and evaluates the public and private means to alleviate them. The Institute disseminates its research findings through publications, its Web site, the media, seminars, and forums.

Through work that ranges from broad conceptual studies to administrative and technical assistance, Institute researchers contribute to the stock of knowledge available to guide decisionmaking in the public interest.

Conclusions or opinions expressed in Institute publications are those of the authors and do not necessarily reflect the views of officers or trustees of the Institute, advisory groups, or any organizations that provide financial support to the Institute.

Contents

Acknowledgments

This volume represents many months of research and would not have been possible without the generous financial support of the Smith Richardson Foundation.

Among our research colleagues, we are particularly grateful to the volume contributors, who originally presented their work at the Urban Institute Conference on Social Security and the Family, held in June 2000. The conference commentators—Yung-Ping Chen (Gerontology Institute, University of Massachusetts-Boston), Heidi Hartmann (Institute for Women's Policy Research), Kilolo Kijakazi (Center on Budget and Policy Priorities), Alicia Munnell (Boston College), Robert Myers (Social Security Administration), Anna Rappaport (William M. Mercer, Inc.), Stanford Ross (Arnold and Porter and the Social Security Advisory Board), Sylvester Schieber (Watson Wyatt Worldwide Co.), Timothy Smeeding (Syracuse University), and Carolyn Weaver (American Enterprise Institute)—helped prompt a lively exchange of ideas and suggestions for further work. We also thank the Honorable Charles Stenholm of the United States House of Representatives (D-TX), whose explanation of his Social Security reform plan helped place the issues in a broader context. Christopher Spiro, a former research assistant at the Urban Institute, contributed greatly to the conference planning and follow-up research.

Many other individuals have contributed to our research plan. Barry Bosworth of the Brookings Institution, Howard Iams of the Social Security Administration, and Sara Rix of AARP have worked closely with us on related projects. Francis Caro of the University of Massachusetts-Boston, Jan Mutchler of the University of Massachusetts-Boston, Lynne Casper of the U.S. Census Bureau, Theresa Devine of the Congressional Budget Office, and Stephen C. Goss and Alice Wade of the Social Security Administration all provided valuable comments and suggestions for this volume early on.

More broadly, we cite the Urban Institute's long-standing commitment to modeling the distributional consequences of social security reform. Although it's not possible to thank all those who have helped engineer the Institute's Dynamic Simulation of Income Model (DYNASIM3), we would like to give special mention to Jillian Berk, Julie Hudson, Paul Johnson, Daniel McKenzie, Douglas Murray, John O'Hare, Kevin Perese, Diane Lim Rogers, Karen Smith, and Sheila Zedlewski. Development of DYNASIM was jointly financed by AARP, the Andrew W. Mellon Foundation, and the Urban Institute. Our final thanks go to the two reviewers who provided extensive advice on the manuscript as well as to two additional organizations that supported key parts of this project—the Social Security Administration and the Center for Retirement Research at Boston College.

Melissa Favreault
Frank Sammartino
C. Eugene Steuerle

1

Introduction

Perspectives on the Structure and Role of Family Benefits

Melissa M. Favreault
Frank J. Sammartino
C. Eugene Steuerle

Social Security, the largest of all federal programs, is likely to undergo many legislative changes early in this century. Governments around the world, forced to deal with the aging of their populations and a corresponding growth in the percentage of adults depending on public transfer programs, must reconsider the nature of their social contracts. In the United States, Social Security expenditures will begin to exceed payroll tax revenues by increasing amounts as each wave of the baby-boom generation ceases to pay Social Security taxes and begins receiving Social Security benefits.

The need for reform has provided policymakers with an opportunity to rethink some of the choices that determined Social Security's original design. Yet the discussion often centers on how the system can accumulate additional savings—either by investing a portion of Social Security taxes in individual accounts or by building up government-held trust fund assets—without considering the more fundamental question of how Social Security benefits might be restructured.

Social Security was modeled on the single-earner, married-couple family. Although more common in the late 1930s, this type of household is not the norm today. Indeed, since Social Security's inception, sweeping social and demographic shifts have radically altered the structure of the American family. Nonetheless, Social Security law still largely reflects the realities of the 1930s. As a result, the program could soon spend hundreds of billions of additional dollars per year without providing a significant number of retirees and their spouses and survivors with a basic level of support.

Social Security, while never designed purely as an antipoverty program, was conceived largely to prevent poverty among the elderly, and it has proved instrumental in reducing poverty in this segment of the population. According to recent demographic and income projections, however, poverty rates among the elderly are likely to remain significant in the next couple of decades, even though real Social Security benefits are scheduled to rise substantially. Social Security already pays out more than enough per person to keep everyone out of poverty, even if some individuals have no other source of income. Yet Social Security falls far short of eliminating poverty and will continue to fall short, despite a planned increase of hundreds of billions of dollars in annual real spending over the next couple of decades. The failure to achieve greater poverty reduction in a system of this type generally stems from the structure of the benefit formulas, which over time fail to concentrate a larger share of resources among those with relatively greater need. The gap between Social Security's structure and the needs of today's families partly explains why the system does not target benefits optimally.

Three factors are contributing to the disconnect between Social Security and America's families. Most significantly, the share of low-income never-married and divorced mothers among retirees has risen. Many of these economically vulnerable women are not eligible for the Social Security income protections provided to widows and long-time spouses.

Second, the number of dual-earner married couples has increased. Roughly speaking, spousal and survivors benefits are add-on features that are not paid for with additional contributions or a reduction in the worker's benefit. A spouse essentially receives either his or her own earner's benefit or, if the amount is higher, a spousal or survivor benefit. This design creates a disadvantage for some couples today—married couples who have the same total household earnings do not always receive the same level of benefits. In general, households where each spouse contributes about the same earnings receive fewer benefits than households where one spouse contributes a larger share of earnings. The decline in the benefits of a two-earner couple relative to those of a one-earner couple with the same total earnings is greater the more evenly divided the couple's earnings are.

Today, most married couples have two earners, and the percentage of spouses with fairly equal earnings is increasing rapidly. Compared with previous decades, more women are earning higher education, entering the labor force, working more hours, and receiving wages comparable with those of men. Consequently, an increasing number of couples participate in a program that provides them with fewer benefits than it provides households with the same total earnings, yet where one spouse brings in all, or much of, the earnings. This unequal treatment goes against Social Security's goal of "horizontal equity," or providing roughly comparable benefits to workers who make the same contributions over their lifetimes.

Another factor that has contributed to the apparent disconnect between Social Security's family benefits and today's families is the work and savings disincentives built into spousal and survivor benefits. In many instances, workers are entitled to spousal or survivor benefits that exceed, or nearly equal, their own potential worker benefits. Hence, they receive little or no return on the payroll tax contributions they make to the Social Security system over their lifetimes. In contrast, the decision of a high-earning spouse to accumulate additional earnings (e.g., through a second job or a salary increase) usually adds to total benefits.

This problem is less about income adequacy—survivors and disability protections are still available—than about how the lack of return on significant payroll contributions might affect work decisions. With demand for different sources of labor likely to be high as baby boomers age and leave the workforce, now is a good time to minimize work disincentives. In fact, the aging of the population provides a strong argument for removing barriers to work. Households that devote extra hours to work typically earn more over their lifetimes and have more resources to support themselves in retirement. Their income tax contributions also reduce the strain on other taxpayers to support other government programs, such as education and defense.

With the system's fiscal balance in jeopardy, Social Security is likely to be reformed in the years ahead, with no one measure likely to achieve all the goals set out by reformers. To ensure meaningful reform at each stage, the Social Security debate must focus not only on creating more savings, but also on how well the system's structure serves the changing profile of the American family. In addition, benefits experts must better inform policymakers about the history of Social Security and reform options affecting the structure of family benefits.

This volume tracks the evolution of family benefits in Social Security and shows how changes in the retired population have affected the nature of these benefits as well as the system's ability to serve the elderly. It examines the current structure, adequacy, and efficiency of spousal and survivors benefits and evaluates specific reform proposals that could improve the living standards of the neediest Social Security beneficiaries. A look at social security systems in other countries, the potential effects of individual account reform options on women's benefits, and other related topics add important perspectives to the Social Security debate.

The History of Family Benefits

In "Family Benefits in Social Security: A Historical Commentary," Edward Berkowitz explains that the evolution of family benefits within Social Security can only be understood as part and parcel of a historical series of enactments pertaining to overall benefits. The Social Security Act of 1935 did not provide benefits for anyone other than workers contributing taxes. But in 1939, right before the government mailed out the first beneficiaries' checks, Congress extended benefits to spouses and survivors of Social Security contributors. In the program's early years, the government collected significantly more payroll taxes than it paid out in benefits. Family benefits were a politically attractive way to reduce this surplus.

Social Security's family benefits resemble pure transfers in that recipients are not required to make additional contributions. That is, unlike private pensions and life insurance plans, Social Security does not reduce a worker's benefit to fund spousal and survivors benefits. The program's formula also assigns larger benefits to higher earners' spouses and survivors rather than allocating benefits evenly among all spouses.

Little attention was paid to this particular design feature in the first few decades of Social Security. Early on, the legislative focus was how to raise spending and cover more workers, with less emphasis placed on ensuring that each dollar was equitably spent or on efficiently pursuing income adequacy goals for families. As time went on, the structure of family benefits took a backseat to legislative debates over provisions that held much larger financial consequences, such as expanding overall benefits (for example, instituting Disability Insurance benefits). Since the 1930s, changes to the structure of Social Security family benefits have been modest. For instance, certain divorced people eventually received coverage, and Congress set the eligibility age for spousal and survivor benefits to correspond to those for retired workers.

Modifying the basic structure of Social Security's family benefits will require significant legislative change. Political concerns have made it difficult to remove inequities, especially because reform typically means lowering one person's benefit while raising another person's. Social Security law uses language built around the idea of entitlement, making support for any reduction in promised benefits or obligations unpopular, even if such measures are necessary to restore equity.

The Changing Retired Population

While the structure of Social Security and family benefits have largely stayed the same, Americans' work, marriage, and education patterns have undergone dramatic changes. As Karen Smith reports in "The Status of the Retired Population, Now and in the Future," recent societal trends are reshaping the profile of the retiree population and the distribution of benefits.

In 1950, less than 40 percent of women aged 20 to 64 were in the labor force; by 2000, more than 70 percent of women held paying jobs. From the 1950s to the 1990s, marriage rates declined, and in recent decades nonmarital cohabitation has increased markedly. From the 1960s to the 1980s, the divorce rate more than doubled, though it has since leveled off. Also dramatic was the rise in the percentage of births to unwed mothers—from 5 percent of all births in 1960 to 33 percent in 1999.

These patterns affect all beneficiaries, but they have the greatest implications for the poor, who marry less and divorce more than the population as a whole. Social Security provides no spousal or survivors benefits to individuals married for fewer than 10 years, regardless of both spouses' earnings contributions to the household. In 1990, more than 63 percent of divorces occurred in marriages lasting fewer than 10 years, which suggests that Social Security does not provide shared benefits in the majority of marriages ending in divorce.[1] Thus, many divorced women do not benefit from the antipoverty protection built into Social Security's spousal and survivor benefits. Black and Hispanic women, in particular, appear vulnerable, because their divorce rates, like those of the poor, are higher than average.

In the past, rising levels of Social Security benefits (and the maintenance of benefits' purchasing power through cost-of-living adjustments)
led to a consistent decline in the poverty rate among the elderly. In the
future, however, the rise in divorced and never-married individuals (particularly women) who do not qualify for spousal and survivor benefits
could prevent the retiree poverty rate from declining significantly. A
decrease in earnings gains among workers with the least education also
clouds some future retirees' income prospects.

In addition to shaping spousal and survivor benefits, societal
changes have important implications for worker benefits, especially
among women. Sheila Zedlewski and Rumki Saha, in "Social Security
and Single Mothers: Options for 'Making Work Pay' into Retirement,"
examine how work trends will affect single mothers' retirement
options. During much of the mid- to late-20th century, the rise in single parenthood was accompanied by an increase in the proportion of
women who received welfare benefits and did not work. Following welfare reform in the mid-1990s, however, the employment rate of single
heads of household rose rapidly. Within a short time, more single
mothers began working, and as a group, they started working more
hours than in the past.

Although this increased work effort means that more former welfare
mothers will qualify for Social Security benefits, many women in this
segment of the population will remain vulnerable to poverty. In particular, the authors' estimates show that single mothers who have spent
more than 10 years on welfare will likely qualify for Social Security benefits equaling only 30 to 60 percent of the poverty level. These women
(as well as a significant share of single mothers receiving welfare for less
than 10 years) will need to turn to Supplemental Security Income (SSI),
a social assistance program available to the elderly. But SSI denies benefits to anyone who has significant unearned income or assets and thus
discourages workers from saving for retirement. In addition, benefits
under SSI, while indexed to inflation, fail to keep pace with average
wages and income levels.

Single mothers who never marry, or only marry for a short time, also
do not qualify for the additional poverty protections Social Security provides spouses and survivors. As a consequence, these low-income working single mothers often pay more in taxes but receive fewer benefits
than do other spouses and survivors.

A Comparison with Other Developed Countries

Policymakers considering how to implement reforms that best serve the retired population will benefit from understanding some of the features of systems in place in other countries. In "Social Security and the Treatment of Families: How Does the United States Compare with Other Developed Countries?" Lawrence Thompson and Adam Carasso look at the U.S. Social Security system and the pension systems of 15 other industrialized countries. The authors also consider how countries calculate benefits for different kinds of households and compare their benefit coverage with that of the United States.

Their analysis shows that the countries use a variety of approaches to balance the two primary goals of retirement programs—individual equity and social adequacy. Many use one public program to address social adequacy concerns and another program to allay individual equity concerns. The United States is unusual in that it relies on a single public program that uses a progressive benefit formula to balance both goals. On the whole, the U.S. system for individual workers (excluding family benefits) tends to be less generous than the other countries' systems, particularly for low and average earners. Supplemental benefits for spouses and survivors, however, tend to be higher in the United States, and thus play an important role in ensuring a minimum level of income protection for qualifying individuals. Although spousal supplements are fairly common in most of the other national systems' adequacy components, they are often structured as an additional flat benefit and, in some cases, are linked to income.

Benefits for surviving spouses tend to be related to earnings in countries that tie worker benefits to earnings (i.e., benefits rise in tandem with the worker's earnings). Still, as a percentage of a worker benefit, a survivor benefit is higher in the United States than in most other countries. As with spousal benefits, the U.S. system supplies relatively generous survivor benefits to offset the impact of its fairly modest worker benefits.

In most countries, survivors benefits reduce the surviving spouse's potential return on additional Social Security tax or contribution payments. The reduction is greatest in the United States as well as in countries with flat benefits, where survivors who work may get exactly the same benefit as those who do not. The more common approach in countries with an earnings-related component is to allow some combining of credits by spouses.

The countries also treat divorce differently. Several countries give each partner equal Social Security credit for earnings accrued during their marriage. Other countries, including the United States, extend spousal benefits only in divorces between couples that were married for a specified number of years. Countries that split the credits between spouses either use a standard formula or rely on court supervised divorce proceedings to determine the benefit. Where there is no flat benefit floor, splitting by itself can create serious adequacy problems, because many divorced spouses, especially women, have low earnings records.

A few countries have pension systems that deal with divorce through pure supplemental benefits (a divorced worker does not relinquish any benefits or make additional contributions to pay for a former spouse's benefits). These plans are subject to many of the same criticisms as the U.S. system. In fact, the U.S. program offers divorced spouses more adequate benefits while the worker is still alive than do pension systems in the small number of other countries using this approach.

Relative to the other countries studied, the U.S. public pension system is the least supportive of child rearing. Thompson and Carasso find that the United States is the only country that does not offer some direct form of compensation to people who temporarily leave the labor force to care for young children.

Assessing Current U.S. Law and Some Alternatives

Research on Social Security's family benefits has been fairly limited and, as in the political arena, the results have often been overshadowed by concerns about workers' primary benefits. Several significant exceptions are important to note, however. In the 1980s, researchers evaluated proposals that would share earnings or benefits between married partners, for example, by granting each spouse half the credit for the taxable earnings of the other (see Burkhauser and Holden [1982]; Congressional Budget Office [1986]; and Zedlewski [1984]). Ross and Upp (1993) provide an overview of the earnings sharing debate and speculate about the factors that led to its ultimate failure. Other family-related proposals surfacing over the years include child care dropout years and homemaker credits, but analyses of the equity and efficiency of these proposals have been fairly rare. (The studies of Iams and Sandell [1994; 1998] and Sandell and Iams [1997] are important exceptions.)

In "Social Security Benefits for Spouses and Survivors: Options for Change," Melissa Favreault, Frank Sammartino, and Eugene Steuerle build on the research that is available, suggesting a variety of ways to rigorously quantify and compare the effects of different reform proposals. The chapter's emphasis on specific tools and evaluation methods gives policymakers an alternative to the anecdotal evidence often trumpeted in particular reform agendas. Unlike many of the earlier studies cited, the chapter also considers how different proposals could be combined to offset the potentially negative effects of any single proposal.

The authors start with four proposals that merely increase benefits—either by raising survivors benefits, introducing child care credits, creating a new minimum benefit, or reducing the length of the marriage requirement for spousal and survivors benefits. They then evaluate three expenditure-neutral packages that combine different aspects of the benefit-increase proposals with benefit cuts for some retirees and assess the performance of the specific proposals (many others could have been chosen) against four efficiency and fairness measures, arguing that these tests should serve as benchmarks for all reforms:

- *Income Adequacy.* Combating poverty among the elderly is one of Social Security's explicit goals. The authors' specific measure of adequacy is the percentage of Social Security benefits that go to individuals with the lowest lifetime earnings.
- *Equal Treatment of Equals.* According to the principle of horizontal equity, Social Security law should treat individuals in similar circumstances the same. The authors quantify the reform proposals' performance against this measure by comparing benefit levels among couples with the same lifetime earnings but different relative shares of earnings, as well as among divorced individuals with marriages lasting for different intervals.
- *Efficiency.* In a system concerned with efficiency, additional taxes paid would bear a strong relationship to additional benefits earned. For each reform option, the authors examine whether spouses and low-earning individuals receive at least the same marginal return as higher earners on each additional tax dollar contributed to Social Security.

- *Support for Single Heads of Household.* Single parents typically have the least income protection in retirement and the worst rates of return among workers with equal earnings levels. The authors assess the reforms' effects on benefits for single heads of household who work and raise children relative to the level for spouses who do not work or raise children. In a sense, this test encompasses several principles, such as income adequacy and equal treatment of equals. Thus, if a provision does not meet the single-head-of-household test, the authors suggest it is not well designed.

Reform Alternatives and Income Adequacy

Congress added spousal and survivors benefits in part to help resolve income-adequacy problems among women. The benefits replace family income lost because of retirement, death, or disability of a worker (and reduce poverty in these workers' families). By the income-adequacy measure, existing spousal and survivors benefits are not well targeted. While the benefits are important for maintaining the income adequacy of many families, they give greater benefits to individuals married to richer people, less support to individuals married to poorer people, and no additional benefits to single heads of household.

Some observers contend that Social Security's spousal and survivor benefits are not meant to support marriage but rather to adjust for a family's child care responsibilities. In fact, the correlation between an individual's potential benefits and the amount of child care he or she provides is weak. For example, spouses and survivors who do not raise children are entitled to the same benefits as those who do.[2]

Examining some alternatives, Favreault, Sammartino, and Steuerle find that proposals that increase survivors benefits by themselves (without lowering spousal benefits at the same time) are also poorly targeted and do not increase the share of benefits to those with the lowest lifetime earnings. In contrast, certain minimum benefit proposals—the minimum benefit can be based upon years of work or have no work requirement— are better targeted and cost-effective in meeting an income adequacy standard among individuals with low lifetime earnings.

Reform proposals that provide limited earnings credit for years spent providing child care also tend to target benefits more precisely to individuals in need, although the effectiveness of these types of proposals varies over time, depending upon work patterns, particularly among women. In particular, the rapid growth in the number of working mothers means that even if child rearing were considered in reforming Social Security law, there is less connection between lack of access to workers' benefits and child rearing today.

Reform Alternatives and Equal Treatment of Equals

The proposals examined have different effects on Social Security's ability to meet the goal of equal treatment of equals. For example, consider a low-wage two-earner couple and a single-earner couple with the same total lifetime earnings. The authors show that some benefit-increase proposals, such as granting higher survivors benefits, would reduce the gap between the two couples' lifetime Social Security benefits. The effect of minimum benefit proposals would vary: under one scenario, the two couples would receive the same total benefits for the same taxes; under another, the two-earner couple who works more years would receive higher benefits than the one-earner couple. The results under the minimum benefit alternatives are not the same for couples at all income levels, making it difficult to generalize the results.

Reform Alternatives and Efficiency/Incentives to Work

A work-related minimum benefit increases lower-income spouses' returns on additional Social Security contributions and thus might add a significant work incentive to the system's structure. Introducing an enhanced, add-on survivors benefit would not add any incentive. And a child credit might discourage work, because the return on additional years worked would likely be zero if an individual could get the same, or a higher number of, Social Security credits without working.[3]

Reform Alternatives and the Single-Heads-of-Household Test

Single heads of household usually fare better under a system that provides minimum benefits. Under such arrangements, single heads of household can qualify for at least some of the additional transfers that only spouses and survivors gain under current law. If a minimum-benefit proposal requires many years of work, but a head of household works for just a few years, SSI might remain the more valuable retirement option. SSI benefits, however, are means-tested and do not increase with growth in economic productivity over time (increasing only with inflation), whereas the minimum benefits examined here would grow over time along with wages (and thus overall productivity). Introducing additional survivors benefits actually hurts single heads of household relative to others in the current system.

Establishing child credits for nonworking spouses creates mixed results, but the credits do the least for single heads of household who already work and thus receive no additional credit. These individuals often get more out of their own earnings contribution than out of an imputed minimum child care supplement. Zedlewski and Saha (this volume) find that minimum benefits with work requirements do the most for individuals who received welfare for a significant number of years.

Women's Benefits and Individual Accounts

One type of reform proposal receiving a great deal of recent attention goes beyond restructuring Social Security's defined benefits and recommends placing a portion of tax dollars in individual accounts whose assets would be invested privately—usually in a limited set of market options. These proposals, recommended by elected officials from both major political parties, raise important questions, such as how the accounts would be financed and administered, what factors determine the size and distribution of transaction costs, and how the strengths and weaknesses of individual accounts compare with those of more collective diversification approaches.[4]

Rudolph Penner and Elizabeth Cove focus on the potential impact of individual accounts on women's benefit levels given a reasonable set of economic and demographic assumptions. The authors look specifically at a "carve-out" proposal that diverts a portion of payroll tax payments into individual accounts.[5] The analysis assumes that traditional benefits are cut proportionately by an amount sufficient both to eliminate the current deficit in the program by 2040 and to finance the diversion of payroll taxes into individual accounts. This type of proposal—a fairly draconian (and, in fact, politically unlikely) scenario in that it finances the accounts entirely through benefit cuts—serves as a useful benchmark for considering whether even the most drastic proposals would have adverse effects on women's retirement incomes. The authors also compare the carve-out option with proposals that "add on" to current-law payroll taxes to finance individual accounts.

The analysis assumes various rates of return on individual accounts and compares the total retirement income under the carve-out and add-on options to a reduced-benefit option, which scales benefits back sufficiently to eliminate the existing deficit by 2040 and does not contain individual accounts. For the carve-out proposal, a particularly interesting question is whether the individual account provides sufficient retirement income to make up for the further cut in traditional benefits necessary to make up for the trust fund's loss in payroll tax revenues.

Under a carve-out proposal that assumes a 5.5 percent net return on individual account investments (after transaction costs), married couples in which the wife works fewer than 25 years do very well compared with the reduced-benefits proposal. Among these couples, annual income would be about one-fourth higher, and nearly all the couples would be better off.

Under a 4 percent rate of return, the majority of couples still do better under the individual account carve-out than under the reduced-benefit option. Even in the bottom quintile of lifetime earnings, about three quarters of couples do better under the reformed system. The reform option, however, looks less favorable as the assumed rate of return is scaled back. The carve-out assuming a 2.7 percent return produces lower benefits than does the reduced-benefit option for more than 70 percent of couples. Still, among those who do worse under the carve-out option, the average benefit is only slightly lower.

In looking at results for nonmarried women, the authors find that most fare better under the carve-out option. For widows, the projections are about as favorable as they are for married couples. For divorced women, the story is more mixed, but under an assumed 4 percent return, the majority of divorced women examined still benefit. As with married couples, however, the 2.7 percent return produces less favorable results. In addition, at the 2.7 percent rate, fewer never-married women than divorced women benefit.

Overall, an individual carve-out would likely help boost women's retirement income relative to a reduced-benefits option if account returns matched historical levels. The lack of improvement in the retirement prospects of some lower-income women, however, suggests that a minimum benefit might be needed to help meet distributional goals and that a single mechanism, such as individual accounts, cannot solve all of Social

Security's problems. Penner and Cove also review research on whether the investment behavior of women differs radically from that of men and conclude that it does not.

Property Rights under Individual Accounts

Individual account proposals have prompted much investigation into the riskiness of certain investment strategies, but almost nothing has been written about the property rights issues attached to such proposals. Upon distribution of an account, important questions of ownership will inevitably surface. Family events such as divorce and death could lead to the early division and distribution of account assets, considerably reducing available retirement income.

Pamela Perun points out that any property rights system for individual accounts must balance an individual's retirement income needs and his or her family members' support needs. Legally, however, there is no sure or standard way to find that balance. The property rights system attached to individual accounts will depend on how legislators answer a series of questions, including, Who should have rights to the assets? At what point should individuals be permitted to exercise those rights? And should account owners' and beneficiaries' rights be restricted?

As it stands, current law treats property rights inconsistently. Social Security uses federal laws to enforce Social Security property rights the same way in all states. But many other property disputes are resolved by state laws that vary widely in how they divide assets among divorced spouses. Given the complexity of state law and the increase in family mobility, Perun concludes that property rights for individual accounts should be based on a coherent, consistent set of federal laws. She reviews several ways of constructing property rights, drawing on existing models, including the private pension system, community property, earnings sharing, IRAs, and common-law approaches.

Perun also discusses the critical decisions that will shape the system. For example, during marriage, should a spouse have no rights over the account, some rights over the account, or equal rights over the account? Current law inconsistently does all three, depending on whether the asset is an IRA, a private pension, or a financial asset in a community property state. If individual accounts become part of the system, lawmakers will need to resolve the question of spousal access, along with many other property rights issues for spouses, survivors, and divorced individuals.

Timing of the Retirement Decision

As more people live into their eighties and nineties and collect benefits for nearly a third of their lives, the factors that surround the choice to retire could provide important clues to optimizing individuals' work efforts and their contributions to the Social Security system. In "The Family, Social Security, and the Retirement Decision," Melissa Favreault and Richard Johnson examine the factors that contribute to a married individual's decision to retire and consider how Social Security reform might influence retirement timing. They find that recent retirement of a spouse, health and functional impairments, and overall retirement wealth (Social Security entitlement, private pension wealth, and other savings) help determine when an individual will retire.

The high rate of joint retirement apparent among husbands and wives is likely to be less relevant in future decades because of women's increased labor force participation. Greater career investment and more employer incentives may make women less likely to follow their husbands into retirement. Their increased retirement wealth also suggests that they will have greater flexibility in choosing their retirement dates. The importance of a spouse's health, however, underscores the fact that marriage itself provides a form of social insurance. While one member of a couple can increase his or her labor supply in response to a spouse's health emergency, single workers do not have this extra economic protection. Accordingly, expanding the marriage bonuses implicit in the Social Security system through increased spousal and/or survivor benefits would not efficiently target benefits to the most vulnerable among the aged. Options to reduce spousal benefits in tandem with expansions of survivors benefits could, however, increase work incentives and thus delay retirement for recipients of Social Security's spousal and survivors benefits (a group overwhelmingly made up of women).

Establishing Standards for Reform

In reforming Social Security to ensure the system's long-term solvency, elected officials and beneficiaries know that there is no simple solution. The reality is that unless taxes are increased significantly, reform almost inevitably will reduce the rate of growth in future benefits simply to restore fiscal balance. This fact creates a difficult legislative road for politicians. The challenges of restoring fiscal balance, however, also present legislators with an important opportunity to address fundamental concerns with the system and to better meet the retirement needs of an aging population. Lawmakers should strive to improve Social Security so that it adheres to principles of fairness and efficiency. In the difficult process of reform, it would be a mistake to ignore features of Social Security that increase real spending annually by hundreds of billions of dollars but provide little additional antipoverty protection, penalize couples simply because both partners have significant earnings, and give minimal protection to many single and divorced mothers who work and raise children, while providing large transfers to individuals who do neither.

Direct benefit increases to one group, the establishment of individual accounts, or other single-goal provisions might achieve worthwhile objectives, but each measure by itself is not enough to correct all the problems or to achieve all the goals of Social Security. To meet various efficiency and antipoverty objectives, policymakers must consider reform "packages"—combinations of proposals that incorporate the positive effects of certain changes, while mitigating or eliminating their negative effects. If reformers on all sides of the debate are willing to confront tough choices and apply rigorous standards, Social Security's family benefits can be restructured to meet the needs of the modern family.

NOTES

1. Of course, some individuals who divorce would not qualify for spousal benefits under current law even if their marriages had remained intact for 10 years or more, because the benefits for which they qualify on the basis of their own earnings exceed the spousal benefits to which they would be entitled. On the other hand, these individuals are still likely to lose out on survivor benefits unless their lifetime earnings exceed those of their former partners. Another complication is that many who divorce remarry and gain entitlement to Social Security spousal and survivor benefits through the subsequent marriage. Regardless, the availability of additional benefits is somewhat arbitrary in its distribution among divorced couples and between those who are or are not divorced.

2. Some might argue that Social Security's practice of averaging earnings over the 35 highest earning years in one's career—thus permitting one to drop out the five lowest earnings years—is a more universal type of subsidy for child rearing. However, the benefit also subsidizes graduate students, early retirees, and many others who do not raise children during their years out of the workforce.

3. Many young people making decisions about whether to work would weight their current income needs more heavily than the marginal changes to pension benefits that they will claim several decades into the future.

4. The already extensive literature on these topics continues to increase. For an overview, including a discussion of the distinction between *privatization, prefunding,*

and *diversification,* see Geanakoplos, Mitchell, and Zeldes (1998). For a discussion of administrative issues associated with individual accounts, see, for example, Thompson (1999). The analysis does not factor in potential macroeconomic feedback and assumes that earlier transition costs have been completely financed by 2040. In 2040, costs that remain are financed by benefit reductions.

5. The authors assume that the reform requires participants to purchase an annuity at the normal retirement age. They also make the following assumptions: participants pay a unisex rate for the annuity, and, if married, must purchase a joint-survivor annuity. Spouses split accounts upon divorce, and survivors inherit accounts upon workers' deaths if death occurs prior to the normal retirement age.

REFERENCES

Burkhauser, Richard V., and Karen C. Holden, eds. 1982. *A Challenge to Social Security: The Changing Roles of Women and Men in American Society.* New York: Academic Press.

Congressional Budget Office. 1986. *Earnings Sharing Options for the Social Security System,* January. Washington, D.C.: Congressional Budget Office.

Geanakoplos, John, Olivia S. Mitchell, and Stephen P. Zeldes. 1998. "Would a Privatized Social Security System Really Pay a Higher Internal Rate of Return?" In *Framing the Social Security Debate,* edited by R. Douglas Arnold, Michael J. Graetz, and Alicia H. Munnell (137–156). Washington, D.C.: Brookings Institution.

Iams, Howard M., and Steven H. Sandell. 1994. "Changing Social Security Benefits to Reflect Child-Care Years: A Policy Proposal Whose Time Has Passed?" *Social Security Bulletin* 57 (4): 10–23.

———. 1998. "Cost-Neutral Policies to Increase Social Security Benefits for Widows: A Simulation for 1992." *Social Security Bulletin* 61 (1): 34–43.

Ross, Jane L., and Melinda M. Upp. 1993. "Treatment of Women in the U.S. Social Security System, 1970–88." *Social Security Bulletin* 56 (3): 56–67.

Sandell, Steven H., and Howard M. Iams. 1997. "Reducing Women's Poverty by Shifting Social Security Benefits from Retired Couples to Widows." *Journal of Policy Analysis and Management* 16 (2): 279–297.

Thompson, Lawrence H. 1999. *Administering Individual Accounts in Social Security: The Role of Values and Objectives in Shaping Options.* The Retirement Project, Occasional Paper No. 1. Washington, D.C.: The Urban Institute.

Zedlewski, Sheila Rafferty. 1984. "The Distributional Consequences of an Earnings Sharing Proposal." Project Report No. 3344. Washington, D.C.: The Urban Institute.

2

Family Benefits in Social Security

A Historical Commentary

Edward D. Berkowitz

Just before Social Security began scheduled operations, Congress changed the program's structure to include family benefits. The 1939 amendments to the Social Security Act of 1935 added benefits for wives, widows, and dependent children. Since then, despite a dramatic rise in women's labor force participation and the divorce rate, the basic structure has remained intact. Indeed, changes made after 1939 tended to reinforce, rather than weaken, the family benefit system's original design.

The balance sheet of the Social Security trust fund and current accounts typically determined when Congress adjusted family benefits. In times of surplus, legislators increased the worth of the family benefits relative to other Social Security benefits and relaxed eligibility criteria. In times of concern over the program's financing, such as the 1973–83 period, policymakers concentrated on ways to raise program revenues and largely overlooked questions related to family benefits. Reforms that would modernize the program to accommodate changes in family structure and female labor market participation tended to be costly, and available funds were often in short supply when family benefit reform reached the political agenda. As a result, Social Security's family benefits structure, put in place in 1939, has persisted both through good times and bad.

Historical Background to the 1939 Amendments

The road to the 1939 amendments began in 1935, the year lawmakers constructed the original financing provisions for Social Security. President Franklin Roosevelt and Treasury Secretary Henry Morgenthau opted to fund the program through payroll taxes without using additional general revenues. The creators of the Social Security Act, understanding that the program's costs would increase as a rising percentage of retirees qualified for benefits, decided to prefund some of the program's future liabilities. This decision meant that the program would initially collect more money than needed to pay current benefits. The excess funds would then be held in a reserve fund for future use. In 1937, when the program began collecting payroll taxes, Congress appropriated $511 million to the Social Security account. Only $6 million of that amount, however, was required to cover current expenses. As set in the original legislation, the program would not begin paying retiree benefits until 1942. Thus, the program only had to pay administrative expenses and lump-sum death benefits to the few Social Security contributors who had died that year (Witte 1963, p. 74; Berkowitz 1996, pp. 151–159; SSA NDa; SSA NDb).

The ailing, deflationary U.S. economy, however, made the large reserve fund an easy target of criticism. In 1936, Republican presidential candidate Alfred Landon called Social Security "unjust, unworkable, stupidly drafted and financed" (Landon 1936, p. 68). In an effort to end such criticism, Social Security administrators created a plan that ultimately led to the 1939 amendments.

The first resolution, put forth by Senator Arthur Vandenberg (R-MI) on January 29, 1937, dismissed the reserve method of Social Security financing as, among other things, "a fiscal and economic menace." Senator Vandenberg argued for not raising the Social Security tax beyond its 1937 rate, increasing initial Social Security benefits, and beginning regular benefit payments before 1942 (U.S. Congress 1937a, p. 548). In February 1937, Arthur Altmeyer, chairman of the Social Security Board, defended the reserve, noting that it kept the ultimate Social Security tax rate, scheduled to take effect in 1949, at 6 percent (divided equally between workers and employers) rather than at 10 percent. But Senator Vandenberg continued to criticize the reserve financing and pressed for a Congressional commission on the matter. Altmeyer had little choice but to agree (U.S. Congress 1937b, pp. 88–89); a 25-member Advisory Council—comprising 6 labor representatives, 6 management workers, and 13 members of the public—

was formed. Part of the Council's charge was to consider extending benefits to "survivors of individuals entitled to such benefits" (Blumberg 1982, p. 191). Hence, family benefits were already on the agenda of the Advisory Council when it convened in November 1937.

The 1937–38 Advisory Council and the Introduction of Family Benefits

Altmeyer and other Social Security officials saw the Advisory Council as a way "not only to offset the attacks on the Social Security Act but really to utilize them to advance a socially desirable program"; Altmeyer wanted to "go off the reserve with our eyes open" (Altmeyer 1966, 90, 295–296). The goal was to increase expenditures in the early years of the program in a way that advanced socially desirable goals while preserving the contributory features of social security financing. Family benefits met this objective; they enhanced benefits and made them more immediate because they were payable to the survivors of younger workers. Family benefits also enjoyed bipartisan support and had historical precedent. Even before passage of the Social Security Act, 45 states had passed mother's pension laws, which were intended to support families after a father's death (Achenbaum 1986, p. 126). When the Advisory Council first met in November 1937, the members agreed on the need for survivors benefits and on the desirability of providing larger benefits for married couples than for single individuals. Over the course of the next year, the Advisory Council worked out the final details.

In February 1938, the Council considered a formal plan prepared by the Social Security Board staff that introduced a benefit for a contributor's wife and another benefit for a contributor's widow. According to the terms of the plan, titled AC-1, a married couple would receive one-and-a-half times the benefit amount of an unmarried male's benefit, while a beneficiary's widow would receive three-quarters of a single male's benefit. Most Advisory Council members reacted with enthusiasm to this proposed change to the original Social Security Act and the implicit retreat from reserve funding.[1]

There was some initial skepticism among the Council's business representatives. Marion Folsom, treasurer of Eastman Kodak at the time and a spokesman for the Council's other management representatives, said that the wives and widows benefits represented too much expansion too early in the program's life. "I think we are trying to get across in two or three years what other countries have taken 30 and 35 years to do," he argued.[2] Gerard Swope, president of General Electric, suggested an alternative that resembled an earnings sharing plan. Of the total wages earned by any married person, half would be credited to his or her account and half to the spouse's account. Old-age benefits levels would be based on the benefits that each had "earned." If a married beneficiary died, his or her spouse would continue to receive the individual benefit, rather than a widow's or widower's benefit. Swope's plan would have saved the system money. For example, most widows would have received half the basic benefit rather than the three-quarters typical under Plan AC-1 (Kessler-Harris 1995, pp. 95–97).

A few months later, the Council reviewed a plan to extend benefits to deceased workers' dependent children. Douglas Brown, a Princeton economist and the Council's chairman, unveiled a plan to cover these children at the April 1938 meeting. His proposal met little opposition, although it included an important change to the benefit formula. The plan altered the earnings calculation on which benefit levels would be based from credited wages, or total wages earned, to average wages in order to pay greater benefits to the children of workers who died at a relatively young age.[3] The Council also agreed to recommend that a woman caring for a dependent child receive a widow's benefit if her husband had died, and a wife's benefit if her husband was alive. The spousal benefits, the formula change, and the treatment of survivors benefits formed the Council's recommended package of family benefits.

The Advisory Council eloquently recommended the package but deliberately left most details vague in its report to Congress. "A democratic society has an immeasurable stake in avoiding the growth of a habit of dependency among its youth. The method of survivors' insurance not only sustains the concept that a child is supported through the efforts of the parent, but affords a vital sense of security to the family unit," the Council wrote (Advisory Council on Social Security 1938, p. 29). The members declined to specify the size of benefits except in the case of married workers, where the Council strongly recommended a 50 percent benefit for the spouse of a retired worker, leaving the other amounts to the Social Security Board and Congress (Brown 1977, p. 23). Ultimately, Congress set the benefit for a widow caring for a dependent child at 75 percent of a basic benefit—the same as a regular widow's benefit—and the benefit for a surviving child at 50 percent (see box 2.A).

Box 2.A. Family Benefits in the 1939 Amendments

Wife's Benefit

- 50 percent

Survivors Benefits

- Widows—75 percent
- Dependent Children—50 percent

Social Tradeoffs in the 1939 Amendments

Social Security officials and Advisory Council members conceded that family benefits would make the system more generous *and* more expensive. But they viewed the greater expense as a social tradeoff. The Advisory Council defended its proposal for a wife's benefit on the grounds that "it would meet the greatest social need with the minimum income in cost" (Advisory Council on Social Security 1938, p. 24). This statement reflected the Council's belief that married couples should receive greater benefits than single individuals. According to figures prepared by the Social Security Board for the Advisory Council, the 1935 version of the law would have granted a retired single man earning an average monthly wage of $50 over 35 years $30 a month from Social Security. Under the terms of the Advisory Council's proposal, the same man would receive only $27.50 a month; if he were married, his benefit would increase to $41.25.[4]

Far from creating controversy, this social judgment was shared by Advisory Council members. "I don't mind taxing the bachelors," said Professor Theresa McMahon of the University of Washington. "I think they ought to take on the responsibility of sharing their income with somebody else."[5] As for the point that women who worked all their lives might have a lower rate of return than those who did not, Paul Douglas, the prominent University of Chicago economist and future Illinois senator, noted, "Of course, wives work too" (Kessler-Harris 1995, p. 101).

Another trade-off was the decision to use the same terms to determine benefits for single female workers and single male workers, although women lived longer, on average, than men. It was determined that men, in the name of social adequacy, would subsidize women. As Douglas Brown later explained, the Council accepted "this costly departure from private actuarial principles . . . without discussion." "There was no reason to believe that an older woman, as a primary beneficiary, did not need as much on which to live as a man nor that protection in old age should be affected by the number of years a person lived," he said (Brown 1977, p. 7).

Still another trade-off was the size of the widow's benefit. In this area, the Council traded equity for a dubious form of social adequacy. Despite Brown's assertion that a woman needed as much money to live on as a man, the Council recommended setting a widow's benefits at approximately 75 percent of a worker's primary benefit. When M. Albert Linton, an actuary from Provident Mutual, questioned the appropriateness of paying a widow 75 percent of her deceased husband's basic benefit, a Social Security Board actuary replied that the widow could "look out for herself better than a man could." After Linton inquired if the actuary's statement was a sociological fact, Brown reframed the question in a way that emphasized the questionable assumptions that lay behind it: "Can a single woman adjust herself to a lower budget on account of the fact that she is used to doing her own housework whereas the man has to go to a restaurant?"[6] The Council apparently decided that the answer to Brown's question was yes and that widows should indeed be given three-quarters of a basic benefit.

According to the Council's reasoning, the simple fact that women lived longer than men meant that many wives became widows. It followed, then, that "Old-age insurance benefits for the husband, supplemented during his life by an allowance payable on behalf of his wife, fall considerably short, therefore, of providing adequate old-age security." The Council deliberately left the percentage a widow should receive vague. "It appears reasonable," the Council stated, that a widow over 65 "should receive an annuity equal to approximately three-fourths of the husband's annuity" (Advisory Council on Social Security 1938, p. 28).

Hard Choices

Setting the age at which a widow's benefits should begin also proved difficult. Altmeyer, speaking to the Council, admitted that uniformity, rather than scientific consideration, was the rationale behind starting a widow's benefits at age 65. "We worked for three months on that problem," he said. "You go from one extreme to the other. You can say that the widows' age shall have to be 65 . . . or you can go to the other extreme and say that widows of any age shall be eligible."[7] The Council ultimately settled on age 65.

The qualifying age for a wife's benefits presented similar problems. In an initial Advisory Council discussion, some Council members argued that benefits should begin at age 60 because many men married younger women. According to these members, delaying the wife's benefit amounted to a benefit cut for many families. "If a married man reaches 65 and his wife is 61, let's say, and you don't give him the wife's allowance until the wife becomes 65, you have virtually reduced his benefit during the years when he is 65 or 69," one member said (Kessler-Harris 1995, pp. 95, 99).

The Council, settling on age 65 as the minimum age for wives to receive benefits, made a rare appeal to gender equity. Because single working women would have to wait until age 65 to claim Social Security, it seemed unfair for married women to receive wife's benefits at age 60 (Kessler-Harris 1995, p. 99). The Council's final report, conceding that many wives were younger than their husbands, said that reducing the eligibility age to 60 would involve "anomalies and inequities between the wives of annuitants and women with wage credits in their own account against which benefits would not be payable until age 65." The report also emphasized that the Social Security system already favored women because of their longer life expectancy (Advisory Council 1938, pp. 26–27).

Moral Hazard

The 1939 amendments resulting from the Advisory Council's recommendations were a product of their era. At the time, with many people out of work, insurance benefits were an attractive source of income. Policymakers, interested in protecting the integrity of the program, built in safeguards against fraud or, in insurance terms, moral hazard, by setting a minimum marriage length of five years before a couple qualified for benefits. The Council wanted to ensure that, for example, a woman did not marry a man just to increase her Social Security benefits. In Douglas Brown's colorful words, the amendments must protect the system from "designing women and old fools."

Policymakers applied a similar restriction to widows' benefits, requiring a minimum period of marital status to prevent "deathbed marriages" and other fraud. In addition, a widow was not permitted to receive benefits after remarrying for fear that Social Security would provide "a prize for the fellow that has looked for it" (Advisory Council 1938, pp. 27–29; Kessler-Harris 1995, p. 95). To avoid making any benefit too attractive, the Council also recommended that a young widow's benefit cease once her children had left her care. "It is normal," the Council wrote despite dire economic conditions, "for a large majority of younger widows without dependent children to reenter employment" (Advisory Council 1938, p. 31).

The Council also believed lump-sum payments, such as payments made to the beneficiary of a private life insurance policy or provided in the original Social Security Act in the form of a death benefit, represented bad social policy. Some Advisory Council members, along with many middle-class reformers of the period, believed that lump-sum payments might tempt poor people, in particular, to spend their retirement funds unwisely. During the Advisory Council's deliberations, Walter D. Fuller, president of the company that published the *Saturday Evening Post*, told a cautionary tale of a "colored man in our employ who died. He was a widower and he had two minor children and he left $2,000 insurance. It was turned over to the family and they immediately tried to run it up in a numbers game and lost it in two weeks."[8]

Persistence in the Face of Change

The Advisory Council's recommendations resulted directly in the 1939 Social Security amendments. Although celebrating this new protection for the American family, few policymakers bothered to explain what they meant by the term "family." At the time, most men and women married for life, and there were few divorces. Once married, a woman usually left the labor force to become a mother and housewife. She and her children became dependent on her husband's earnings. Thus, a married man's retirement and death posed the greatest risk to his family's support system. Policymakers in 1939 could not have anticipated the revolution in female labor force participation. In the 1930s, an estimated 15 percent of married women worked (Blumberg 1982, p. 194; King 1985, p. 64). Although World War II drew record numbers of women into the labor force, within a year of the war's end, 2.25 million female workers had given their jobs back to men. Another million were laid off during the economic uncertainty of reconversion. Still, about 2.75 million female workers drawn into the labor force by the war continued working. By 1947, about 29 percent of the labor force was female. The most dramatic change, however, occurred over the next few decades, when 6 out of 10 additions to the labor force were female (Achenbaum 1986, p. 1). Policymakers also did not anticipate the steep rise in the divorce rate. At the time of the 1939 amendments, about one in six marriages ended in divorce; by 1975 about half of all marriages led to divorce. Among women 26 to 40 in 1979, a third could expect to be divorced (U.S. Department of Health, Education, and Welfare 1979, p. 2).

These social trends put a great deal of strain on the 1939 amendments and its idealized family, and ultimately sparked extensive criticism. In 1974, Congressman Martha Griffiths (D-MI) charged that, "The income security programs of this Nation were designed for a land of male and female stereotypes, a land where all men were breadwinners and all women were wives and widows; where men provided necessary income for their families but women did not: in other words, where all the men supported all the women. This view of the world never matched reality but today it is further than ever from the truth" (King 1985, p. 65).

In fact, Griffiths shortchanged the policymakers of the 1930s. For one, recognizing that a significant number of women never married and continued to work, they granted single women Social Security benefits under the same terms as single male workers. Moreover, they realized that many women worked before marriage and sometimes during it, and used this fact in selling their plan to Congress. In the official Social Security ideology, a wife who qualified for a benefit based on her wage record always received it; the benefit was, however, sometimes topped off at 50 percent of her husband's benefit in the form of a wife's benefit. Viewed that way, part of the wife's benefit would be funded through contributions made by women who ultimately married and became housewives or who worked after their children were grown. The Ways and Means Committee, echoing the conclusions of the Social Security Board, noted that wives' benefits would cost relatively little: "Because most wives, in the long run, will build up wage credits on their own account, as a result of their own employment" (Reno and Upp 1983, p. 144).

Family benefits survived from the time of Douglas Brown to the era of Martha Griffiths because policymakers were able to introduce incremental changes to respond to changing conditions (see box 2.B). Some of these changes reflected second thoughts about the details of the 1939 amendments on the part of those who designed the amendments. Other changes reflected Social Security administrators' efforts to expand the program by

---

Box 2.B. Incremental Expansion of Family Benefits

1950: Husband and widower benefits introduced (with conditions)

1956: Survivors benefits for a disabled child extended beyond the age of 18

1958: Benefits for dependents of disabled worker beneficiaries begin

1965: Benefits for divorced wives with stringent conditions

1967: Benefits go to disabled widows, disabled widowers, disabled surviving divorced wives

1972: Dependency requirement for divorced wives eliminated

1977: A divorced wife's required length of marriage reduced

1983: Restrictions on divorced wife's benefits eased further

---

expanding family benefits, or, in the parlance of Social Security, making them more adequate. Still other alterations resulted from feminist criticisms of the program, legal imperatives produced by Supreme Court decisions, or conservative critiques that deemed family benefits too costly.

The Beginning of Incremental Change

Almost as soon as the 1939 amendments were passed, Douglas Brown questioned setting the widow's benefit at 75 percent. Over the next decades, the percentage of the widow's benefit became a subject of concern and an object of reform, and in 1959, Social Security administrators considered the effects of raising the widow's benefits to 80, 85, and 100 percent of a basic benefit.[9]

Such preparation paved the way for Congress to raise the widow's benefit 10 percent in 1961. Although ways to stimulate the economy and cope with the consequences of automation were of immediate concern that year, favorable legislative conditions enabled Congress to raise the widow's benefit. In 1972, Congress expanded the benefit further, setting it at the same level as a basic benefit. In that year, the automatic adjustment of Social Security benefits and welfare and Medicare reform dominated the policy agenda. The adjustment to the widow's benefit was a minor part of the second piece of Social Security legislation passed that year. The long campaign that began with Brown's uneasiness in 1939 and culminated in a full-scale widow's benefit in 1972 illustrates how Congress typically expanded family benefits alongside other Social Security benefits.[10]

The 1938 Council's decision about the age a wife or a widow begins to receive benefits was also reevaluated. The initial decision to start the benefits at age 65, as specified in the Advisory Council's report and the 1939 law, was reconsidered and subsequently lowered. Social Security officials no longer felt comfortable with the gender equity argument it had used to support starting a wife's benefits at age 65. Instead, they emphasized society's obligation to treat women differently than men and to allow women to retire at an earlier age. Arthur Altmeyer, speaking before the Advisory Council that met in 1948 and laid the groundwork for the 1950 amendments, suggested that the age at which women qualified for retirement benefits or a wife's benefit be lowered to 60 years.

Altmeyer based his recommendation on precedents from other countries and other public retirement systems as well as on demographic and labor force participation data. He noted, as some committee members had 10 years earlier, that the wives of less than 20 percent of the married men reaching retirement age each year were 65 or older. Altmeyer's data, compiled by his staff, also showed that 21 percent of males between 60 and 64 were not in the labor force; for women, the corresponding figure was nearly 86 percent. He presented further evidence that women needed benefits earlier: Although women made up 30 percent of the workers who received wage credits in 1940, they accounted for only 13 percent of workers age 60 to 64. At age 20, half of all covered workers were women; at age 60, one covered worker in eight was female. This data meant that lowering women's eligibility age to 60 would make more than half of the married men reaching age 65 eligible for the spousal benefit and a quarter of all widows eligible for benefits. Presented in that way, the data suggested that Social Security administrators should change the terms of the 1939 amendment to permit early retirement for women and grant widows and wives benefits at an earlier age.[11] The Advisory Council that reported in the spring of 1948 recommended lowering the qualifying age for wives and widows benefit to 60 years. But the recommendation was listed as the 20th among 22 recommendations. Extensions of coverage and a rise in the benefit formula took precedence (Advisory Council 1948, p. 43).

The item remained on Social Security's agenda for expansion until Congress acted in 1956, lowering the minimum age for women's retirement benefits, wives' benefits, and widows' benefits to 62 (with an actuarial reduction for taking benefits before age 65). Congress prevailed despite opposition from the Eisenhower administration and despite member's preoccupation with the debate over introducing disability insurance. Social Security Commissioner Charles Schottland later hinted that the lower retirement age for women was inserted to "sweeten" legislation, making passage of disability insurance more palatable (Achenbaum 1986, p. 128).

Family Benefits and the 1950 Amendments

Before these adjustments could be made, the Social Security program had to overcome challenges to its very existence. In 1939, Social Security applied to only about half the labor force and paid lower benefits than did many state welfare programs for the aged. The program risked becoming irrelevant, replaced by a public assistance program or a Townsend-style program that paid benefits to every elderly person, regardless of his or her work history.[12]

One advantage of the Townsend Plan was in the area of family benefits. Under the plan, married couples would have received twice the benefits of single individuals (because benefits would go to the elderly individual rather than to the family), and widows would have received 100 percent of a basic benefit. Critics of Social Security that supported the idea of noncontributory benefits behind the Townsend Plan also argued that gender anomalies in the Social Security program detracted from its effectiveness.

In the 1940s, Social Security officials, such as Arthur Altmeyer, attempted to respond to these criticisms, but other items, such as raising the benefit level and expanding coverage, took precedence. In 1948, for example, Altmeyer talked about raising the wife's benefit to 75 percent of the basic benefit. He pointed out that critics of the Social Security program, such as Senator Downey (D-CA), criticized the program for giving only half the basic benefit to the wife. Because the Council's priority was expanding the basic benefit, the issue was dropped, although Congress ultimately did liberalize the structure of dependent children benefits.

In 1948, the Social Security Advisory Council recommended raising benefits for dependent children to three-quarters of the basic benefit for the first child and one-half of the basic benefit for each additional child. In making the recommendation, the Council cited studies from the Bureau of Old Age and Survivors Insurance, which found that 44 percent of widows with young children did not have sufficient income for what the Bureau called a "maintenance level of living" (a forerunner of the SSA's poverty level). The Council argued that, in addition to helping pull families headed by women out of poverty, the proposal would make the various types of Social Security benefits more uniform. As matters stood, families consisting of a husband and wife might receive 150 percent of the basic benefit, while a family consisting of a widow and child might receive 125 percent of the basic benefit (Advisory Council 1948, p. 37). In 1960, more than a decade later, Congress responded to the Council's request and raised a surviving child's benefit to 75 percent of the basic benefit.

By that time, some of the program's gender-related inequities had been solved. Under the terms of the 1939 amendments, for example, the program paid benefits to widows, but not to widowers. In 1946, Brookings Institution Analyst Lewis Meriam wrote that the program neglected the case of the wife who worked because "her husband is unable to make a living; he is physically or mentally disabled or mentally incompetent as a provider. Under these conditions he is not taken care of by his wife's insurance in the event of her death but must depend on other savings or on relief payments." In general, "the state assumes that husbands support wives and does not allow for conditions that may reverse the normal situation." According to Meriam, the program's failure to pay benefits to widows under 65 with no children, divorced wives, or deserted wives detracted from its effectiveness (Meriam 1946, pp. 122, 649–52).

In 1948, the Council instructed the staff, headed at the time by future Social Security Commissioner Robert Ball, to draft new proposals that "would more nearly equalize the benefit rights of women and men workers." The Council worried, in particular, about survivors benefits and wanted children to be able to receive benefits on the mother's wage benefit. The Council also supported benefit payments to aged dependent husbands and to widowers who were "currently and fully insured" at the time of their wives' retirement or death. Congress followed the Advisory Council's advice a couple of years later. In 1950, it created husband's and widower's benefits and made surviving dependent children eligible to receive benefits based on a woman's wage record. Congress, however, imposed more stringent eligibility conditions for benefits tied to a woman's wage record. A husband, for example, had to prove he was economically dependent on his wife to receive benefits, although a wife was automatically entitled to benefits based on her husband's wage record.

Congress also made its first attempt to deal with divorce. A divorced widow caring for a former husband's child could receive a widow's benefit if she could prove he was providing half the child's support before he died. The 1950 amendments marked an important, and relatively uncontroversial, step toward the incremental reform of family benefits (Blumberg 1982, p. 193; Reno and Upp 1983, p. 145).

Expanding Family Benefits in an Expanding System

Between 1950 and 1972, Congress tackled several controversial topics. Disability insurance, the lead issue from 1951 to 1956, was only passed after Social Security officials made numerous concessions, including restricting such benefits to people with severe disabilities and not making the families of workers with severe disabilities eligible. But two years later Medicare was the most visible, controversial issue, and Congress succeeded in amending the law to provide benefits for the dependents of disabled worker beneficiaries on the same terms as retired worker beneficiaries. Disabled workers were more likely than retired workers to have dependents in their care, and Congress's recognition of these children represented a vote of confidence in the family benefits system. Once the disability category was established, Congress applied it to other forms of family benefits. For example, in 1956 it determined that a disabled child could receive survivors benefits past the age of 18. Legislation in 1967 established benefits for disabled widows, disabled widowers, and disabled surviving divorced wives (Berkowitz 1987, p. 109).

Next, Congress turned its attention to Medicare and, after many bruising battles, passed the controversial measure in 1965. In addition to enacting Medicare, the 1965 law liberalized the definition of disability, increased Social Security benefits 7 percent, eased the earnings test, and introduced a rehabilitation program for Social Security Disability Insurance beneficiaries. It also contained extensive sections relating to public assistance and child and maternal health. Finally, a provision buried in this omnibus legislation allowed a divorced woman meeting certain conditions to collect a wife's benefit based on her former husband's wage record. As was customary when the program began a new type of benefit, Congress attached many conditions. In this case, a woman needed to have been married to her former husband for at least 20 years; she could not be married at the time she received the benefit, and she had to demonstrate financial dependence on her ex-husband (Achenbaum 1986, p. 129).[13]

Over time, Congress eased the restrictions on this benefit. A series of benefit increases in the late 1960s and early 1970s culminated in a 1972 law that featured a 20 percent average benefit increase and shifted to automatic benefit increases based on the Consumer Price Index.[14] Later that same year, Congress passed another comprehensive Social Security bill that eliminated the dependency requirement for divorced wives. Five years later, even though fiscal relief had become a top priority, Congress halved the marriage length required for a woman to receive a divorced wife's benefit. In 1983, Congress further liberalized the divorced wife's benefit, despite the fiscal problems of the Social Security system.

Feminist Critiques of Social Security and the Courts

Movements to change family benefits acquired strong momentum in the 1970s and the early 1980s. Social Security's treatment of women was of particular concern, but the Advisory Councils that met during these years continued to take relatively conservative positions, arguing in 1971, for example, that "men are generally not dependent upon their wives for support, and a presumption of dependency that is reasonable for a wife or widow does not seem reasonable for a husband or widower." In 1975, the Council reversed this decision and explicitly recommended revising Social Security laws that treated men and women differently. Still, although a Subcommittee on the Treatment of Men and Women had been established as part of the 1975 Council, gender equity remained a relatively minor issue. A few years later, however, priorities had changed: The 1979 Council spent more time on Social Security's treatment of working and nonworking women than on any other issue (Burkhauser and Holden 1982, pp. 11–12).

Changing economic, social, and political conditions precipitated the shift. With the 1972 amendments marking the completion of an expansionist agenda established in 1950, only the goal of introducing national health insurance remained. Despite initial optimism, particularly with the promising 1974 appearance of the Kennedy-Mills bill, the likelihood of successful legislation on this issue faded as the decade progressed (Randal 1974, p. c-5). Proposals that included mandated benefits financed by private employers and the removal of the Medicare program from the Social Security Administration in 1977 made national health insurance less of a Social Security issue and more of a general social policy issue (Berkowitz 1998, pp. 283–288). As for Social Security, in 1973 then Commissioner Robert Ball announced "it is more important from the standpoint of the health of the program to focus on the correction of inequities" than it was to devote attention to general benefit increases (Derthick 1979, p. 262). The treatment of women topped the list of inequities that required correction.

The feminist movement helped put the treatment of women at the top of the Social Security Administration's agenda. Congress's attention to women's Social Security benefits in the 1970s reflected not only the successful expansion of the program and the era's political tenor, but also changes in the tightly controlled policymaking system. During his tenure, Wilbur Mills presided over the Ways and Means Committee without aid of permanent subcommittees.[15] After a series of public humiliations forced him to step down as committee chair in 1975, all Congressional committees were required to have subcommittees, creating more openings through which advocates could influence Congress.

The courts served as another reform avenue for feminist causes during the 1970s. In the seminal Supreme Court case of *Weinberger* v. *Weisenfeld,* decided on March 19, 1975, the justices awarded widower's benefits to a man whose wife had died in childbirth. This decision made a widowed father caring for an eligible child under 18 eligible for benefits on the basis of his wife's contributions, regardless of whether he had been dependent on his wife for support. In its reasoning, the Court dismissed the idea that the earnings of male workers were vital to supporting families, while women's earnings contributed little. In other words, the Court argued that a woman's Social Security contributions should count as much as a man's.

Other decisions acknowledging women's contributions followed the *Weisenfeld* case. The 1978 Supreme Court decision in *Cooper* v. *Califano* permitted husbands who were caring for an eligible child to receive benefits based on the benefits of their retired wives (Kessler-Harris 1995, p. 130; Holden 1997, p. 94). Congress and the Social Security Administration followed the Court's lead. For example, in 1983 Congress wrote widowed father's benefits and other Court adjustments into the statute.

The women's rights movement sought equality of labor force opportunities and outcomes. The importance of work in women's lives was impossible to dismiss by the 1970s. In 1975, for the first time in history, a majority of the nation's mothers with school-age children held jobs outside the home. Female labor participation had become the norm. The nation reached another symbolic milestone in its bicentennial year when the number of divorces exceeded 1 million (U.S. Census Bureau 1987).

One of the first outside groups to examine Social Security's effects on women was the President's Commission on the Status of Women, created by President Kennedy in late 1961. Part of the commission's task was to look at federal social insurance and tax laws as they affect the net earnings and other income of women. The commission's research committee, headed by Senator Maurine B. Neuberger (D-OR) consisted of at least two members with close connections to the Social Security Administration; the technical secretary heading up the staff was a former SSA employee. Thus, the committee, although it might have prodded SSA on particular issues, was not likely to take a critical attitude toward Social Security.

The committee supported the passage of Medicare—SSA's primary legislative objective—and defended the program's treatment of working wives. The program's primary goal was adequate social security for workers and their families, with individual equity a secondary consideration. Conceding that the notion that working wives should receive more in benefits than nonworking wives had merit, the committee considered such remedies as imputing earnings to a woman's work as a homemaker, which it put aside as too complicated to implement. The committee did recommend that the wife's benefit be reduced on a sliding scale in proportion to her own benefit (the one she earned by working). In addition, the committee took up the cause of divorced women, suggesting that a divorced woman qualify for a wife's or widow's benefit (Committee on Social Insurance and Taxes 1963, p. iv, 3, 30–35).

The full Commission did not adopt all of the committee's recommendations. In general, it took a permissive stance toward the Social Security system of family benefits. The Commission even stated that it would not "be appropriate for the social insurance program to provide a benefit so that the father could stay at home to care for the child" (President's Committee on the Status of Women 1963, p. 42). At the same time, the Commission pursued what might be described as an adequacy agenda on behalf of women, citing the need for increased payments to widows and divorced women. The only formal recommendation that emerged was that a widow's benefit under the federal old-age insurance system should be equal to the amount that her husband would have received at the same age had he lived. Nothing in this recommendation, or in the Commission's other suggestions, conflicted with the wishes of the Social Security Administration (Harrison 1988, pp. 156, 226). In fact, the Advisory Councils that met in 1965 and 1971 took up the cause of raising the widow's benefits (Reno and Upp 1983, p. 145).

Although the system eventually corrected most of the problems cited by the President's Commission on the Status of Women, certain inequities persisted. A widow's qualifying age was lowered to 60, but homemakers under that age still could not receive benefits unless they were disabled (and over 50) or caring for children. Under these rules, younger widows suffered from a "widow's gap." Moreover, older widows, used to living with their husbands on one-and-a-half times his basic benefit, found it difficult to live on two-thirds of that benefit, particularly because Social Security benefits often served as their only source of income.

The Social Security system, originally designed to ease the burden of married people, proved least helpful to single individuals. For example, even once benefits for divorced women were introduced, they were often inadequate as a means of support, because they represented 50 percent of a living former husband's benefit (U.S. Department of Health, Education and Welfare 1979, p. 3). Divorced women's needs, like other adequacy issues, pitted women's rights groups against groups focused on expanding disability benefits, cutting auxiliary benefits to save the system money, or on other priorities.

Arguments over Equity

In addition to adequacy claims, feminist groups critiqued the Social Security system's equity features. This straightforward campaign aimed to end the double standards that applied to men's and women's benefits, such as the failure to provide husbands with benefits based on their wives' income record, as outlined in the *Weisenfeld* case. For the most part, efforts to close gender equity gaps elicited favorable responses from expansionists, including Robert Ball, and from conservative critics, such as President Ford's Domestic Policy Council. Ball, in congressional testimony just after he left the Commissioner's office in 1973, noted that a husband or widower could receive benefits on his wife's record only if he had been receiving at least one-half of his support from his wife. Ball argued that this provision should be changed, anticipating the later court case and the SSA's favorable response to it (Ball 1973). In 1975, James Cannon, one of President Ford's chief domestic councilors, recommended that most of the 1975 Advisory Council's recommendations be opposed, except for those that dealt with male-female equity issues in the granting of benefits.[16]

Other equity issues raised by women's groups proved more difficult either because they could not be solved inside the Social Security system or because their solution involved restructuring the program in a time of fiscal austerity. For example, making the system's rules the same for men and women—a task basically completed by 1983—did not eliminate gender-based differences. Females continued to receive a lower average monthly retired worker benefit, worth only about three-quarters of a man's benefit at the end of 1993, despite the fact that male and female benefits "were calculated in precisely the same manner." To eliminate that inequity would mean, under the current system, equalizing male and female average wages and requiring men to spend as much time outside the labor force as women. Alternatively, solutions that radically restructure Social Security, such as moving toward a universal uniform benefit, violate the fundamental principles of the Social Security system and how it ties benefits to wages (Holden 1997, p. 94).[17]

The fact that more women than men worked as homemakers, and that homemakers received no Social Security credits, aggravated the disparity between men's and women's benefits. For example, if a young, married homemaker became disabled, she received no benefits from Social Security. To recognize the role of homemakers, the National Commission on the Observance of the International Women's Year recommended in 1976 that the homemaker be covered in her own right under Social Security. The National Women's Conference held in Houston, Texas, adopted a similar resolution the next year (Reno and Upp 1983, p. 150; King 1995, p. 3). Unlike the widowers' benefits extended to men caring for children, homemakers' benefits had no clear analogue in the original system. Thus, they were more controversial and were never implemented.

Like benefits for women who did not work outside the home, equity issues related to the return on working women's Social Security contributions sparked controversy. Unlike discussions of homemakers' needs, which mostly stayed within women's policy and Social Security networks, the unequal treatment of two-earner couples relative to single-earner couples attracted a great deal of media attention. In 1973 testimony, Robert Ball observed that, "Under the present social security law, a working couple may be paid less in total retirement benefits than another couple with the same total earnings where only the husband worked . . . there is no good reason in social insurance theory for this difference in treatment. Both couples in the example have paid the same in contributions and both have had the same level of living and should get the same replacement of past earnings in retirement or disability" (Ball 1973, p. 20).

Economists cited other examples: The family of a married man who earned $12,000 per year on average received more in social security benefits than did a family with combined husband-wife earnings of $12,000. Benefits disparities tended to grow as the wage differential between the husband and wife became larger. Indeed, a family in which one member earned $12,000 and the other earned $4,800 received benefits that were only marginally greater than a one-earner family earning $12,000, despite having contributed much more to social security. Furthermore, differences between one- and two-earner families were even more pronounced for survivors benefits than for retirement benefits (see Gordon 1979, p. 224–226).

Gender equity issues were officially aired in a 1968 report from the Task Force on Social Insurance and Taxes, which reported to the Citizens Advisory Council on the Status of Women. Despite being dominated by Social Security Administration employees, the task force proposed fundamental reforms, recommending that "Earnings for couples who both have reached retirement age and have a long period of wage credits under social security be combined for benefit computation purposes." In policy parlance, this proposal, suggested as far back as 1938 by Gerard Swope, became known as earnings sharing. By the time of the task force's 1968 report, Congresswoman Griffiths had already introduced earnings sharing in Congress. In addition, the Task Force suggested that the 1969 Advisory Council consider "a system that would provide a benefit based on social need with supplementation of this benefit by a contributory wage-related benefit." This idea, known as a double-decker plan, had been discussed since the 1940s, often by critics of Social Security who pointed to the program's low benefit levels. Now, policymakers wanted to use this old device to assure "a more equitable return for the provisions of the working wife" (Committee on Social Insurance and Taxes 1968).

System's Fiscal Problems Take Precedence

The gender equity problems reflected the effects of applying 1939 rules to modern family life, where female labor force participation was on the rise. Solutions, though relatively easy to devise, were much harder to implement, particularly if policymakers accepted the constraint that costs could not be added to the system. That constraint pressed heavily on President Gerald Ford and President Jimmy Carter, who presided at a time when the Social Security system faced severe fiscal problems.

Both Ford and Carter decided that maintenance of the system should take precedence over reshaping the system in a potentially costly way. Neither wanted to risk the political fallout of eliminating family benefits or face the problems of restructuring the benefits in a way that would add costs. From the right, conservative politicians and economists criticized the program for making too many promises that would, in the long run, undermine the program's solvency and produce serious economic problems (Boskin 1986). According to this view, family benefits needed to be cut back. For example, staffers, in a memo to Arthur Burns, listed reducing benefits to spouses as a possible option. In citing this option, the staffers relied upon reasoning that had become standard in policy discussions. "Under the current benefit structure," they explained, "non-working wives of retired beneficiaries are entitled to additional benefits equal to 50 percent of their husband's benefits. As a result, the replacement rates (ratio of benefits to preretirement earnings) of one-worker families are significantly larger than those of families with working wives. Thus, benefits paid to two-worker families are not much larger than those of one-worker families, even though the two-worker families pay a much larger amount in payroll taxes."

Liberal participants in the debate did not entirely disagree with this benefits-cutting approach, although they would have gone about it in a different way. Even Robert Ball, one of the ultimate defenders of Social Security, initially suggested cutting the spousal benefit. Early in the decade, he told Congress that, "Apparently the only practical way to correct this problem is to base the benefits for the working couple on their combined earnings" (Ball 1973, p. 21). Soon, however, he offered a different solution, one in the incremental expansionist tradition. He wanted to help the 8.6 million women who were getting benefits based on their own wage records at the beginning of 1977 (nearly 1.7 million of these women were also receiving wives' or widows' benefits based on their husband's wage records). Specifically, he proposed that legislators raise the individual benefit by 12.5 percent and reduce the spouse's benefit to a third of the basic benefit. This change would have kept the family benefit the same but would have increased benefits based on the wage records of single workers (Ball 1978, p. 322).

This clever but costly solution gained little support as policymakers became more and more focused on correcting the "double-indexing" problem created by the 1972 amendments and saving the system from short- and long-term deficits. President Ford was faced with a long litany of criticisms of Social Security ending with a plea to put most of the problems aside and shore up Social Security financing. At the end of 1975, Caspar Weinberger, then secretary of Health, Education and Welfare (HEW), advised President Ford that people were more worried about many features of Social Security than at any other time in the nation's history, but that stabilizing and financing the system for the future must take priority.[18] Thus, solutions to problems created within family benefits tended to be set aside.

James Cardwell, who served as President Ford's commissioner of Social Security, put the matter in perspective during a long, rambling press conference announcing President Ford's plan to solve the double-indexing problem. He described the problem of giving equity to women as overwhelming. "The solutions to that problem turn out to be very expensive, if you try to round everybody upward," he noted.[19] He went on to say that, "If you leave the wife's benefit in place and if you try to also give the working wife an equivalent benefit opportunity, that increases the cost of the system. Another advocacy on the part of women these days is that housewives should get a fuller benefit, even though they do not pay directly into the system. You have all these points and counterpoints flooding in for consideration at a time when we see the long-term cost of the System rising at a very rapid rate. We think that by putting the System on a firm footing—which we think the President's proposal would do—you improve the opportunity for policymakers to later rationally approach these kinds of questions. The answers are not going to be easy to come by" (Ibid).

President Carter expressed interest in family problems, but he also tended to become absorbed in financing issues. Carter hoped to use family policy to anchor domestic policy. The President mentioned, in particular, that the government should give working married couples the same tax benefits as single working people who lived together. At the top of the President's domestic policy concerns was welfare reform; he hoped to create incentives within the system to keep fathers from deserting their families.[20]

Despite the rhetoric, family policy remained separated from discussions of Social Security policy. Although the 1977 Social Security Amendments contained a number of gender-equity components, such as eliminating the dependency requirement for widowers, they dealt mostly with financing issues. Later in the administration, HEW Secretary Califano advanced proposals, with only limited success, to cut back some family benefits, such as the survivors benefits for students between the ages of 18 and 21 (Berkowitz 1995, pp. 300–303; Califano 1981, p. 387). Carter, like Ford, ended up doing little about the apparent inequities between one- and two-wage earner couples.

For the most part, the policy stalemate over family benefits continued during President Reagan's tenure. Despite Reagan's conservatism, the adequacy side of the feminist agenda culminated in important legislative victories during his presidency. The 1983 "rescue" legislation incorporated a measure allowing a divorced spouse to draw spouse's benefits at age 62, whether or not the former spouse had retired (Berkowitz 1988, pp. 59–60). In addition, the 1983 amendments brought "gender rights" decisions into the statute. But the equity side of the feminist agenda stalled. The country did not adopt a double-decker or an earnings-sharing plan.

In the 1990s, the Social Security debate took a new turn. In response to a long-term crisis in Social Security funding, advocates along the political spectrum proposed measures that would "privatize" part of Social Security. These ideas were not new, nor were they totally outside the design of the Social Security system. The system already contained private features, such as the private insurance companies that helped administer the Medicare program. The 1990s proposals, however, including those advanced by some Advisory Council members between 1994 and 1996, would run part of the Social Security program as a defined *contribution* program, rather than as a defined *benefit* program (Advisory Council 1997).

The idea of privatizating parts of Social Security created uncertainty about the fate of the system's well-established, defined benefit structure. In the face of this possible step, some groups that had previously criticized Social Security for not being generous enough began to defend the program. For example, in congressional testimony presented in early 1999, the National Council of La Raza contended that the Social Security program disproportionately benefited Latinos. Thus, according to the La Raza testimony, if the program were changed, a guaranteed and defined benefit would be an essential feature. Furthermore, the statement pointed out that Hispanic women were more likely than other women to work in the home. Consequently, reform plans that changed the survivors benefits system would have a disproportionately harmful effect on Hispanic women (National Council of La Raza 1999).

Other groups interested in issues affecting women also defended Social Security and its structure of family benefits. The Institute for Women's Policy Research, arguing that women constitute 60 percent of Social Security beneficiaries and depend more heavily than men on Social Security in their later years, argued for preserving the life insurance or survivors features of the program. In 1999, a task force of the National Council of Women's Organizations argued for an increase in the widow's benefit to 75 percent of the couple's combined benefits. It also supported increasing benefits for divorced spouses from 50 percent to 75 percent of a worker's benefit. The task force cited the preservation of survivors benefits on its checklist of items that any reform proposal must contain (Institute for Women's Policy Research 2000; Task Force on Women and Social Security, National Council of Women's Organizations 1999, pp. 8, 27).

Whatever the flaws, the Social Security program had evolved to include a definite set of rules concerning family benefits. Newer plans incorporating privatization must do the same. In the debate over privatization, questions related to the nation's savings rate and the long-term solvency of the Social Security trust fund tend to overshadow concerns about family benefits. Social Security surpluses and a generally robust economy in the 1990s stimulated more proposals to increase the adequacy of family benefits in the existing system rather than proposals to tackle the hard questions of folding family benefits into a partially privatized system.

Conclusion

The incremental changes made to Social Security family benefits and the financing crises experienced after 1974 have not changed the basic outline of the 1939 Amendments to the Social Security program. Wives continue to receive a 50 percent supplement to their husbands' basic benefit, even though labor force participation patterns have made this benefit less relevant than in the late-Depression era. Survivors benefits, particularly for widows, are still paid much the same way they were paid when family benefits went into effect in 1940. It is true that legislators have lowered the qualifying ages and altered the percentages of benefits; divorce and disability have also become legal categories in the family benefits system. Nonetheless, members of the 1939 Advisory Council would have little trouble seeing their handiwork in the modern program.

In some respects, the persistence of family benefits reflects the fact that the benefits have met real social needs. In other respects, their persistence demonstrates the program's resistance to change, perhaps because of its great popularity between 1950 and 1972, and because its fiscal problems since 1972 have made change very difficult to enact. Given modern developments in the family and in the labor force, we undoubtedly would create a different system were we able to start over today. The state of the Social Security system today reflects historical circumstances as much as the designer's original social goals.

NOTES

The author thanks Virginia Reno and Cynthia Harrison for their help and generosity in providing useful historical documents and helpful advice. Any errors in the institutional detail or in the description of women's history are the responsibility of the author.

1. Advisory Council Minutes, February 18, 1938, morning session, p. 6, RG47; "Summary of Provisions of Present Title II and Proposed AC-1," (n.d.), RG 47.

2. Advisory Council Minutes, February 18, 1938, afternoon session, pp. 35–36, RG 47.

3. Advisory Council Minutes, April 29, 1938, morning session, pp. 17–19, RG 47; "Description of Proposed Plan AC-12," (n.d.), RG 47.

4. "Average Monthly Annuities under Proposed Plan AC-1 and under Present Title II, 1940–1980," (n.d.) and "Illustrated Monthly Annuities Under Plan AC-1" n.d., RG 47.

5. Advisory Council minutes, February 18, 1938, morning session, pp. 41–42, RG 47.

6. Colloquy among Linton, W. R. Williamson and Brown, Advisory Council Minutes, February 18, 1938, afternoon session, p. 12, RG 47.

7. Advisory Council minutes, October 21, 1938, morning session, p. 57, RG 47.

8. Walter Fuller, Advisory Council Minutes, February 18, 1938, afternoon session, p. 34, RG 47.

9. Alvin David to Victor Christgau, Robert Ball, and Jack Futterman, March 10, 1959, transmitting "Level-Premium Cost Estimates on Intermediate-Cost Basis for Var-

ious Proposed Changes in OASDI System," Robert Ball Papers, Wisconsin State Historical Society, Madison, Wisconsin.

10. For details on the expansion of widows' benefits, see Achenbaum (1986, p. 129). For information on the expansion of the Social Security program more generally, see Derthick (1979).

11. Arthur Altmeyer, "Statement before the (1948) Advisory Council," *Ball Papers;* O. C. Pogge to Mr. A. J. Altmeyer, December 2, 1947, "Material for Advisory Council Meeting," *Ball Papers.*

12. For the relevant background, see Berkowitz (1997, pp. 22–38).

13. For more background on the 1965 legislation, see Berkowitz (1995).

14. For information on the adoption of the cost-of-living adjustments, see Derthick (1979), Weaver (1988), and Zelizer (1999).

15. For more on Mills's influence, see Zelizer (1999); for a look at Mills's dealing with social security policymakers, see Berkowitz (1995, pp. 294–295).

16. James Cannon to the President, May 2, 1975, Cannon Files, Box 33, Gerald Ford Library, Ann Arbor, Michigan.

17. For a succinct list of the basic principles of social insurance see Advisory Council (1997, p. 94).

18. Caspar Weinberger to the President, December 9, 1974, Pamela Needham Files, Box 5, Gerald Ford Library, Ann Arbor, Michigan.

19. All quotes here are from the transcript of Bruce Cardwell's Press Conference, June 17, 1976, Spencer Johnson Files, Box 11, Gerald Ford Library.

20. *New York Times,* June 15, 1977, p. 32. For a good overview of the domestic policies of the Carter administration, see Fink and Graham (1978).

REFERENCES

Achenbaum, W. Andrew. 1986. *Social Security: Visions and Revisions.* New York: Cambridge University Press.

Advisory Council on Social Security. 1938. *Final Report of the Advisory Council on Social Security.* Washington, D.C.: Government Printing Office.

———. 1948. *Old-Age and Survivors Insurance: A Report to the Senate Committee on Finance from the Advisory Council on Social Security.* Document 149. 80th cong., 2d sess. Washington, D.C.: Government Printing Office.

———. 1997. *Report of the 1994–1996 Advisory Council, Volume I: Findings and Recommendations.* Washington, D.C.: Government Printing Office.

Altmeyer, Arthur. 1966. *The Formative Years of Social Security.* Madison: University of Wisconsin Press.

Ball, Robert M. 1973. "The Treatment of Women under Social Security." In *Robert Ball Papers,* statement before the Joint Economic Committee, U.S. Congress, July 25.

———. 1978. *Social Security: Today and Tomorrow.* New York: Columbia University Press.

Berkowitz, Edward D. 1978. Interview with Charles Schottland. Waltham, Massachusetts.

———. 1987. *Disabled Policy: America's Programs for the Handicapped.* New York: Cambridge University Press.

————. 1988. "Public History, Academic History and Policy Analysis: A Case Study with Commentary." *The Public Historian* 10 (fall): 59–60.

————. 1991. *America's Welfare State from Roosevelt to Reagan.* Baltimore: Johns Hopkins University Press.

————. 1995. *Mr. Social Security: The Life of Wilbur Cohen.* Lawrence, Kansas: University Press of Kansas.

————. 1996. "Social Security and the Financing of the American State." In *Funding the Modern American State, 1941–1995,* edited by W. Elliot Brownlee (151–159). New York: Woodrow Wilson Center and Cambridge University Press.

————. 1997. "The Historical Development of Social Security in the United States." In *Social Security in the 21st Century,* edited by Eric Kingson and James Schulz (22–38). New York: Oxford University Press.

————. 1998. "The Health Care Financing Administration." In *A Historical Guide to the U.S. Government,* edited by George T. Kurian (283–288). New York: Oxford University Press.

Blumberg, Grace Ganz. 1982. "Adult Derivative Benefits in Social Security: A Woman's Issue." In *Women and the Law: A Social Historical Perspective, Volume II: Property, Family and the Legal Profession,* edited by D. Kelly Weisberg (194). Cambridge, Mass.: Schenkman Publishing Company.

Boskin, Michael J. 1986. *Too Many Promises: The Uncertain Nature of Social Security.* Homewood, Illinois: Dow-Jones Irwin.

Brown, J. Douglas. 1977. *Essays on Social Security.* Princeton, N.J.: Industrial Relations Section.

Burkhauser, Richard V., and Karen C. Holden. 1982. "Introduction." In *A Challenge to Social Security: The Changing Roles of Women and Men in American Society,* edited by Richard V. Burkhauser and Karen C. Holden (11–12). New York: Academic Press.

Califano, Joseph A. Jr. 1981. *Governing America.* New York: Simon and Schuster.

Committee on Social Insurance and Taxes. 1963. *Report to the President's Commission on the Status of Women.* Washington, D.C.: Government Printing Office, pp. iv, 3, 30–35.

————. 1968. *Report to the Citizens Advisory Council on the Status of Women.* Washington, D.C.: Government Printing Office, pp. 68–76.

Derthick, Martha. 1979. *Policymaking for Social Security.* Washington, D.C.: Brookings Institution.

Fink, Gary M., and Hugh Davis Graham, eds. 1978. *The Carter Presidency: Policy Choices in the Post-New Deal Era.* Lawrence, Kansas: University Press of Kansas.

Gordon, N. M. 1979. "Institutional Responses: The Social Security System." In *The Subtle Revolution: Women at Work,* edited by Ralph E. Smith (224–226). Washington, D.C.: The Urban Institute Press.

Harrison, Cynthia. 1988. *On Account of Sex: The Politics of Women's Issues 1945–1968.* Berkeley: University of California Press.

Holden, Karen C. 1997. "Social Security and the Economic Security of Women." In *Social Security in the 21st Century,* edited by Eric R. Kingson and James H. Shulz (94). New York: Oxford University Press.

Institute for Women's Policy Research. 2000. "Why Privatizing Social Security Would Hurt Women." *Research in Brief,* March.

Kessler-Harris, Alice. 1995. "Designing Women and Old Fools: The Construction of the Social Security Amendments of 1939." In *U.S. History as Women's History:*

New Feminist Essays, edited by Linda K. Kerber, Alice Kessler-Harris, and Kathryn Kish Sklar (95–97). Chapel Hill: University of North Carolina Press.

King, Gail Buchwalter. 1985. "Social Security and the Changing Role of Women." In *Fifty Years of Social Security: Past Achievements and Future Challenges: An Information Paper Prepared for Use by the Special Committee on Aging,* edited by Andrew W. Achenbaum (64). Washington, D.C.: Government Printing Office.

Landon, Alfred. 1936. "Text of Governor Landon's Milwaukee Address on Economic Security." *New York Times,* September 26.

Meriam, Lewis. 1946. *Relief and Social Security.* Washington, D.C.: The Brookings Institution.

National Council of La Raza (NCLR). 1999. "Social Security Reform: Issues for Hispanic American." Http://www.nclr.org/policy/socialsecurity/socialsecurityreform1.htm. (Accessed February 10, 1999).

President's Commission on the Status of Women. 1963. American Women: Report of the President's Commission on the Status of Women. Washington, D.C.: Government Printing Office.

Randal, Judith. 1974. "National Health Insurance Gets New Lease on Life." *Washington Star News,* April 7.

Reno, Virginia P., and Melinda M. Upp. 1983. "Social Security and the Family." In *Taxing the Family,* edited by Rudolph G. Penner (144). Washington, D.C.: American Enterprise Institute.

Social Security Administration (SSA). NDa. *Cumulative Tax Collections, Benefit Payments, Net Excess of Tax Collections.* File 025, Records of the Social Security Administration, RG 47, National Archives, Washington, D.C.

———. NDb. *Annual Appropriations, Benefit Payments and Reserves.* File 025, Records of the Social Security Administration, RG 47, National Archives, Washington, D.C.

Task Force on Women and Social Security, National Council of Women's Organizations. 1999. "Strengthening Social Security for Women: A Report from the Working Conference on Women and Social Security," July 19–22, Airlie House, mimeo.

U.S. Census Bureau. 1987. *Statistical Abstract of the United States, 1986.* Washington, D.C.: U.S. Census Bureau.

U.S. Congress. 1937a. *Reserves Under Federal Old-Act Benefit Plan—Social Security Act.* Senate Committee on Finance. 75th cong., 1st sess., Feb. 22. Washington, D.C.: Government Printing Office.

———. 1937b. Senate. *Congressional Record.* 75th cong., 1st sess. Washington, D.C.: Government Printing Office.

U.S. Department of Health, Education, and Welfare. 1979. *Social Security and the Changing Roles of Men and Women.* Washington, D.C.: Department of Health, Education, and Welfare.

Weaver, R. Kent. 1988. *Automatic Government: The Politics of Indexation.* Washington, D.C.: Brookings Institution.

Witte, Edwin. 1963. *The Development of the Social Security Act.* Madison: University of Wisconsin Press.

Zelizer, Julian. 1999. *Taxing America: Wilbur D. Mills, Congress, and the States.* New York: Cambridge University Press.

3

The Status of the
Retired Population,
Now and in the Future

Karen E. Smith

Sweeping demographic changes have reshaped the U.S. population since the inception of the Social Security program in 1935. The population today is aging rapidly, with a much larger percentage of people expected to live well into their 80s and 90s. Compared with previous decades, more people today remain single, marriages do not last as long, and people remarry less frequently. In addition, women are having fewer children and are having them at later ages, and more children are being raised outside of traditional two-parent families.

The American workforce has also changed dramatically. Although less than a third of women participated in the paid workforce in 1935, a majority of women today work. This increased participation, as well as a narrowing in the gap in hourly male-female earnings, has pushed up women's average earnings relative to men's. Although most men in their prime working years continue to participate in the paid labor force, early retirement has lowered participation rates among men over age 55. Early retirement erodes the financial base of the family both by reducing Social Security benefits and by limiting earnings, wealth, and pension accumulation.

These demographic and work life changes are remaking the current and future profile of the U.S. retiree population. This chapter summarizes recent demographic and economic trends that will affect retirement income, explores how these trends may evolve in the future, and reviews the implications for the Social Security system.

The Aging of the Population

Perhaps the most salient trend affecting the Social Security program, as well as most societal structures, is the aging of the population. Increased life expectancy and a decline in fertility rates have altered the age distribution of the population. In the mid-1960s, the end of the baby-boom era, the age distribution exhibited the pyramidal shape typical of a growing population, with the number of people at each age somewhat larger than the population a few years older (see figure 3.1, panel 1). As the baby-boom generation has aged, however, the pyramidal shape of the age distribution has taken on a more rectangular form, that is, with more equal numbers of young, middle-aged, and old individuals.

The legacy of the baby-boom generation will persist for many years to come. Baby boomers not only live longer but have had fewer children than past generations, and the continued decline in birth rates means that they will also have fewer grandchildren. Consequently, the age distribution will maintain an almost rectangular shape through about age 55 (see figure 3.1, panel 6). The sections that follow outline how longevity and fertility trends have shaped the age distribution.

Longevity Trends

Throughout much of the world, death rates steadily declined over the 20th century. Explanations for the decline in mortality vary. Control of infectious diseases, improved public health, and sophisticated medical technology have been important contributors. Many researchers also attribute part of the U.S. decline to Medicare's introduction in 1965, which gave nearly all senior citizens access to health care and may have stimulated advances in medical technology. Whether the declines in mortality, which have varied for men and women and for individuals at different ages, will continue to fall is debated widely among population experts. Some demographers anticipate further "rectangularization" in mortality, with death rates at the younger part of the age spectrum declining and most people surviving into old age. Wilmoth and Horiuchi (1999), however, argue that U.S. mortality rates are highly variable and cannot be easily anticipated. Lee and Tuljapurkar (1997) suggest that differences between death rates in the United States and other highly economically developed countries (especially Japan, which has

Figure 3.1 *Population by Age, Gender, and Year*

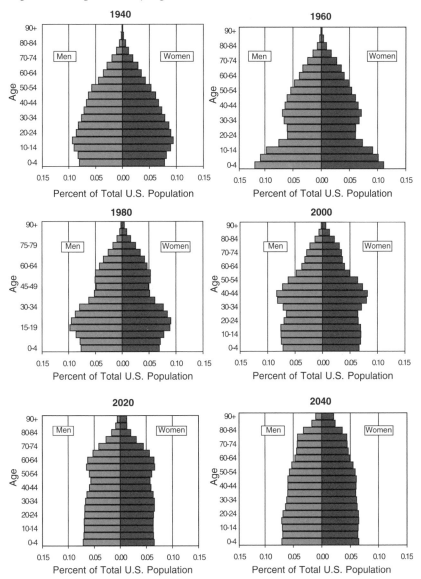

Source: Urban Institute tabulations from 1940, 1960, 1980 Decennial Census, and 2000, 2020, 2040 U.S. Bureau of the Census projections.

significantly lower mortality rates than the United States) suggest a like-lihood of rapid mortality declines in the coming decades.

Social Security Administration (SSA) actuaries project that the U.S. decline in age-adjusted mortality rates for both men and women will slow substantially from the rates of the second half of the 20th century (see table 3.1). Even with this assumption, life expectancy for individuals who reach age 65 is projected to increase markedly. In 1970, a 65-year-old woman could expect to live about another 17 years. By 2040, a 65-year-old woman is projected to live an additional 21 years. Although men's life expectancy will continue to lag women's, the increase in men's longevity is projected to be greater than that for women, causing the male-female mortality differential to decline. In 1970, a 65-year-old man could expect to live another 13 years or so; by 2040, mortality experts project a 65-year-old man will live 18 more years.

The expected increase in longevity will swell the 65-and-over population, with the very old making up an increasing portion of that group. In 2000, 11 percent of the over-65 population was 85-years-old or older. By 2040, that share is expected to grow to 18 percent. As long as the retirement age stays the same (and even if it rises slightly), the length of time that men and women will receive Social Security retirement will continue to increase, pushing the costs of the system up. At the same time, because Social Security benefits are indexed to prices after first receipt (rather than to wages, as they are at first receipt), the retired population, especially the oldest, will experience a decline in living standards relative to that of the working population.

Table 3.1 *Life Expectancy by Sex: 1970–2040*

	At Birth		At Age 65	
Year	Female	Male	Female	Male
1970	74.9	67.2	17.1	13.1
1980	77.5	69.9	18.4	14.0
1990	78.9	71.8	19.0	15.0
2000	79.6	73.9	19.2	15.9
2010	80.7	75.4	19.4	16.4
2020	81.1	76.4	19.8	16.9
2030	82.0	77.4	20.7	17.5
2040	82.7	78.3	21.0	18.1

Source: Board of Trustees (2001).

While the overall trend in life spans shows that all types of people are living longer, longevity at any point in time still differs by race and gender. Not only do women on average live longer than men, but whites live considerably longer than blacks. A significant number of black males do not survive to retirement age. In 1997, life expectancy at birth was 67 years for black men, compared with 74 years for white men and 80 years for white women. Although longevity is increasing in all racial groups, black men are more likely than women and members of other races to pay into Social Security without ever receiving a retired worker benefit. On average, white women receive Social Security benefits for the greatest number of years.

Trends in Hispanic mortality are less clear. Some researchers estimate that Hispanics have higher mortality rates than non-Hispanic whites (see, for example, Hayward and Heron 1999). Others suggest the opposite (Sorlie et al. 1993). The National Center for Health Statistics' (1995) estimates indicate that age-adjusted Hispanic death rates were 16 percent lower than those of the white population in the early 1990s.[1] Measurement errors may explain part of the discrepancy and may also account for other unusual patterns in mortality by race and ethnicity (Sorlie et al. 1992).

In addition to differentials by race, large mortality gaps, especially at younger ages, are apparent among different socioeconomic groups, with wealthier individuals on average living longer than poorer individuals (Kitagawa and Hauser 1973). Research by Hurd, McFadden, and Merrill (1999), which relies on data for the oldest segment of the over-65 population, suggests that the socioeconomic differential declines with age. Other researchers (McCoy, Iams, and Armstrong 1994; Manton, Stallard, and Corder 1997) present evidence that the differential may persist later into life. Socioeconomic differentials in mortality play an important role in determining the individual equity and progressivity of Social Security. Aaron (1977), Garrett (1995), Panis and Lillard (1996), and Caldwell et al. (1999) suggest that mortality rates have a potentially regressive effect on lifetime Social Security redistribution. Most researchers conclude that although mortality differentials dampen Social Security redistribution, they do not make it regressive (Cohen, Steuerle, and Carasso 2001).

Fertility Rates

The theory of demographic transition, formed by Davis et al. (1986) and others, posits that in industrialized nations, birth rates will fall to below replacement levels as mortality rates decline and children become less of an economic asset. Lower fertility rates reflect many other factors, including changing social attitudes and the greater availability of reliable birth control methods. The U.S. experience since the 1800s generally shows declining fertility rates, with the exception of the baby-boom period, when fertility rates soared. Drawing on data from Vital Statistics (Ventura et al. 2000) and estimates of the Social Security Administration (Board of Trustees 2001), figure 3.2 tracks the U.S. total fertility rate from 1930 to 2000.[2] The high fertility rates from 1940 to 1970 contrast sharply with the rates from 1970 through 1999. The Social Security Administration projects that the 2000 birth rate of 2.05 births per woman will decline slightly to 1.95 births per woman in 2014.

A decline in births today has huge implications for economic well-being tomorrow. Social Security is a pay-as-you-go system—that is, current workers support current beneficiaries. As the relatively large number of people born during the baby-boom period retire, they will be supported by people born during a lower fertility period. Indeed, experts project that the number of beneficiaries per worker will rise by more than 60 percent between 2000 and 2040 (see figure 3.3). This increase in beneficiaries per worker, along with increased life expectancy trends, is

Figure 3.2 *Total Fertility Rate by Year: 1930–2000*

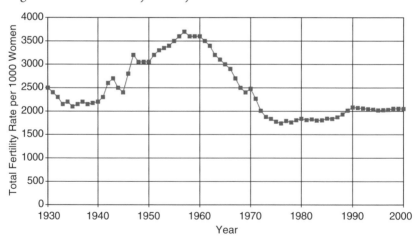

Source: Ventura, Stephanie J., Joyce A. Martin, Sally C. Curtin, T.J. Matthews, and Melissa M. Park (2000) and United States Bureau of the Census (1992).

Figure 3.3 *Number of Social Security Beneficiaries per 100 Covered Workers, by Year*

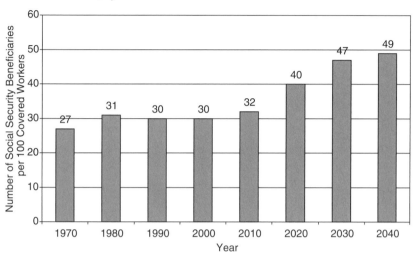

expected to increase the Social Security cost rate (benefits paid divided by payroll taxes) by almost 70 percent over the same time span. According to Social Security actuaries, payroll taxes will no longer cover expected Old-Age and Survivors Insurance and Disability Insurance (OASDI) and Medicare benefits after 2016, and Social Security trust fund balances will not cover all promised benefits after 2038 (Board of Trustees 2001). Social Security and Medicare already compete with other federal programs for government resources. Without reform, benefit cuts, increased taxes, or reduced spending on other government services will be necessary to cover benefit payments.

In addition to reducing the working-age population, low birth rates may also make some retirees more vulnerable to poverty in old age. Research has consistently shown the importance of interfamily transfers for well-being in old age. Families who are having fewer children today will have fewer children to help support them as they grow older.

While birth rates have declined since 1960, the proportion of children born out of wedlock has increased. From 1960 to 1998, the share of nonmarital births rose dramatically, from just over 5 percent to 33 percent. The increase in nonmarital births suggests that more children are being raised by single mothers. These mothers, who do not have the added benefit of a spouse's earnings to augment family income during their working years or to qualify them for a spousal benefit during retirement, are at greater risk of economic hardship throughout their lives. Zedlewski and Saha (this volume) describe the economic consequences of single parenthood on labor force participation and well-being in more detail.

The Changing Role of Marriage

Dramatic changes in family formation have occurred in the last four decades. Three family formation behaviors—marriage, cohabitation, and divorce—are critical to determining Social Security outcomes and adequacy. Eligibility for certain forms of Social Security benefits is explicitly based on marital status. Married couples, and divorced spouses married for at least 10 years, are eligible for Social Security benefits based on their own lifetime earnings or their spouse's—whichever is higher. This entitlement helps provide financial security to low-earning and nonworking spouses (primarily women) throughout retirement. Compared with families, who can generally spread risk among working-age members, single-headed households are more vulnerable to income losses due to earnings cuts, health problems, or other unforeseen events. Together, decreasing marriage rates and increasing cohabitation and divorce rates mean that more individuals will enter retirement without access to spousal benefits and at greater risk of hardship, particularly if hardships is defined as income well below the average.

Marriage Declines

Marriage rates have varied over time because of both demographic and behavioral changes. Between 1960 and 1970, the age-adjusted marriage rate, at about 100 marriages per 1,000 unmarried individuals, was fairly stable.[3] From 1970 to about 1988, the rate fell dramatically, to just over 50 marriages per 1,000 unmarried individuals of each sex (see figure 3.4). Since 1989, the rate has risen slightly and leveled off at 55 marriages per 1,000 unmarried individuals.

The recent declines in marriage rates have been accompanied by dramatic increases in nonmarital cohabitation. The number of unmarried-couple households more than tripled between 1978 and 1998, from

Figure 3.4 *Age-Adjusted Marriage Rates: 1957–1995*

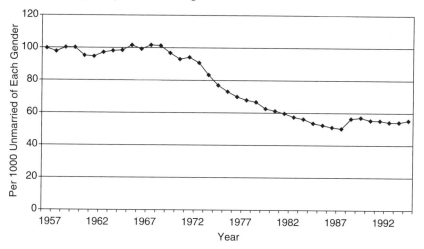

Source: Bell (1997).

1.3 million to 4.9 million (Bianchi and Casper 2000). In the late 1990s, three-fifths of recently married couples lived together before marriage (Bumpass and Lu 1999). Because entitlement to Social Security spousal benefits requires couples to be married for at least 10 years, the decline in marriage rates and the rise in cohabitation suggest that fewer women will be entitled to spousal benefits.

Divorce Rates

Divorce rates increased rapidly from 1960, peaked in 1979, and have remained flat since the mid-1980s (see figure 3.5). Much of the increase occurred as the baby-boom generation entered its prime divorce years, but age-specific divorce rates confirm that rates more than doubled in all age groups between 1960 and 1980 (see figure 3.6). Between 1980 and 1990, the age-adjusted divorce rate declined slightly (Bell 1997). Divorce rates are marked by significant differentials across groups. The likelihood of divorce decreases with age, income, and duration of marriage. Poor, less-educated individuals experience higher rates of divorce than do those who are more advantaged.

Social Security provides benefits to divorced spouses as long as a marriage lasted for 10 years. Of all divorces finalized in 1990, more

Figure 3.5 *Divorce Rates per 1000 Married Women Age 15 and Older, by Year: 1960–1990*

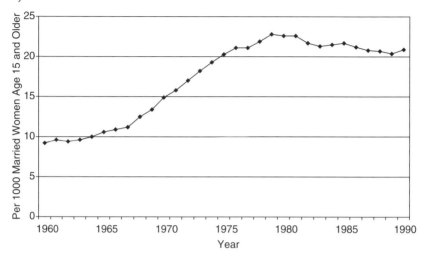

Source: Clarke (1995).

Figure 3.6 *Divorce Rates, by Age and Year, 1960–1990*

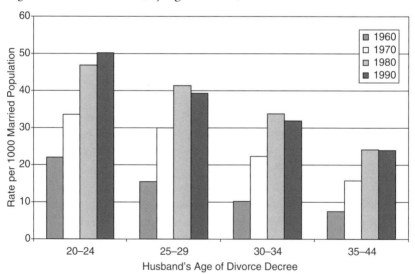

Source: Clarke (1995).

than 63 percent were among couples married fewer than 10 years, indicating that the majority of divorced spouses did not qualify for spousal Social Security benefits. The median duration of marriage for divorcing couples in 1990 was 7.2 years, longer than the median during the previous two decades, but still shy of the 10-year eligibility requirement (Clarke 1995).

As a result of trends in marriage, divorce, and cohabitation, a higher percentage of women are likely to enter retirement without having married or having been married only for a short time. With a greater percentage of women ineligible for spousal or survivors benefits in retirement, a greater share of older women could be at risk of poverty.

Changes in Work Patterns and Work Participation

Social Security benefits are based on lifetime earnings. Thus, changes in the pattern of work directly affect the adequacy and distribution of benefits. Four key trends are shaping the current and future workforce: increased participation among women, earlier retirement by men, a narrowing of the gap between men's and women's earnings, and increased inequality of earnings among both men and women.

Women's Labor Force Participation

Female labor force participation has risen dramatically over the last four decades in all age groups (see figure 3.7). While 37 percent of women age 20 to 64 worked in 1950, more than 71 percent worked by 1995. Women born between 1926 and 1945 led the way in changing female labor force participation (Fullerton 1999). After 1925, all cohorts of women born started working earlier than their predecessors and continued to work at higher rates at all ages. Indeed, the once-prevalent dip in participation throughout the childbearing years has all but disappeared (figure 3.8).

The increase in women's labor force participation has occurred mostly among mothers. For women with school-age children (ages 6 to 17), labor force participation increased from 44 percent in 1970 to 76 percent in 1995. For women with children under age 6, labor force participation increased from 29 percent in 1970 to 62 percent in 1995 (see figure 3.9). Women with no children, who mostly fall in the under-25 and over-55 age categories, have lower-than-average participation rates.

Figure 3.7 *Labor Force Participation Rates for 20- to 64-Year-Old U.S. Residents, by Gender and Year: 1950–1995*

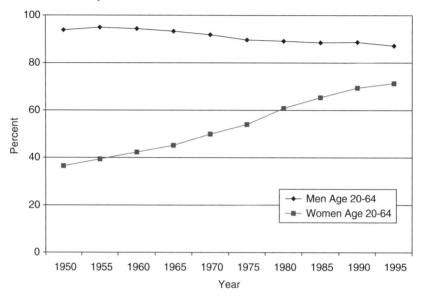

Source: U.S. Bureau of Labor Statistics (1999).

Figure 3.8 *Female Labor Force Participation Rates, by Age and Cohort*

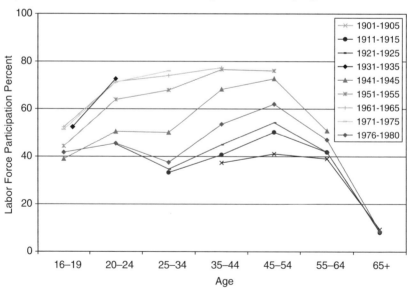

Source: The Urban Institute tabulations based on data from U.S. Bureau of Labor Statistics (1999).

Figure 3.9 *Female Labor Force Participation Rate, by Age of Youngest Child: 1970–1995*

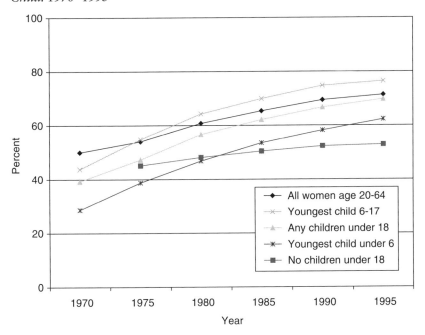

Source: Hayghe (1997).

Men's Labor Force Participation

Male labor force participation, especially among prime-age males, remains fairly high, but it has declined over the last four decades. In 1950, 94 percent of men age 20 to 64 worked, but by 1995, 87 percent of these men worked. This decrease in participation largely reflects work patterns among 55- to 64-year-olds; in this category, male labor participation declined from about 87 percent in 1950 (for those born in 1900) to 68 percent in 1998 (for those born in 1941), or by more than 20 percent (see figure 3.10). In addition to social and economic trends, the passage of various Social Security amendments have contributed to the reduction in male labor force participation (Fullerton 1999). For example, legislators changed the laws regulating disability benefits to make individuals under age 50 eligible for benefits beginning in 1960. Legislators also reduced the minimum retirement age from 65 to 62 for women in 1956 and for men in 1961 (see Berkowitz, this volume).

Figure 3.10 *Male Labor Force Participation Rates, by Age and Cohort*

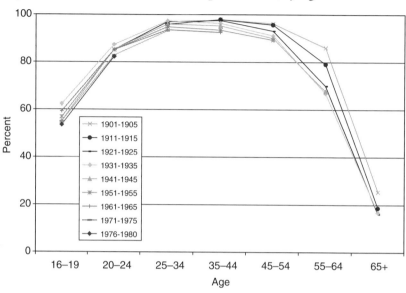

Source: Urban Institute tabulations based on data from U.S. Bureau of Labor Statistics (1999).

The labor force participation rate for women at all ages remains below that of men, but the gap has closed considerably. The Bureau of Labor Statistics assumes that female labor force participation will continue to increase in all age groups, although at a decreasing rate, until 2015, and that the participation rates for men will remain stable. The aging of the U.S. population, however, is expected to offset the increase in the number of working women. Thus, although the size of the overall labor force will grow, the aggregate participation rate (including individuals over age 65) is projected to fall 6 percent (from 67.1 percent to 63.2 percent) between 1998 and 2025 (Fullerton 1999).

The participation rates among older individuals could change as the retirement age goes up. In 2000, the normal retirement age for Social Security started to rise from 65 to 67 in two month increments. The normal retirement age will hold steady at age 66 for people born from 1943 to 1954. For people born after 1954, the age will increase incrementally until 2022, so that the normal retirement age will be 67 for individuals born in 1960 or later (Committee on Ways and Means 2000).[4] Social Security retirement benefits will still be available to qualified individuals

at age 62, but with an increasing actuarial reduction as the normal retirement age rises to 67. As long as the normal retirement age is 65, the maximum actuarial reduction for benefits received at an earlier age is 20 percent. This maximum rate, however, increases to 30 percent when the
normal retirement age is 67. Greater benefit reductions, along with
increases in longevity, could encourage increased labor force participation among older individuals. The increase in the actuarial reduction,
however, may put people in poor health and in physically demanding
jobs at higher risk of poverty in old age.

The Gap in Men's and Women's Earnings

Although men continue to earn more than women, the gap has closed
significantly. In 1950, women's average real earnings were about 44 percent of men's (figure 3.11). By 1995, the differential had shrunk to 66 percent of men's earnings. Unlike women's average real earnings, which have
increased in almost every year since 1940, men's real earnings increased
from 1940 to 1970, but have declined since then. Part of the decline in

Figure 3.11 *Median Wage and Salary Earnings for Workers by Gender:
1940–1995*

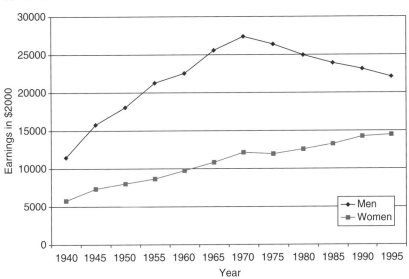

Source: Social Security Administration, Office of Research, Evaluation and Statistics (1999).

men's average earnings reflects the effect of baby-boom workers entering the early part of their careers, when earnings tend to be low. But, on average, men in all age groups have experienced real earnings declines beginning in the 1970s (see figure 3.12). Age-specific earnings for women have generally increased every year for all groups, except younger workers, who experienced a slight decline in real earnings in the 1990s, in part because of the 1990–91 recession and increased college enrollment (Hayghe 1997) (see figure 3.13).

Because of the increasing female labor force participation and earnings, the share of total earnings attributable to women has risen over time. In 1950, men earned 82 percent of total wage and salary income (U.S. Bureau of the Census 1998). By 1998, this proportion had declined to just under 64 percent. And with more women working more years at higher wages, women have increasingly qualified for their own Social Security benefits. In 1960, 44 percent of women age 62 and over received Social Security based in part on their own earnings (either as a worker only or as a worker *and* wife or widow).[5] By 1998, this share had risen to more than 65 percent (see figure 3.14) (Social Security Administration

Figure 3.12 *Median Wage and Salary Earnings of Male Workers, by Age: 1940–1995*

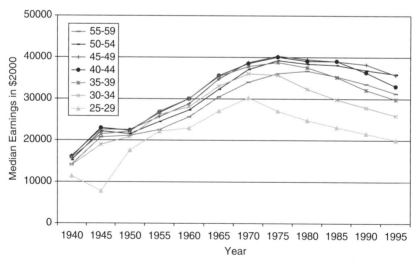

Source: Social Security Administration, Office of Research, Evaluation and Statistics (1999).

Figure 3.13 *Median Wage and Salary Earnings of Female Workers, by Age: 1940–1995*

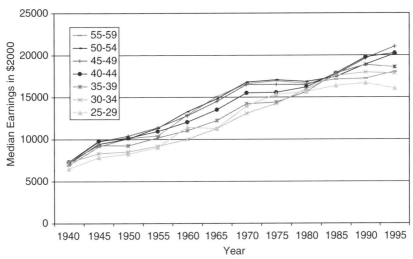

Source: Social Security Administration, Office of Research, Evaluation and Statistics (1999).

Figure 3.14 *Distribution of Female Social Security Beneficiaries Age 62 and Older, by Type of Benefit and Dual Status: 1960–1999*

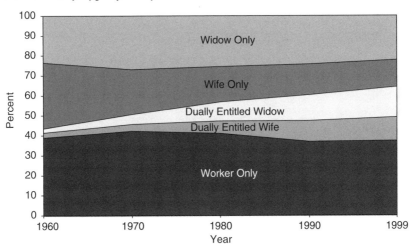

Source: Social Security Administration, Office of Research, Evaluation and Statistics (1999).

1999). Given the higher labor force participation and greater earnings of women today, this share will certainly increase over time. As women's earnings increase relative to their husbands', and as more women enter retirement unmarried, more women will qualify for worker-only benefits. The proportion of women receiving only a widow's or a wife's benefits should thus dwindle over time. For more information on different types of benefits and the implications for women's well-being, see Favreault, Steuerle, and Sammartino (this volume).

Income Inequality

Over the past three decades, family income has become increasingly unequal, with the richest segment of the population accounting for an increasing share of income. Jones and Weinberg (2000) show that, based on gini coefficients, the inequality among families at all income levels fell between 1947 and 1968, but it has increased almost every year since (see figure 3.15).[6] Although some alternative measures show income inequality decreasing in the 1970–80 period, most measures show a clear rise in

Figure 3.15 *Gini Coefficient for Family Income: 1947–1998 and Earnings of Men and Women Full-Time, Year-Round Workers: 1967–1998*

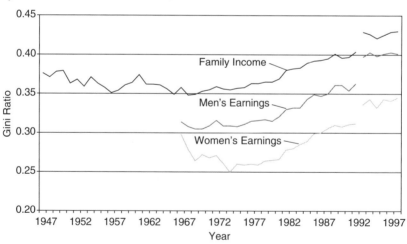

Source: Jones and Weinberg (2000).
Note: The discontinuity between 1992 and 1993 are due to inconsistencies in the CPS that make the series not comparable.

income inequality from 1980 to 1990 (Jones and Weinberg 2000). The increase in income inequality mirrors trends in earnings, the largest component of income. For male full-time year-round workers, earnings inequality remained fairly stable between 1967 and 1980, and then increased rapidly. Female full-time, year-round workers experienced a decline in earnings inequality between 1967 and 1974, but the level has since increased.

Increased income inequality has implications for family poverty. As the U.S. economy has grown, wage growth has typically outpaced price growth. Poverty thresholds are updated by prices, so real wage growth should reduce poverty, at least for workers. This may not happen, however, if wages are stagnant or fall in real terms for some segments of the population. Increased inequality is a concern when families at the bottom of the income distribution are falling further behind.

The decreased inequality between 1959 and 1969 mostly came from gains by those in the bottom half of the income distribution (Karoly and Burtless 1995). Between 1969 and 1979, people in the lower end of the income distribution experienced little to no gain, and between 1979 and 1989, people in the bottom 30th percentile experienced real income losses. Low-skilled men, in particular, experienced serious reductions in real wages. The rise in inequality partly reflected several factors, including an increase in the number of single-headed families, greater male earnings inequality, and increased female earnings in high-income families.

Another reason for the widening disparity in earnings is increased returns to education. Earnings for men with a college degree have historically been above those of men with less education, and the gap widened beginning in the 1980s (see figure 3.16). In 1980, full-time wage and salaried men age 25 and older with a college degree earned about 30 percent more than the same men with only a high school degree. Men with less than a high school degree earned about 22 percent less than men with a high school degree. These differences have widened over time, and in 1999, college-educated, male, full-time workers earned 68 percent more than high-school-educated men, and men with less than a high school education earned about 47 percent less than high-school-educated men. As with men, college-educated women have historically earned more than lesser-educated women, and the returns to education have widened since the 1980s.

Since 1940, when the Census Bureau first collected information on education, educational attainment has increased (see figure 3.17). The

Figure 3.16 *Median Earnings of Full-Time Workers by Educational Attainment and Gender: 1979–1999*

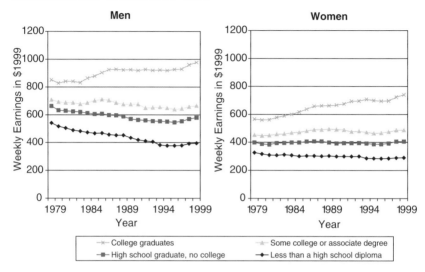

Source: U.S. Department of Labor, Bureau of Labor Statistics (2000).

Figure 3.17 *Percent Distribution of Years of School Completed by 25- to 34-Year-Olds: Selected Years 1940 to 1999*

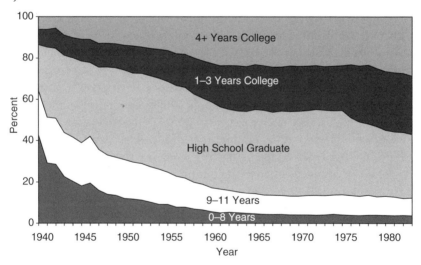

Source: U.S. Census Bureau (2000a).

proportion of 25- to 34-year-olds with less than a high school education has fallen dramatically, decreasing from 64 percent in 1940 to 12 percent in 1999. The proportion with a college degree rose from 6 percent in 1940 to 29 percent in 1999.

More women now pursue a higher education than in the past, and they make up the majority of college attendees and college degree recipients (see figure 3.18). The increase in female educational attainment is an important factor in the rise in family income inequality, because people with similar educational attainment tend to marry (Mare 1991; Winkler 1998; Qian, 1998; Pencavel 1998; Lewis and Oppenheimer 2000). As women's education levels have increased, so has the percentage of men with a college education who have married college-educated women. In 1940, 46 percent of college-educated (13 or more years of education) newlywed husbands married college educated wives. By the mid-1980s, the proportion had increased to 74 percent (Mare 1991). College-educated women also have higher earnings potential, especially in light of increased female labor force participation. Together, the increase in marriages between college-educated partners and the higher returns to education have led to a greater correlation between husbands' and wives' earnings among higher-educated couples. Cancian

Figure 3.18 *Percent of Individuals Age 25 to 35 with a Bachelor's Degree or Higher, by Gender: Selected Years 1940 to 2000*

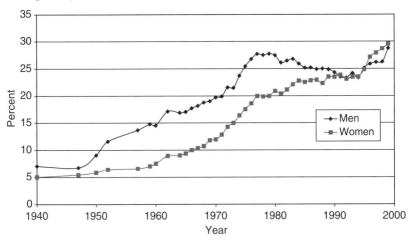

Source: U.S. Census Bureau (2000a).

and Reed (1999) report an increasing correlation of all husbands' and wives' earnings beginning in the early 1970s.

The Composition of the American Family

The nature of the American family has changed dramatically since Social Security began. In 1940, almost 70 percent of families were headed by a working husband and a nonworking wife. By 1998, this fraction had dropped to about 15 percent (see figure 3.19). The traditional male-breadwinner family has been largely replaced by the dual-worker family. At the same time, greater longevity, earlier retirement by men, and receipt of Social Security benefits have allowed retired workers to remain independent, increasing the proportion of elderly families maintaining their own households. Increased divorce rates and out-of-wedlock births have increased the proportion of single adults heading up working families, particularly among female heads of household. Although the increased labor force participation of married women has made dual-earner couples commonplace, such couples still make up less than 50 percent of all families.

Figure 3.19 *Percent of Families, by Composition and Employment Status: 1940–1998*

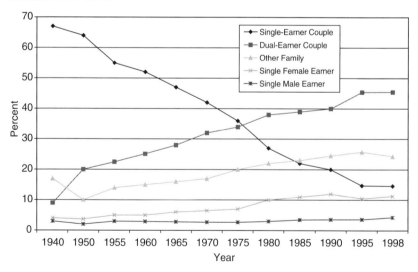

Source: Hayghe (1990); U.S. Bureau of Labor Statistics (1999).

Not surprisingly, among working families, dual-earner couples earn more than single-earner couples, and single-earner couples earn more than single-headed families. But the median real family income of two-earner couples has increased, while the median real family income of single-earner families has decreased, particularly among male-headed families (see figure 3.20). These differences reflect the choices families make about the number of hours they work, differences in education, and other factors, but the rising disparity in earnings today imply a rising disparity in retirement income tomorrow.

Because Social Security pays benefits to families according to earnings, the changing composition of the family and its members' wage profiles will change the future size and distribution of benefits. Benefits to couples will likely increase as couples' incomes rise. Given current marriage rates, however, couples will become a smaller share of the retired population. Benefits to single men, whose earnings are declining, will likely fall relative to overall average earnings. Single males, however, will continue to make up a small share of families in retirement. Benefits for single women will likely stay about the same. Despite greater labor force participation among women, single women's incomes have

Figure 3.20 *Median Family Income by Family Type and Year: 1967–1997*

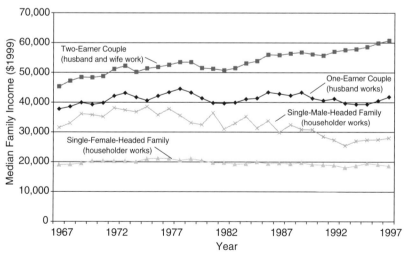

Source: U.S. Bureau of Labor Statistics (1999; 1989).

stayed fairly flat. Married women have made the most earnings gains in recent years.

Many married women, however, will continue to see no added Social Security benefit from their work contribution. Social Security pays a couple 1.5 times the higher-income worker's benefit (in most cases, the husband's) or the sum of the husband's and wife's worker benefit. Because wives' earnings tend to be below their husbands', even after their earnings gains, many working women will receive the same Social Security benefit they would have received without any earnings (see Favreault, Sammartino, and Steuerle, this volume). While Social Security benefits of married women may not increase much, greater labor force participation of wives should increase pension and the other savings of future married retirees.

The Future Retiree Population

Numerous trends will shape the profile of future generations of retirees and their benefit needs. In 2040, Social Security beneficiaries will have dramatically different characteristics than today's beneficiaries. To gauge these trends' combined effects, and to evaluate the characteristics of the future retiree population at the individual level, we employ microsimulation model techniques using an updated version of the Urban Institute's DYNASIM model, originally built by Orcutt, Caldwell, and Werthheimer (1976). Microsimulation models, while not perfect predictors, provide a good measure of the direction of important effects and the sensitivity of outcomes to certain assumptions.

In constructing our profile of future retiree populations, we simulate birth, education, marriage, divorce, labor force participation, wages, hours worked, retirement, disability, and death over the 1992–2040 period. In addition to applying different assumptions to measure the robustness of our results, we manipulate Social Security program rules to see how certain changes influence the distribution of benefits supplied to future retiree populations. We begin our simulation in 1992, using data from the Survey of Income and Program Participation. Our model projects population changes, earnings, Social Security benefits, pension income, private savings, and home equity out to 2040, just beyond the year that the Social Security trust fund will be sufficient to pay all benefits promised under the current system (Board of Trustees 2001). See the appendix for more details about the simulations.

Table 3.2 shows the age distribution of the population at or above the normal retirement age, assuming the retirement age increases as scheduled from 65 to 67 between 2000 and 2002. Over time, the model projects that the retirement-age population will be older, more educated, more equally divided in the number of men and women, and more racially diverse than it was in the 1990s. It will also likely consist of more individuals who are divorced or were never married than in previous decades. Note, in particular, that the proportion of this population age 80 and older should rise from 21 percent in 1992 to 35 percent in 2040.

The simulations show interesting patterns in projected earnings histories. First, most families' estimated average indexed earnings (AIE) fall below projected economywide average earnings. The earnings distribution as a whole, however, is expected to shift to higher earnings levels as more women with higher wages enter the labor force. Second, the share of women with more than 30 years of Social Security–linked earnings should increase dramatically. Increased earnings and years of employment mean that more women will receive higher Social Security benefits and more of these benefits will be based on their own earnings over time.

To calculate AIE, we divide individuals' annual earnings between the ages of 25 and 62 by the economywide average earnings.[7] We then calculate the average AIE for the couple. For a single individual with lifetime earnings equal to economywide average earnings, AIE equals 1. For a married couple with a nonworking wife and a husband with lifetime earnings equal to the average, the AIE equals 0.5. In 1992, 34 percent of the retirement age population had projected AIE below 0.32; 7 percent had AIE above 1.01. By 2040, only 10 percent of retirees will have AIE in the lowest group, and 32 percent will have AIE in the highest group. This finding reflects women's increasing contribution to family earnings and the effect of greater earnings inequality.

The simulations project that women will dramatically increase their number of years of Social Security–covered employment. In 1992, only 7 percent of retirement-age women had 30 years or more of Social Security–covered earnings. By 2040, this proportion will likely increase to 60 percent (34 percent of the retirement population including men). While women will continue to have fewer years of Social Security–covered earnings than men, they are more likely to be eligible for Social

Table 3.2 *Percent of Individuals At or Above the Normal Retirement Age, by Individual Characteristics and Year*

	Year					
	1992	*2000*	*2010*	*2020*	*2030*	*2040*
Total	100	100	100	100	100	100
Educational Attainment						
High School Dropout	38	31	22	14	11	10
High School Graduate	49	53	57	59	60	57
College Graduate	13	16	21	27	29	33
Race and Ethnicity						
Non-Hispanic White	86	83	81	78	75	72
Hispanic	4	5	7	9	10	12
Non-Hispanic Black	8	8	8	9	10	11
Other	2	3	4	5	5	5
Average Indexed Earnings (AIE)						
<.32	34	32	27	19	13	10
.32–.57	23	23	20	20	20	19
.57–.77	25	20	18	18	19	19
.77–1.01	12	15	18	18	19	20
1.011	7	9	16	24	28	32
Gender						
Male	41	41	42	43	43	44
Female	59	59	58	57	57	56
Gender by Years of Covered Earnings (age 25–62)						
Male, 0–9 Years	5	4	3	3	2	1
Male, 10–29 Years	18	11	5	5	4	4
Male, 30 Years or More	18	27	33	35	37	39
Female, 0–9 Years	25	20	13	7	4	4
Female, 10–29 Years	30	31	31	28	23	18
Female, 30 Years or More	4	8	14	23	30	34
Marital Status and Gender						
Married Men	31	29	29	28	27	25
Widowed Men	5	7	7	6	7	8
Divorced Men	3	4	5	5	5	5
Never-Married Men	2	2	2	3	4	6
Married Women	25	21	21	23	22	20
Widowed Women	25	29	26	21	20	21
Divorced Women	4	6	8	10	10	10
Never-Married Women	4	2	2	3	5	6

Table 3.2 *Percent of Individuals At or Above the Normal Retirement Age,*
by Individual Characteristics and Year (Continued)

	Year					
	1992	*2000*	*2010*	*2020*	*2030*	*2040*
Gender by Social Security						
Benefit Type						
Male Uncovered	3	1	2	3	1	1
Male Worker	38	40	39	40	42	43
Female Uncovered	3	2	2	2	1	1
Female Worker Only	19	21	22	26	29	31
Female Dual Worker	6	8	10	10	8	6
Female Dual Survivor	8	12	14	15	15	15
Female Wife Only	9	7	4	2	1	1
Female Survivor Only	13	10	7	3	2	2
Age						
65–69	33	28	27	28	19	16
70–74	27	26	26	30	30	26
75–79	20	22	19	20	23	23
80 and older	21	24	28	22	28	35

Source: Urban Institute tabulations of DYNASIM3.
Notes: AIM is the average earnings from age 25 to age 62 divided by the year-specific average earnings. It is then averaged between husbands and wives. The normal retirement age increases from 65 in 1992 to 67 in 2040.

Security benefits based, in part, on their own earnings—with a rise in female beneficiaries from 60 percent in 1992 to 95 percent in 2040.

Despite the rise in the normal retirement age, many retirees are still expected to collect Social Security at age 62. In 1998, about 57 percent of men and 64 percent of women collected Social Security at age 62, although the normal retirement age was 65 (Social Security Administration 1999, tables 6.A4 and 6.D3).[8] The simulations project that for individuals born between 1961 and 1965, about 49 percent of men and 57 percent of women will begin to collect Social Security benefits at age 62. The combination of continued early retirement and increased longevity will increase the average length of retirement. Under the current Social Security system, the increasing length of retirement means that benefit outlays will increase dramatically over the coming decades.

Although more women are projected to be working at higher wages over time, the persistent, though decreasing, gap between male-female

Table 3.3 *Average per Capita Family Social Security Income Divided by the Economy-Wide Average Earnings for Individuals At or Above the Normal Retirement Age, by Individual Characteristics and Year*

	Year					
	1992	*2000*	*2010*	*2020*	*2030*	*2040*
Total	0.27	0.27	0.26	0.27	0.28	0.28
Educational Attainment						
High School Dropout	0.25	0.24	0.21	0.20	0.21	0.21
High School Graduate	0.28	0.28	0.26	0.26	0.27	0.26
College Graduate	0.28	0.32	0.31	0.32	0.34	0.34
Race and Ethnicity						
Non-Hispanic White	0.28	0.28	0.27	0.28	0.29	0.29
Hispanic	0.20	0.21	0.21	0.22	0.24	0.25
Non-Hispanic Black	0.21	0.23	0.21	0.23	0.23	0.24
Other	0.19	0.21	0.21	0.24	0.28	0.29
Average Indexed Earnings (AIE)						
<.32	0.24	0.22	0.18	0.17	0.17	0.17
.32–.57	0.26	0.26	0.24	0.23	0.23	0.21
.57–.77	0.28	0.29	0.27	0.26	0.26	0.25
.77–1.01	0.30	0.32	0.31	0.30	0.30	0.29
1.011	0.31	0.36	0.37	0.37	0.37	0.36
Gender						
Male	0.26	0.28	0.28	0.28	0.28	0.28
Female	0.27	0.27	0.25	0.26	0.28	0.28
Gender by Years of Covered Earnings (age 25–62)						
Male, 0–9 Years	0.24	0.16	0.08	0.07	0.08	0.07
Male, 10–29 Years	0.28	0.28	0.22	0.21	0.22	0.21
Male, 30 Years or More	0.25	0.30	0.31	0.31	0.30	0.29
Female, 0–9 Years	0.25	0.25	0.21	0.19	0.20	0.20
Female, 10–29 Years	0.29	0.27	0.25	0.25	0.25	0.25
Female, 30 Years or More	0.28	0.30	0.30	0.31	0.31	0.31
Marital Status and Gender						
Married Men	0.25	0.26	0.26	0.26	0.27	0.26
Widowed Men	0.31	0.35	0.32	0.33	0.32	0.31
Divorced Men	0.31	0.32	0.33	0.33	0.31	0.30
Never-Married Men	0.23	0.29	0.30	0.30	0.28	0.27
Married Women	0.27	0.27	0.26	0.27	0.28	0.28
Widowed Women	0.29	0.28	0.26	0.27	0.29	0.29

Table 3.3 *Average per Capita Family Social Security Income Divided by
the Economy-Wide Average Earnings for Individuals At or Above the Normal
Retirement Age, by Individual Characteristics and Year (Continued)*

	Year					
	1992	2000	2010	2020	2030	2040
Divorced Women	0.24	0.22	0.22	0.25	0.27	0.29
Never-Married Women	0.22	0.24	0.20	0.22	0.25	0.26
Gender by Social Security Benefit Type						
Male Worker	0.28	0.29	0.29	0.30	0.29	0.28
Female Worker Only	0.29	0.26	0.24	0.26	0.28	0.29
Female Dual Worker	0.30	0.30	0.28	0.27	0.27	0.26
Female Dual Survivor	0.32	0.31	0.30	0.31	0.31	0.31
Female Wife Only	0.26	0.25	0.23	0.24	0.23	0.22
Female Survivor Only	0.26	0.25	0.23	0.24	0.23	0.22
Age						
65–69	0.24	0.25	0.27	0.27	0.28	0.29
70–74	0.27	0.27	0.27	0.28	0.29	0.29
75–79	0.29	0.27	0.25	0.28	0.29	0.28
80 and older	0.28	0.30	0.26	0.25	0.26	0.27

Source: The Urban Institute tabulations of DYNASIM3.

Notes: AIM is the average earnings from age 25 to age 62 divided by the year-specific average earnings. It is then averaged between husbands and wives. The normal retirement age increases from 65 in 1992 to 67 in 2040.

earnings will likely keep married women from realizing higher total family benefits from Social Security (see table 3.3). Because so many women receive benefits partly on the basis of their own earnings history and partly on their spouse's earnings record, only women whose own primary insurance amount (PIA) exceeds half of their husband's PIA during their husbands' lifetimes receive extra income from Social Security. And only widows whose PIA exceeds their former husband's PIA get any extra income from Social Security from their own work. Our simulations show that average per capita family income from Social Security for married women was 27 percent of the economywide average earnings in 1992. This percentage is projected to increase slightly, to 28 percent in 2040.

Never-married and divorced women eventually realize larger gains in their Social Security income. Initially, all per capita benefits decline because of a number of factors. Besides composition changes, the share of surviving beneficiaries whose Social Security payment was based on the older, more generous average monthly wages compared with the more recent average indexed monthly earnings (AIME) formula declines. Second, the increase in the normal retirement age increasingly reduces benefits for a larger share of beneficiaries. After these initial declines, benefits for never-married women should increase from 20 percent of average earnings in 2010 to 26 percent of average earnings in 2040, and benefits for divorced women increase even more.

Family Well-Being in Retirement

Social Security is an important source of income in retirement, but it is only one aspect of family assets. Other important components are private pensions, private savings, and earnings (both earnings in retirement and earnings of other family members). DYNASIM3 projects each of these assets separately to calculate total family income in retirement and finds that the economic well-being of the overall future retired population should improve relative to that of current retirees. While this improvement is inevitably the result of projected income growth, some subgroups, especially single women and high school dropouts, will continue to see relatively high poverty rates. Moreover, if we adjust for economic growth, DYNASIM3 projects that these subgroups will stay in the same relatively poor position they held in the 1990s, and sometimes will be worse off.

We measure well-being in terms of family total income relative to the family's poverty threshold. Poverty thresholds take into account the economies of shared resources, including the accommodations enjoyed by married couples compared with those of singles.[9] Poverty-adjusted income allows us to compare the well-being of a married couple and a single individual on an equivalent basis.

DYNASIM3 projects that the ratio of average family income relative to poverty for all individuals at or above the normal retirement age will increase about 50 percent from 1992 to 2020 (from 3.14 to 4.65 times poverty) and about 75 percent by 2040 (to 5.45 times poverty) (see table 3.4). The persistent increases in wages relative to prices (leveling out at 1 percent per year according to the Board of Trustees' 2001 economic assumptions), along with the increase in female labor force participation and earnings, cause family retirement income to rise relative to the poverty threshold, which is indexed only by prices.

The simulations show that as the lifetime earnings of women rise, families with women realize more economic gains than do families without women. Economic status will improve faster for divorced women than for never-married women. The average poverty-adjusted income of divorced women is projected to rise from 1.73 times poverty in 1992 to 4.25 times poverty in 2040, almost a 150 percent increase. The poverty-adjusted income of never-married women will increase only 91 percent (from 2.21 to 4.23) between 1992 and 2040. This difference reflects the dramatic compositional changes among the female population over time. Today, never-married women are more likely to have had children, to be less educated, and to have more interruptions in their work histories than in the past. By contrast, divorced women today are more likely to have worked and to have access to a pension than in the past. Poverty-adjusted income of never-married men, however, will increase only 61 percent (less than the rate of wage growth) between 1992 and 2040. This relatively small advance reflects the decline in men's real earnings after 1970, as women's earnings increased.

While retirement income rises in the simulations, its distribution among lifetime earnings quintiles becomes increasingly uneven. Families in the top lifetime earnings quintile had, on average, 2.35 times the poverty-adjusted income of families in the bottom lifetime quintile (4.85 divided by 2.06) in 1992. This ratio is projected to increase to 2.97 by 2020 and to 2.86 by 2040. Still, the increased female earnings and the progressive Social Security payment formula make the retirement income distribution more equal than it would be otherwise. Largely because of recent trends, the poverty-adjusted income of families in the bottom 20 percent of the earnings distribution is expected to fall relative to that of other families.

DYNASIM3 projects that absolute poverty rates for individuals at or above the normal retirement age will fall from 12 percent in 1992 to 6 percent in 2020, and to 3 percent in 2040. Although the rates will decline, never-married women, high school dropouts, and older retirees remain at risk of absolute poverty in the future.

When poverty thresholds are shown to increase with wage growth, relative poverty rates remain at about 12 percent over the coming

Table 3.4 *Average Family Income as a Percent of Poverty and Percent of Retirees Below Absolute and Relative Poverty, by Individual Characteristics and Year*

	Family Income/Poverty			Percent in Absolute Poverty			Percent in Relative Poverty[a]		
	1992	2020	2040	1992	2020	2040	1992	2020	2040
All	3.14	4.65	5.45	12	6	3	12	13	12
Education									
Less than High School	2.24	2.97	4.05	20	17	9	20	30	26
High School Graduate	3.28	4.18	4.73	8	5	3	8	13	15
College Graduate	5.37	6.51	7.09	5	1	1	5	3	3
Race									
White non-Hispanic	3.30	4.88	5.74	9	4	2	9	10	9
Black non-Hispanic	1.95	3.42	4.09	32	15	9	32	26	28
Hispanic	2.33	3.67	4.94	33	12	5	33	22	18
Other	3.06	5.00	5.38	27	7	3	27	15	13
Gender									
Male	3.66	5.35	6.13	9	2	2	9	6	8
Female	2.78	4.12	4.93	15	9	4	15	18	16
Marital Status by Gender									
Male Married	3.97	6.04	7.42	5	1	0	5	3	2
Male Widowed	2.73	4.35	4.67	17	5	2	17	12	14
Male Divorced	2.82	3.74	4.22	19	5	3	19	14	18
Male Never-Married	2.62	3.79	4.23	22	6	5	22	17	18
Female Married	3.70	5.57	6.65	5	1	0	5	3	2
Female Widowed	2.13	3.15	3.83	21	11	4	21	25	22

Female Divorced	1.73	3.17	4.25	37	16	6	37	32	23
Female Never-Married	2.21	3.27	4.23	22	22	11	22	32	26
Age									
65–69[b]	3.73	5.48	6.71	9	3	3	9	7	8
70–74	3.17	4.94	6.11	11	5	2	11	11	8
75–79	2.87	4.39	5.37	14	6	2	14	14	12
80–84	2.47	3.87	4.77	16	8	3	16	17	15
85+	2.40	2.91	4.13	20	15	5	20	28	20
Average Family Lifetime Earnings Quintile (ages 25 to 62)									
1	2.06	2.57	3.02	28	23	12	28	40	38
2	2.51	3.34	4.10	14	5	1	14	16	15
3	2.88	4.32	5.16	10	1	1	10	6	6
4	3.42	5.38	6.35	7	1	0	7	2	2
5	4.85	7.63	8.63	4	0	0	4	1	1

Source: The Urban Institute projections.

Notes: Total family income includes Social Security, pension income, family earnings, and co-resident income. It excludes imputed rental income.

[a] Relative poverty rates are based on 1992 wage adjusted poverty thresholds.

[b] This table includes all individuals at or above the normal retirement age.

decades. Older retirees are still more likely than younger retirees to live in absolute or relative poverty, and single women are more likely than married women and men to be impoverished. Never-married women, high school dropouts, and retirees in the bottom lifetime earnings quintile have higher relative poverty rates in 2040 than in 1992. Although all long-term projections are tentative, these results show that Social Security is not using its substantial growth in benefits and revenue to improve the relative standing of more vulnerable groups over time.

While certain subgroups remain economically vulnerable, their contribution to overall poverty depends on their size relative to the overall population. High school dropouts have higher poverty rates than more educated retirees. However, because high school dropouts make up a smaller share of the future population, they contribute 0.9 percent to absolute poverty in 2040, while high school graduates contribute 1.7 percent to absolute poverty in 2040 (not shown in table). Even though the poverty rates of female widows decline substantially over time, and the group declines as a share of the retired population, these women still contribute more to poverty than do all other marital groups in all years. Despite dramatic gains in female earnings and labor force participation, women will continue to be about twice as likely as men to be both in absolute and in relative poverty.

Conclusion

The retired population will consist of many more individuals and will make up a greater share of the total population in the coming decades. Future retirees will be more educated than past retirees, fewer individuals will enter retirement married, and the retiree population will be more racially and ethnically diverse.[10] Overall, women retirees, especially women who have had children, will have gained more experience in the labor force, and thus will have contributed a greater amount to family income. As the traditional single-earner couple typical in the 1940s becomes increasingly rare, the presence of more dual-earner couples and single-earner families will change the makeup of family resources and Social Security benefit entitlement.

Despite increased female labor force participation and earnings, working women are not expected to realize increasing returns on contributions to the Social Security system, even as they pay substantially more into the system. This paradox reflects the continued gap in women's earnings relative to men's, as well as the larger share of women who will enter retirement with no claim to a spousal or survivor benefit.

The percentage of women qualifying for retirement benefits based on their own earnings will increase rapidly. Projections indicate that 90 percent or more of all retired women will receive at least some benefit based on their own earnings. Nonetheless, the percentage of widows receiving a full or partial survivor benefit should continue to be higher than those who do not. A woman's own retirement benefit would need to exceed her deceased spouse's benefit in order to disqualify her from being dually entitled. In the next few decades, relatively few women are expected to have higher lifetime earnings than their spouses.

Family earnings are projected to increase at a faster rate than inflation, causing retirement incomes to rise. Retirement income is also projected to become more unevenly distributed over time. As family incomes rise, *absolute* poverty rates are expected to decline, but *relative* poverty rates are not expected to drop. Moreover, despite Social Security's current schedule to distribute thousands of extra dollars per person over the next few decades, some subgroups continue to have both high absolute and relative poverty rates. In particular, families headed by high school dropouts; by never-married, divorced, or widowed women; and by never-married men remain at risk of being poor.

APPENDIX 3A

Dynamic Microsimulation as a Method for Integrating Trends and Differentials

DYNASIM3 is a dynamic microsimulation that integrates all of the important trends and differentials in life course processes that we describe.[11] DYNASIM3 starts with a self-weighting sample from the 1990 to 1993 Survey of Income and Program Participation (SIPP). Synthetic earnings records, which enable the user to calculate Social Security benefits, are attached to each person's record using a statistical matching algorithm described in Smith, Scheuren, and Berk (2001). The model then ages this population year by year using parameters estimated from longitudinal data sources. DYNASIM3's mortality parameters, for example, are estimated from the National Longitudinal Mortality Study and calibrated to Vital Statistics estimates. The appendix table describes other model parameters. The model contains a detailed Social Security benefit calculator that we use to calculate the implications of current law and distributional consequences of various reform proposals.

DYNASIM3 projects pension and asset income using the same methodology as that used in the Social Security Administration's MINT model. A fuller discussion of the various components in MINT is available in Toder et al. (1999), Panis and Lillard (1999), and Butrica et al. (1999). A more detailed comparison of MINT and DYNASIM is available in Toder et al. (2000).

Appendix Table 3.A1 *Core Processes Modeled in DYNASIM3*

Process	Data	Form and predictors
Birth	Estimation: NLSY; VS; Target: OACT	Seven equation marital status-specific parity progression model; predictors include age, marriage duration, time since last birth; uses vital rates after age 39; sex of newborn assigned by race; probability of multiple birth assigned by age and race
Death	Estimation: NLMS; VS; target: OACT	Three equations; time trend from Vital Statistics 1982–1997; includes socioeconomic differentials; separate process for the disabled based on age, sex, and disability duration derived from Zayatz (1999)
Schooling	NLSY, CPS (Oct. 1995)	Ten cross-tabulations based on age, race, sex, and parent's education
Leaving Home	NLSY	Three equations; family size, parental resources, and school and work status are important predictors
First Marriage	NLSY	Eight equations; depend on age, education, race, earnings, presence of children (for females); use vital rates at older ages
Remarriage	VS	Table-lookups, separated by sex for widowed and divorced

Appendix Table 3.A1 *Core Processes Modeled in DYNASIM3 (Continued)*

Process	Data	Form and predictors
Divorce	PSID	Couple level outcome; depends on marriage duration, age and presence of children, earnings of both spouses
Labor Supply and Earnings	Estimation: PSID; NLSY Target: OACT	Separate participation and hours decisions, wage rates for 16 age-race-sex groups; all equations have permanent and transitory error components; some wage equations correct for selection bias; key predictors include marital status, education level, age splines, region of residence, disability status, job tenure, whether currently in school, unemployment level, and education level interacted with age splines. Also number and ages of children.
Retirement		Unrevised model from DYNASIM2
Disability	PSID	Separate entry and exit equations; incorporate socioeconomic differences

Source: Author's compilation from surveys listed in notes.
Notes: CPS = Current Population Survey. NLMS = National Longitudinal Mortality Study. NLSY = National Longitudinal Survey of Youth. OACT = Intermediate assumptions of the OASDI Trustees. PSID = Panel Study of Income Dynamics. VS = Vital Statistics.

NOTES

1. National Center for Health Statistics (1995).
2. The total fertility rate for the period equals the sum of the age-specific fertility rates from the first age that a woman is generally considered able to have a child (14) to an estimate of the latest age (45). One can interpret the total fertility rate as the number of children the average woman could expect to have if she experienced current period fertility over the entire span of her childbearing years.
3. Age-adjusted marriage rates are a weighted average of the age-specific rates (Bell 1997).
4. Committee on Ways and Means U.S. House of Representatives (2000, Table 1-20).
5. An individual may be entitled to Social Security benefits both as a worker, based on his or her own earnings, or as a dependent of another worker. Social Security does not pay the full amount of both benefits. Rather, it first pays the individual's worker benefit and then supplements the payment to the extent the worker benefit is below the dependent benefit. Such individuals are considered *dually entitled.*
6. The discontinuity between 1992 and 1993 is due to changes in the survey that make the series not comparable between periods.

7. $AIE = \dfrac{1}{62 - 25 + 1} \displaystyle\sum_{y=b+25}^{b+62} \dfrac{E_y}{A_y}$ where b is the year of birth, E is social security covered earnings, A is the economywide average earnings, and y is the year. Note that this measure differs from what the Social Security Administration calls "AIME," in that the computation does not include any dropout years and does not allow workers to substitute earnings accrued before age 25 or after age 62.

8. This figure includes people who first receive survivor benefits at age 60 or 61.

9. In 1999, the poverty threshold for a married couple age 65 and older was $10,075. For a single individual age 65 and older, the poverty threshold was $7,990 (U.S. Census Bureau 2000b). These poverty thresholds are updated each year for increases in the current price index for urban workers (CPI-U).

10. Immigration rates have steadily increased since the 1940s. In addition, the changing mix of countries of origin and increasing diversity, will change the population.

11. Zedlewski (1990) describes how DYNASIM evolved through the late 1980s. A new version of DYNASIM is under development.

REFERENCES

Aaron, Henry J. 1977. "Demographic Effects on the Equity of Social Security Benefits." In *The Economics of Public Services: Proceedings of a Conference Held by the International Economic Association at Turin Italy,* edited by Martin S. Feldstein and Robert P. Inman (151–173). London: MacMillan.

Bell, Felicitie C. 1997. *Social Security Area Population Projections: 1997.* Actuarial Study no. 1/2. Baltimore, Md.: Office of the Chief Actuary, Social Security Administration.

Bianchi, Suzanne M., and Lynne M. Casper. 2000. "American Families." *Population Bulletin* 55 (4): 1–44.

Board of Trustees. 2001. *2001 Annual Report of the Board of Trustees of the Federal Old-Age and Survivors Insurance and Disability Insurance Trust Funds.* Washington, D.C.: Board of Trustees.

Bumpass, Larry, and Hsien-Hen Lu. 1999. "Trends in Cohabitation and Implications for Children's Family Contexts in the U.S." Paper presented at the 1998 Annual Meetings of the Population Association of America. CDE WP-98-15. Madison, Wisc.: Center for Demography and Ecology: University of Wisconsin.

Butrica, Barbara A., Steven H. Sandell, and Howard M. Iams. 1999. "Using Data for Couples to Project the Distributional Effects of Social Security Policy Changes." *Social Security Bulletin* 62 (3): 20–27.

Caldwell, Steven B., Melissa Favreault, Alla Gantman, Jagadeesh Gokhale, Laurence J. Kotlikoff, and Thomas Johnson. 1999. "Social Security's Treatment of Postwar Americans." In *Tax Policy and the Economy,* edited by James M. Porteba, (109–148). Cambridge, Mass.: MIT Press.

Cancian, Maria, and Deborah Reed. 1999. "The Impact of Wives' Earnings on Income Inequality: Issues and Estimates." *Demography* 36 (2): 173–184.

Clarke, Sally C. 1995. "Advance Report of Final Divorce Statistics, 1989 and 1990." *Monthly Vital Statistics Report* 43 (9, March supplement).

Cohen, Lee, C. Eugene Steuerle, and Adam Carasso. 2001. "Social Security Redistribution by Education, Race, and Income: How Much and Why?" Paper presented at the Third Annual Joint Conference of the Retirement Consortium. May 17–18. Washington, D.C.

Committee on Ways and Means, United States House of Representatives. 2000. *Overview of Entitlement Programs: 2000 Green Book Background Material and Data on Programs within the Jurisdiction of the Committee on Ways and Means.* Washington, D.C.: U.S. Government Printing Office.

Davis, Kingsley, Mikhail S. Bernstam, Rita Ricardo-Campbell, eds. 1986. *Below Replacement Fertility in Industrial Societies: Causes, Consequences, Policies. Population and Development Review, A Supplement to Volume 12.* New York: The Population Council.

Fullerton, Howard N., Jr. 1999. "Labor Force Participation: 75 Years of Change, 1950–98 and 1998–2025." *Monthly Labor Review,* December: 3–12.

Garrett, Daniel M. 1995. "The Effects of Differential Mortality Rates on the Progressivity of Social Security." *Economic Inquiry* 33 (3): 457–475.

Hayghe, Howard V. 1990. "Family Members in the Work Force." *Monthly Labor Review,* March: 14–19.

———. 1997. "Developments in Women's Labor Force Participation." *Monthly Labor Review,* September: 41–46.

Hayward, Mark D., and Melonie Heron. 1999. "Racial Inequality in Active Life among Adult Americans." *Demography* 36 (1): 77–91.

Hurd, Michael D., Daniel McFadden, and Angela Merrill. 1999. "Predictors of Mortality among the Elderly." National Bureau of Economic Research Working Paper W7440.

Jones, Arthur F., Jr., and Daniel H. Weinberg. 2000. "The Changing Shape of the Nation's Income Distribution." *Current Population Reports,* P60-204. June. Washington, D.C.: Government Printing Office.

Karoly, Lynn A., and Gary Burtless. 1995. "Demographic Change, Rising Earnings Inequality, and the Distribution of Personal Well-Being, 1959–1989." *Demography* 32 (3): 379–405.

Kitagawa, Evelyn M., and Philip M. Hauser. 1973. *Differential Mortality in the United States: A Study in Socioeconomic Epidemiology.* Cambridge, Mass.: Harvard University Press.

Lee, Ronald, and Shripad Tuljapurkar. 1997. "Death and Taxes: Longer Life, Consumption, and Social Security." *Demography* 34 (1): 67–81.

Lewis, Susan K., and Valerie K Oppenheimer. 2000. "Educational Assortative Mating across Marriage Markets: Non-Hispanic Whites in the United States." *Demography* 37 (1): 29–40.

Manton, Kenneth G., Eric Stallard, and Larry Corder. 1997. "Education-Specific Estimates of Life Expectancy and Age-Specific Disability in the U.S. Elderly Population 1982 to 1991." *Journal of Aging and Health* 9 (4): 419–450.

Mare, Robert D. 1991. "Five Decades of Educational Assortative Mating." *American Sociological Review* 56 (February): 15–32.

McCoy, John L., Howard M. Iams, and Timothy Armstrong. 1994. "The Hazard of Mortality among Aging Retired and Disabled-Worker Men: A Comparative Sociodemographic and Health Status Analysis." *Social Security Bulletin* 57 (3): 76–87.

National Center for Health Statistics. 1995. "Annual Summary of Births, Marriage, Divorces, and Deaths: United States, 1994." *Monthly Vital Statistics Report* 43 (13).

———. 1999. *Vital Statistics of the United States, 1993, Volume 1, Natality.* Hyattsville, Md.: U.S. Department of Health and Human Services.

Orcutt, Guy H., Steven Caldwell, and Richard Wertheimer II. 1976. *Policy Exploration through Microanalytic Simulation.* Washington, D.C.: Urban Institute Press.

Panis, Constantijn W. A., and Lee A. Lillard. 1996. "Socioeconomic Differentials in the Returns to Social Security." RAND Labor and Population Program Working Paper Series.

———. 1999. "Near-Term Model Development." Final Report to the Social Security Administration. Santa Monica, Cal.: RAND.

Pencavel, John. 1998. "Assortative Mating by Schooling and the Work Behavior of Wives and Husbands." *AEA Papers and Proceedings* 88 (2, May): 326–329.

Qian, Zhenchao. 1998. "Changes in Assortative Mating: The Impact of Age and Education, 1970–1990." *Demography* 35 (3): 279–292.

Smith, Karen E., Fritz Scheuren, and Jillian Berk. 2001. "Adding Historical Earnings to the Survey of Income and Program Participation (SIPP)." In *2001 Proceedings, Statistical Computing Section,* American Statistical Association *[CD-ROM].*

Social Security Administration, Office of Research, Evaluation and Statistics. 1999. *Annual Statistical Supplement, 1999* to the *Social Security Bulletin.* Washington, D.C.: Social Security Administration.

Sorlie, Paul D., Eric Backlund, Norman J. Johnson, and Eugene Rogot. 1993. "Mortality by Hispanic Status in the United States." *JAMA* 270 (20): 2464–2468.

Sorlie, Paul D., Eugene Rogot, and Norman J. Johnson. 1992. "Validity of Demographic Characteristics on the Death Certificate." *Epidemiology* 3 (2): 181–184.

Toder, Eric, Cori Uccello, John O'Hare, Melissa Favreault, Caroline Ratcliffe, Karen Smith, Gary Burtless, and Barry Bosworth. 1999. *Modeling Income in the Near Term—Projections of Retirement Income through 2020 for the 1931–1960 Birth Cohorts.* Final Report to the Social Security Administration. Washington, D.C.: The Urban Institute.

Toder, Eric, Melissa Favreault, John O'Hare, Diane Rogers, Frank Sammartino, Karen Smith, Kent Smetters, and John Rust. 2000. "Long-Term Model Development for Social Policy Analysis." Final Report to the Social Security Administration. Washington, D.C.: The Urban Institute.

U.S. Bureau of the Census. 1992. "Households, Families, and Children: a 30-Year Perspective." *Current Population Reports Population Characteristics,* P23-181. Washington, D.C.: Government Printing Office.

———. 1994. "How We're Changing Demographic State of the Nation: 1995." *Current Population Reports Special Studies Series,* P23-188. Washington, D.C.: Government Printing Office.

———. 1998. "Measuring 50 Years of Economic Change Using the March Current Population Survey." *Current Population Reports,* P60-203. Washington, D.C.: Government Printing Office.

———. 2000a. "Educational Attainment in the United States, March 1999." *Current Population Reports* P20-528. Washington, D.C.: Government Printing Office.

————. 2000b. "Poverty in the United States: 1999." *Current Population Reports.* P60-210. Washington, D.C.: Government Printing Office.

U.S. Bureau of Labor Statistics. 1989. *Handbook of U.S. Labor Statistics,* 3rd ed. Washington, D.C.: U.S. Bureau of Labor Statistics.

————. 1999. *Handbook of U.S. Labor Statistics,* 3rd ed. Washington, D.C.: U.S. Bureau of Labor Statistics.

————. 2000. "Highlights of Women's Earnings in 1999." Report 943, May. Washington, D.C.: U.S. Bureau of Labor Statistics.

Ventura, Stephanie J., Joyce A. Martin, Sally C. Curtin, T. J. Matthews, and Melissa M. Park. 2000. "Births: Final Data for 1998." *National Vital Statistics Report* 48 (3): 1–99.

Wilmoth, John R., and Shiro Horiuchi. 1999. "Variability of Age at Death Within Human Populations." *Demography* 36 (4): 475–495.

Winkler, Anne E. 1998. "Earnings of Husbands and Wives in Dual-Earner Families." *Monthly Labor Review,* April: 42–48.

Zayatz, Tim. 1999. *Social Security Disability Insurance Program Worker Experience.* Actuarial Study no. 114, June. Baltimore, Md.: Office of the Chief Actuary of the Social Security Administration.

Zedlewski, Sheila R. 1990. "The Development of the Dynamic Simulation of Income Model (DYNASIM)." In *Microsimulation Techniques for Tax and Transfer Analysis,* edited by Gordon H. Lewis and Richard C. Michel, (109–136). Washington, D.C.: Urban Institute Press.

4

Social Security and Single Mothers

Options for "Making Work Pay" into Retirement

Sheila R. Zedlewski
Rumki Saha

Many American families today consist of a single parent (usually a mother) and her children. Never-married parents constitute an increasing share of this group, especially among low-income families. Historically, Social Security protection has been relatively limited for these families. A single parent relying on welfare was not part of the paid labor force, and her children went without Social Security protection in the event of her disability or death. In addition, many of these women did not have enough calendar quarters of Social Security coverage to earn a significant Social Security retirement benefit for themselves. Instead, many relied on means-tested benefits provided by Supplemental Security Income (SSI) for the aged, blind, and disabled.

The strong economy and recent policies to "make work pay" have increased the number of single mothers working and should increase Social Security insurance protection for single parents and their children. State and federal welfare reform efforts have increased employment within this population by requiring work after two years for most welfare recipients and by limiting the number of years mothers can spend on welfare. For example, between 1995 and 1999, labor force participation rates for single mothers with children increased by an unprecedented 16 percentage points (U.S. Census Bureau 2000, table 653). The continuation of these trends will increase single mothers' quarters of covered employment, and, consequently, increase their protection against income loss in the event of severe disability or retirement. The insurance will also protect children in case of their mothers' disability or death.[1]

This chapter explores the potential implications of recent labor market trends and legislation affecting low-income single-mother families for their long-run retirement income adequacy. We estimate Social Security benefits for a small cohort of single mothers who had some experience with the welfare system between 1968 and 1993 using data from the University of Michigan's Panel Study of Income Dynamics (PSID). We also estimate benefits for these women under alternative labor market and welfare experience assumptions that follow those recently observed for younger mothers. Using PSID, we observe 25 years of earnings and welfare experience for the cohort of women born between 1942 and 1946. Because our sample sizes are small, however, the results can only be considered illustrative. We show retirement benefits under current Social Security law and under two alternatives (see table 4.1). The first alternative increases benefits for women who take time out of the labor force to care for their children. The second provides a minimum benefit for all workers with substantial years in covered employment at low wages. The second proposal is designed to increase Social Security benefits for those who "play by the rules," but do not achieve an adequate retirement benefit. Projected benefits include Social Security and SSI.

Our results suggest that single mothers with limited (up to 5 years) and moderate (6 to 10 years) welfare use should do better under Social Security in the future if recent trends in labor market participation con-

Table 4.1 *Six Simulated Scenarios for Single Mothers with Welfare Experience*

	Benefit Simulations		
Earnings History Assumption	*Social Security, Current Law*	*Alternative I: New Minimum*	*Alternative II: Up to 5 years of Additional Wage Credits for Child Care Years*
Historical			
Wage Pattern	X	X	X
Increased Work	X	X	X

tinue. However, single mothers with extensive welfare use (11 years or more) are a group that still raises significant concern, even under the assumption of increased labor market participation. Under current law, they will need to turn back to welfare when they retire, or try to live on a Social Security benefit of 60 percent of poverty if they retire at age 62. Their benefits still fall substantially below poverty even if they can continue working until the normal retirement age of 66. The minimum-benefit alternative would target this group particularly well, increasing their retirement benefit to 85 percent and 117 percent of poverty, depending on whether they retired at age 62 or 66, respectively.

Background: Single Mothers and Trends in Labor Force Participation

Single mothers, especially those who have children out of wedlock as teenagers, are one of the most disadvantaged groups in our society. They tend to have high poverty rates relative to other families (in 1998, 30 percent were poor, compared with 10 percent of all families[2]); work less because of single-parent child care responsibilities and low education status; typically receive little or no child support from the noncustodial parent; and at least historically, rely on welfare as their primary means of support. The size of this group swelled during the 1980s and mid-1990s, suggesting that a growing proportion of women will arrive at retirement without enough covered earnings to receive an adequate Social Security benefit. However, more recently, government policies and changing societal norms appear to be having a positive effect on these trends. The rise in out-of-wedlock childbearing has at least leveled off,[3] and new government policies have focused on increasing single mothers' labor force participation and child support.

Still, single-mother families make up an increasing share of all American families. The percentage of children living in single-parent families, usually with a single mother, has risen sharply over the past few decades—from 13 percent in 1970 to 32 percent in 1998 (Council of Economic Advisers 1999). While part of the increase has been due to high divorce rates, more recently, the share of single-mother families has increased because of a rise in out-of-wedlock childbearing. For example, the percentage of births to unmarried mothers rose from 5 percent in 1960 to 18 percent in 1980 and 33 percent by 1994 (U.S. Department of

Health and Human Services 2000). This trend has leveled off, however, remaining around 33 percent through 1999.

According to recent research, single-parent, never-married families are quite common, with half of the 15 million children living in single-mother families born to unmarried parents (Halpern 1999). The same study showed that never-married mothers with children had higher poverty rates than all single-mother families (60 percent compared with 48 percent). In addition, never-married mothers were less likely to have year-round full-time work.

A recent surge in labor force participation among single, never-married female-headed families could counter this trend and potentially *increase* the share of women arriving at Social Security age with limited covered earnings in the future. While the labor force participation rates of mothers in this group were relatively flat during the 1980s and early 1990s, dramatic increases have been evident since 1995 (figure 4.1). The labor force participation rate for single, never-married mothers with children under age 6 increased by 15 percentage points, from 53 percent in 1995 to 68 percent in 1999. Increases in participation rates for single, never-married mothers with older children were also steep, rising from 67 percent in 1995 to 83 percent in 1999. Labor force participation rates

Figure 4.1 *Labor Force Participation: Single, Never-Married Mothers versus all Mothers, 1980–1999*

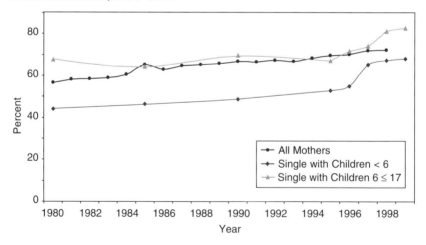

Source: U.S. Census Bureau (2000, table 653); U.S. Bureau of Labor Statistics (1999).
Note: The never-married category excludes mothers who are widowed, divorced, or separated, but are living alone.

for widowed, separated, or divorced single mothers (not shown separately in figure 4.1) rose somewhat less dramatically than those for never-married single mothers—from 75 percent in 1995 to 80 percent in 1999. The trend in participation for married mothers during the same period was relatively flat.

Unemployment rates (measuring the percentage of all women in the labor force who were unable to find work) have declined steeply, from a high of nearly 30 percent in 1985 for single, never-married mothers with children under age six to about 14 percent in 1999 (figure 4.2). Unemployment rates for single, never-married mothers with older children were somewhat lower, about 10 percent in 1999.

Several factors have contributed to the increase in labor force participation among single mothers, including increases in the earned income tax credit (EITC), the hike in the minimum wage, welfare reform, expansions in Medicaid coverage to low-income children not tied to welfare, and expansions of child care programs for low-income parents. In recent years, the tighter labor market has made employers more willing to hire welfare recipients and has made it easier for single mothers to find jobs.

Studies have shown that the 1993 expansion of the EITC and welfare reform have been particularly significant in increasing labor force

Figure 4.2 *Unemployment Rates for Single, Never-Married Mothers versus All Single Women, 1980–1999*

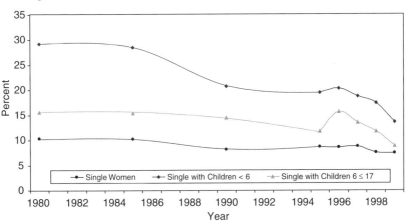

Source: U.S. Census Bureau (2000, table 653).

Note: The never-married category excludes mothers who are widowed, divorced, or separated, but who are living alone.

participation rates for single mothers (Council of Economic Advisors 1999). In fact, one recent study concluded that as much as 60 percent of the increase in employment of single mothers since 1984 can be attributed to expansions in the EITC (Meyer and Rosenbaum 1999). The EITC explained 33 percent of the 1992–96 increase in annual employment of this group. The real value of the EITC increased by 38 percent for workers with one child and by 116 percent for those with two or more children between 1992 and 1998. A worker with one child received a credit of 34 cents per dollar of earnings up to a maximum of $2,271 in 1998. A family with two or more children received 40 cents per dollar up to a maximum of $3,756. (These amounts are indexed to the Consumer Price Index.)

Federal welfare reform enacted Temporary Assistance for Needy Families (TANF) in August 1996. TANF substantially strengthened work requirements for parents in the welfare system relative to its predecessor, Aid to Families with Dependent Children (AFDC). The 1996 federal law requires most parents to participate in work activities within two years of receiving welfare benefits. Many states go beyond this federal minimum by requiring participation immediately unless the mother is caring for a child under three months of age.[4] The federal law also limits welfare assistance to five years during an individual's lifetime. Some states have adopted even shorter lifetime benefit time limits, although a handful guarantee some state-funded assistance beyond the five-year limit (often in the form of vouchers). These new rules, coupled with new policies to increase the payoff from working and a strong economy throughout much of the 1990s, led to plummeting welfare rolls. Nationwide, the number of families on welfare dropped by one-half between 1994 and 1999.

Implications for Social Security Benefits

The long-run implication of the increasing labor force participation of single mothers is that they will have substantially longer lifetime attachments to the labor force than their predecessors. Many should also have substantially higher Social Security benefits when they reach retirement age. However, the long-term Social Security payoff from working is not totally clear because many of these women are still likely to have a significant number of years without earnings, and most, when they do work, earn relatively low wages. The benefit formula, which is constructed to replace a higher share of the wages of low-wage workers than higher-wage workers, does tilt benefits toward these women. Loprest (1999; 2001) has published the only nationally representative portrait of two cohorts of women—those who left welfare between 1995 and 1997 and those who left between 1997 and 1999. She found that about two-thirds of single mothers were working in both cohorts and that those who were working earned about $7.00 per hour (in 1999 dollars). More than two-thirds of employed former welfare recipients worked 35 hours per week or more.

RETIREMENT BENEFITS. Social Security was designed to reward long-term work, and it provides a significantly higher replacement rate for low-wage workers than for higher-wage workers. Social Security's progressivity benefits never-married single mothers (because of their relatively low wages). However, historically, many of these single mothers have had a significant number of adult years outside the labor force caring for children and, in many cases, relying on welfare as a means of support. While recent trends should improve this outcome, current statistics still indicate that many single, never-married mothers will have some years out of the labor force.

Social Security benefits are calculated based on average earnings during most of a worker's adult years—generally including annual taxable earnings attained after age 21, or 1950, if later, and up until the worker reaches age 62, less five dropout years. (Earnings in years before age 21 or after reaching age 62 can count by replacing zero or low earnings years.) Average earnings before age 61 are indexed to reflect the growth in average earnings levels. For an individual first eligible to receive benefits in 2000, the full benefit (or primary insurance amount) is equal to 90 percent of the first $531 of average indexed monthly earnings, plus 32 percent of the next $2,675, plus 15 percent of the remainder over $3,202.

Workers who retire before the full retirement age (in 2000, early retirement for cohorts born in 1938 was 65 and 2 months) receive a reduced benefit to account for additional benefit payments. Early retirement is common among workers—for example, 75 percent of retired women received benefits with a reduction for early retirement in 1999 (Social Security Administration 2000a, table 5B.8)—and can make a significant difference in retirement income adequacy for single mothers with potentially low primary insurance amounts. For individuals who retired at age 62 before 2000, the reduction was 20 percent. The reduction will increase to 30 percent by 2022 (as the normal retirement age increases from 65 to 67). The reduction declines proportionately with each additional year of benefit deferral.

Workers with low earnings but steady attachment to the workforce over most of their adult years may qualify at retirement for monthly benefits based on a special minimum computation. This formula does not depend on average earnings but on the number of covered years above a specified amount. In 1998, the special minimum formula provided a maximum benefit of $567 per month for workers with 30 years of earnings meeting the threshold and $284 per month for workers with 10 years of earnings meeting the threshold. These benefits amount to 87 and 44 percent of poverty for an elderly person, respectively. The threshold amount is 15 percent of the annual taxable maximum—for example, an annual earnings requirement of $8,055 in 1999.

DISABILITY INSURANCE. While the focus here is primarily on retirement income, it is important to remember that additional work in covered employment will qualify more single, never-married mothers for disability benefits. Workers qualify for disability insurance if they are fully insured and meet Social Security's test of "substantial recent work activity."[5] At ages 21 through 31, a special insurance status requires a minimum number of credits (quarters of coverage) equaling the number of calendar years elapsing between age 21 and the year the individual becomes disabled. For example, a disabled worker would meet the eligibility test at age 30 if she acquired nine credits. Full insurance status for persons becoming disabled at ages older than 31 requires having 20 credits from the 40-quarter period that ends with the onset of disability (for example, working 5 out of the last 10 years). The minimum number of credits required to earn a disability insurance benefit (for workers under age 24) is six. Benefits for the disabled are calculated based on earnings averaged over the number of calendar years elapsing after age 21, or 1950, if later, and up to the year of first eligibility, less up to five dropout years.[6] Disabled workers receive 100 percent of their primary insurance amount.

SURVIVORS BENEFITS. If a covered worker dies before becoming fully insured, he or she needs six quarters of coverage over the 13 years preceding his or her death to leave a survivor benefit. Thus, with increasing labor force participation, more single, never-married mothers will gain insurance coverage for their children (until age 18 or 19 if in secondary school), but only in the unlikely event that they die.

Additional Protection from Supplemental Security Income

SSI provides a floor of protection for those who become disabled or reach age 65 and have very low wages or relatively few credits. It has served as a safety net for many women who do not qualify for an adequate Social Security benefit. SSI benefits for an individual equal 76 percent of the poverty threshold for a person age 65 or older (the threshold was $8,200 in 2000).[7] SSI also disregards $20 of an individual's monthly Social Security benefit. That is, the total SSI and Social Security benefit increases to about $6,470 per year (79 percent of poverty).[8] The $20 "disregard" was set at a fixed level in 1972 and has eroded in real value over time. In current 2000 dollars the original disregard would be about $80 per month (Social Security Administration 2000b).

SSI also requires beneficiaries to pass an assets test. Individuals' financial assets cannot exceed $2,000.[9] The assets test was increased only once since the inception of the program in 1972 (from $1,500 to $2,000 for an individual). Had the financial assets threshold been indexed with the cost of living since 1972, it would be about $6,000 (Social Security Administration 2000b).

The number of aged SSI beneficiaries has been declining. In 1982, they accounted for 40 percent of the caseload compared with 20 percent in 1998 (Ibid). Fewer elderly individuals qualify for SSI because Social Security benefits tend to rise with growth in the economy until they are paid out, while SSI benefits, which are indexed to inflation, do not. In addition, as mentioned earlier, the asset limits and unearned income disregards have not been indexed with the consumer price index and discourage many elderly from applying for benefits. In fact, the participation rate is relatively low for the elderly. For example, the Urban Institute's Transfer Income Model estimated a participation of 62 percent for aged singles in 1998.[10]

The Wage Histories of Single, Never-Married Mothers

In our analysis, real wage histories are used to calculate Social Security benefits for an actual cohort of women with characteristics similar to those of women who have been the focus of recent policies to encourage work. We selected women who have children and some experience with welfare and who were not married a sufficient number of years to qualify for a Social Security spousal benefit. These women will need to rely on their own wage credits to earn a Social Security benefit that will provide them with a reasonable standard of living in retirement. We base Social Security benefits on the historical pattern of labor force participation for this group and simulate an alternative earnings history scenario that assumes increased work effort consistent with more recent trends.

We compare the Social Security benefits of this group under current law to benefits under two alternatives that should increase their retirement benefits. The first alternative is modeled after the Kolbe-Stenholm minimum benefit proposed in H.R. 1793. The new minimum benefit is $7,818 in 1998 (set at the poverty threshold for an elderly person in nominal 1998 dollars). The benefit is price indexed until 2010, and each year thereafter the benefit is wage indexed. Individuals receive 100 percent of the minimum after 40 years of work, and the amount is prorated depending on the number of years of covered work. When fully phased in, workers who have at least 20 years of work (80 quarters) receive 60 percent of the minimum benefit and receive an additional 2 percent of the minimum for each additional year of work. Since the women in the age profile examined would retire at age 66 in 2011 (or at age 62 in 2007), we show the effect of this type of minimum benefit by assuming that it was fully phased in by 1998. That is, the benefit is wage indexed after 1998, and workers can qualify for the full or partial minimum as outlined earlier.

The second alternative is modeled after the proposal of former Vice President Gore to offset low or zero earnings during years spent caring for a child. This alternative grants individuals caring for children younger than six credits of one-half the average Social Security wage for up to five years, if it is higher than their own covered earnings.

We calculate Social Security benefits under the three alternatives—current law, the minimum benefit, and credits for child care years—for historical and alternative wage profiles. The alternative wage profiles assume that mothers have a maximum of five years on welfare and some probability of working in those years during which they historically had zero earnings. We also compare benefits to the SSI benefit guarantee and show these comparisons, assuming retirement at age 62 and age 66. Note that the normal retirement age for this group will be age 66 in 2011, since the normal retirement age will begin slowly increasing in 2001 until it reaches age 67 in 2022. The SSI eligibility age for the elderly, however, remains age 65. Table 4.1 summarizes the set of benefit options.

The comparisons show the likely Social Security benefits for a group of women who have relied on welfare to some extent during their adult years. In addition to comparing their benefits with the SSI benefit guarantee, the analysis shows how well alternative Social Security benefits target this particular group. It also presents estimates of the retirement benefit payoff likely from the additional work effort expected among future, younger cohorts of never-married single mothers. Also considered is the extent to which new patterns of employment will increase retirement benefit adequacy and reduce their future reliance on SSI. Finally, the analysis explores whether changes to the Social Security benefit structure and/or changes in the SSI program will be required to ensure an adequate retirement income at least for some of these women.

Data

We examine lifetime earnings histories of single mothers who do not qualify for a spousal benefit and have had some experience with welfare during their adult years to highlight the current pattern of Social Security benefit protection for this group. Social Security benefit qualifications of single mothers are difficult to examine in the context of large models such as the Social Security Administration's Modeling Income in the Near Term (MINT) and the Urban Institute's Dynamic Simulation of Income model, version 3 (DYNASIM3) because they represent a relatively small proportion of all women, and they historically have had unusual lifetime labor market experience that is difficult to capture in models designed to simulate the labor market experiences of all women. We rely instead on the Panel Study of Income Dynamic (PSID), which provides the demographic and economic characteristics of a sample of women, including their marital histories, whether children were in the family, their annual earnings, and whether the family received benefits from AFDC.

The University of Michigan's PSID began in 1968 as a longitudinal study of individuals (men, women, and children) as well as respondents' family units.[11] The survey addresses various economic and demographic data as well as sociological and psychological factors. The PSID began with a nationally representative sample of 3,000 U.S. households plus an oversample of 2,000 low-income households; respondents have been re-interviewed every year. Members of the original 1968 sample, including children who have since become adults, are observed throughout the years despite changes in the family unit, such as divorce or the presence of a new spouse. Information is gathered on the respondent as well as on all current co-residents.

Attrition has been low among PSID respondents, and re-contact efforts have been very successful.[12] Consequently, the sample size has continued to grow over the years. In 1990, approximately 7,000 core households were surveyed, and the number rose to 8,700 in 1995. By 2000, the PSID had collected data on more than 50,000 individual respondents over its 28-year history.[13]

The analysis focuses on the age cohort of women born between 1942 and 1947 because we could follow them from age 22 to 26 in 1968 through age 47 to 51 in 1993. This time span allows us to take advantage of all of the available years of the PSID for a group of women in their prime earnings years. An unweighted total of 403 women fell in this age cohort on the PSID. Of those, 331 (82 percent) had raised a child, and only 56 women (14 percent) were unlikely to qualify for a spousal benefit—i.e., they did not have a marriage lasting at least 10 years, and they were not married at the time they were interviewed in 1993. (We included currently married women in the potential spousal benefit group even if they had not already accumulated 10 years of marriage, assuming that most would eventually qualify for a spousal benefit.)

We further divided the group of single mothers who did not qualify for a Social Security spousal benefit into those with limited, moderate, and high welfare use. About half (27 observations) of the women in this group had some welfare experience during their prime-age years. Limited experience was defined as up to 5 years on welfare, moderate as 6 to 10 years on welfare, and high as more than 10 years on welfare. Of those with some welfare experience, 44 percent (12 observations) were in the limited use group; 30 percent (8 observations) were in the moderate use group; and 26 percent (7 observations) were in the high use group.

Methods

These sample observations formed the basis of synthetic wage profiles for single-mothers in the three welfare usage groups. Confirming Toder et al.'s (1999) findings, the individual wage profiles for women in our sample showed considerable variability across the 25 years. The three welfare usage groups had very different wage profiles. Median years out of the labor force (since age 22) increased from 3 in the limited use group to 11 in the moderate use group and 16 in the high use group. We calculated the ratio of each individual's annual earnings to the average social security wage for each year of observation. Relative to average covered Social Security wages, the limited welfare use group's 25-year earnings were, on average, 0.566 of the Social Security wage; average earnings for the moderate use group were 0.381; and the average for the high use group was 0.108. (Full wage profiles are provided in appendix table 4.A1.) Average earnings increased significantly over time for the limited and moderate welfare use groups (figure 4.3). The earnings were relatively flat, however, for the high welfare use group, typically remaining below 20 percent of average covered wages.

As mentioned earlier, earnings patterns for single, never-married mothers may look substantially different in the future because of recent increasing trends in labor force participation for this group. While the weakening economy could dampen this trend, reformed policies that have increased the payoff from work at the low-end of the wage distribution seem permanent. Therefore, we estimate the effect of increased labor force participation and reduced welfare participation on lifetime wage profiles and Social Security benefits.

The simulations of alternative wage profiles for this same cohort of women essentially assume that more recent policies and the favorable economic environment had been in place during the cohort's prime earnings years. Recent findings about individuals leaving welfare guide

Figure 4.3 *Mean Earnings Ratios for Single Mothers, Age 47–51 in 1993, Who Have Been on AFDC: Historical Results*

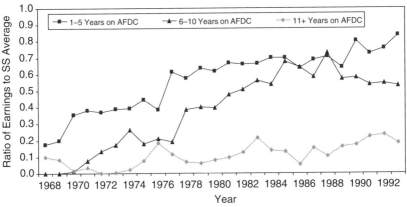

Source: University of Michigan's Panel Study of Income Dynamics.
Note: Sample excludes single mothers who would qualify for a Social Security spousal benefit (owing to a marriage lasting 10 years or more).

these simulations and result in somewhat different assumptions for the three welfare usage groups. Members of the limited welfare use group are assumed to have had no years on welfare and are assigned a 0.66 probability of working in lieu of their years out of the labor force. For the moderate- and high-welfare-usage groups, we assume a maximum of five years of welfare receipt, following the new federal lifetime limit, and a 0.66 probability of working in lieu of years not working. For additional simulated years of work, a 35 hour workweek and a 50-week year at 115 percent of the prevailing minimum wage apply to the limited welfare usage group, and a wage rate of 110 and 105 percent of the minimum wage apply to the moderate and high usage group, respectively. These work and wage assumptions were modeled after findings reported in Loprest's (1999) study of people leaving welfare. Alternative wages are simulated individually for each year and each observation in our sample.

Figure 4.4 shows these alternative wage profiles. While all three groups have higher average wages under this scenario, the increases are, of

Figure 4.4 *Mean Earnings Ratios for Single Mothers, Ages 47–51 in 1993, Who Have Been on AFDC: Assuming an Increased Probability of Working*

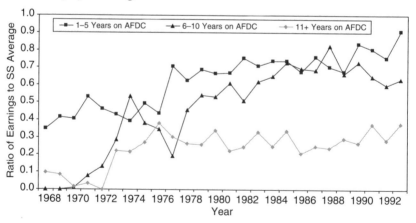

Source: Source: University of Michigan's Panel Study of Income Dynamics.

Notes: Sample excludes single mothers who would qualify for a Social Security spousal benefit (owing to a marriage lasting 10 years or more).

Alternative work history assumptions are 0.66 probability of working in lieu of zero earning years beyond five years for moderate and high AFDC participation and for all years for limited usage group.

course, particularly significant for the moderate- and high-welfare-usage groups. On average, Social Security wages rise to 0.629 of the average Social Security wage for the limited use group, 0.465 for the moderate use group, and 0.237 for the high-welfare-usage group (from 0.566, 0.381, and 0.108, respectively, as shown earlier).

The historical and the alternative wage profiles use the average wage observed (between ages 22–26 and 47–51) for each group relative to the average covered wage to project these earnings profiles into the future.[14] (That is, 57 percent of the average Social Security wage for the limited welfare use group, 38 percent for the moderate welfare use group, and 11 percent for the extensive welfare use group.) The analysis assumes that these women work continuously until they retire and projects average lifetime wages, instead of final average wages, because the usual humped profile is likely to occur as real earnings decline with age. To a large extent, this pattern compensates for the extreme assumption that these women work continuously until retirement. These synthetic profiles probably assign more years of earnings than are likely to occur at older ages, but they also assume that some years of earnings will be lower than one might expect given that the final wages observed are generally higher than lifetime wages.

For each scenario, the potential federal SSI benefits for women at ages 62 and 66 are presented. The benefits potentially could supplement their Social Security benefits. The calculations only take into account federal benefits, omitting the benefits supplements available in some states.[15] These hypothetical benefit calculations assume that individuals with incomes below the eligibility limits would not have assets in excess of current law limits. As noted later, the SSI benefit would be available at age 62 only for individuals totally and permanently disabled.

Single Mothers' Projected Retirement Benefits

Figures 4.5a through 4.7b report annual Social Security benefits relative to the poverty threshold for an elderly, single person to indicate likely retirement income adequacy for each of the three welfare-usage groups using the historical and alternative earnings history assumptions. Outcomes vary significantly across the three groups, reflecting differences in their historical wage patterns. In general, the alternative benefit options do not target single mothers in the limited welfare-usage group, and their Social Security benefits exceed the SSI threshold. The picture is

Figure 4.5a *Benefits as a Percentage of the Poverty Threshold, Group A: Limited Welfare Use, Historical Pattern*

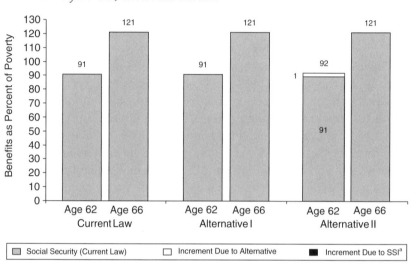

Source: Authors' calculations.

Notes: Analysis computes annual Social Security and SSI benefits relative to poverty threshold for a single, elderly person.

Alternative I is a minimum benefit similar to Kolbe-Stenholm proposal (H.R. 1793).

Alternative II credits individual with one-half of the average wage for up to five years when caring for a young child.

ᵃ The chart does not register an SSI increment because Social Security benefits for single mothers with limited welfare use are higher than the SSI benefit guarantee.

more complex, however, for the moderate and extensive usage groups. Income adequacy will be affected dramatically by the retirement age assumption, increased labor force participation, the alternative benefit formula, and SSI, as detailed in the following section.

Limited Welfare Use Group

Current law benefits for single mothers with historically limited welfare usage are projected to be 91 percent of poverty for retirement at age 62 and reach 121 percent of poverty for those who retire at age 66 (figure 4.5a). Benefits remain the same under Alternative I because their earnings histories already exceed what would be provided under the alternative minimum benefit. Alternative II (additional wage credits for child care years) provides only a slight increment for women in this group who retire at

Figure 4.5b *Benefits as a Percentage of the Poverty Threshold, Group A: Limited Welfare Use, Increased Work*

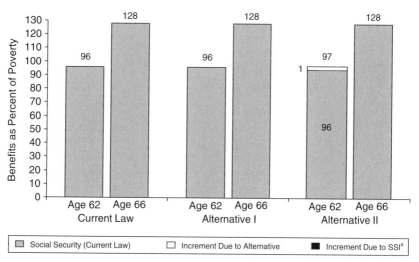

Source: Authors' calculations.

Notes: Analysis computes annual Social Security and SSI benefits relative to poverty threshold for a single, elderly person.

Alternative I is a minimum benefit similar to Kolbe-Stenholm proposal (H.R. 1793).

Alternative II credits individual with one-half of the average wage for up to five years when caring for a young child.

[a] The chart does not register an SSI increment because Social Security benefits for single mothers with limited welfare use are higher than the SSI benefit guarantee.

age 62. Basically, women in the limited welfare use group, representing 3 percent of our entire 47–51 age cohort and 40 percent of those who used any welfare, had earnings sufficient to achieve a benefit close to the poverty level. As noted above, average earnings for the group were 0.566 of Social Security average wages. They had few zero earning years (a median of three since age 22); on average, they earned wages in excess of the poverty threshold in all years. They also benefited from the progressivity of the Social Security benefit formula, experiencing a 90 percent replacement rate in the bottom bracket.

Figure 4.5b shows that retirement benefits for women in the limited welfare use group under the higher work assumption would reach 96 percent of poverty at age 62 and 128 percent of poverty at age 66. Again, with few years out of the labor force, the alternative work assumption does not make a large difference in final benefits. On the other hand, their

Figure 4.6a *Benefits as a Percentage of the Poverty Threshold, Group B: Moderate Welfare Use, Historical Pattern*

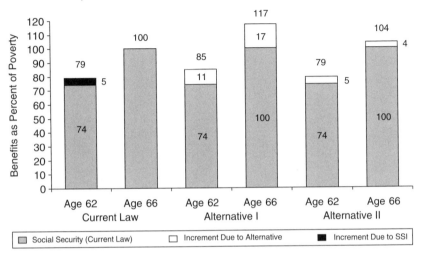

Source: Authors' calculations.

Notes: Analysis computes annual Social Security and SSI benefits relative to poverty threshold for a single, elderly person.

Alternative I is a minimum benefit similar to Kolbe-Stenholm proposal (H.R. 1793).

Alternative II credits individual with one-half of the average wage for up to five years when caring for a young child.

reliance on welfare for up to five years did cost these women about 5 to 7 percent of poverty in annual retirement benefits, depending on their choice of retirement age. These results indicate that single, never-married mothers will have somewhat higher retirement incomes in the future if recent labor market trends continue.

Moderate Welfare Use Group

Women who spent 6 to 10 years on welfare have significantly lower annual Social Security retirement benefits than those with limited use. Under current law, these women would receive a benefit of 74 percent of poverty at age 62, below the 79 percent of poverty guarantee provided by SSI (assuming the $20 monthly increment for unearned income) should the woman become disabled or when she reaches age 65 (see figure 4.6a). Women who can work until age 66, however, would attain a benefit equal

Figure 4.6b *Benefits as a Percentage of the Poverty Threshold, Group B: Moderate Welfare Use, Increased Work*

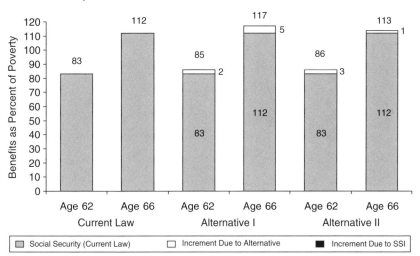

Source: Authors' calculations.

Notes: Analysis computes annual Social Security and SSI benefits relative to poverty threshold for a single, elderly person.

Alternative I is a minimum benefit similar to Kolbe-Stenholm proposal (H.R. 1793).

Alternative II credits individual with one-half of the average wage for up to five years when caring for a young child.

The chart does not register an SSI increment because Social Security benefits for single mothers with limited welfare use are higher than the SSI benefit guarantee; they would not receive an increment from SSI.

to the poverty threshold for an elderly single person. (Note that the SSI eligibility age was not increased to track the increase in the normal retirement age for Social Security. Thus, this cohort would be eligible for SSI at age 65 even though their normal retirement age will be 66.)

Benefits are higher for this group under both benefit alternatives. The minimum benefit alternative increases their benefits at age 62 to 85 percent of poverty, but the alternative that provides credits for up to five years to a mother caring for a young child raises the benefit only by the amount of the SSI supplement the woman could receive at age 65 (or at age 62 if disabled). Thus, to some extent, the child care credit alternative simply shifts the cost of this incremental benefit from general revenues to the Social Security system. Of course, it would eliminate the hassle and stigma attached to applying for SSI benefits, and individuals would

Figure 4.7a *Benefits as a Percentage of the Poverty Threshold, Group C: High Welfare Use, Historical Pattern*

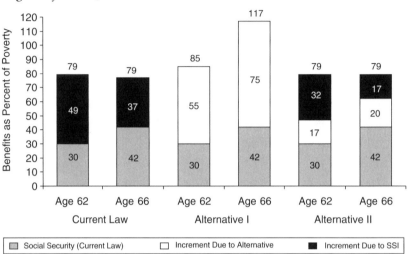

Source: Author's calculations.

Notes: Analysis computes annual Social Security and SSI benefits relative to poverty threshold for a single, elderly person.

Alternative I is a minimum benefit similar to Kolbe-Stenholm proposal (H.R. 1793).

Alternative II credits individual with one-half of the average wage for up to five years when caring for a young child.

receive the additional benefit regardless of the level of their savings. Since few elderly individuals apply for SSI when the payoff is so limited, this alternative would ensure that these individuals' incomes would reach 79 percent of poverty in retirement.[16]

Both alternatives would also increase benefits for those who work until age 66. The minimum benefit would provide a benefit equal to 117 percent of poverty, showing the power of wage indexing until retirement age. The alternative that provides higher earnings credits for up to five child care years would increase incomes to 104 percent of poverty.

The higher work assumption (figure 4.6b) shows that this group of single mothers will fare significantly better in retirement than their predecessors. Under higher labor market assumptions that limit welfare use to five years, women retiring at age 62 would have annual Social Security benefits of 83 percent of poverty, and those who can work until age 66 will have benefits at 112 percent of poverty. Their benefits are likely to exceed the SSI benefit guarantee regardless of their retirement age.

Figure 4.7b *Benefits as a Percentage of the Poverty Threshold, Group C: High Welfare Usage, Increased Work*

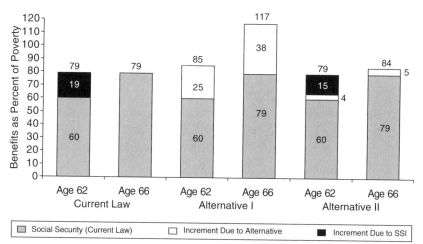

Source: Author's calculations.

Notes: Analysis computes annual Social Security and SSI benefits relative to poverty threshold for a single, elderly person.

Alternative I is a minimum benefit similar to Kolbe-Stenholm proposal (H.R. 1793).

Alternative II credits individual with one-half of the average wage for up to five years when caring for a young child.

Under the higher work assumption, the two benefit alternatives have minimal effects at age 62—increasing benefits by 2 and 3 percent of poverty, respectively. However, the increment from the alternative minimum is somewhat higher for those who reach age 66 because it is wage indexed until this age (providing an incentive to delay retirement). The additional wage credits for child care years have only a minor effect on annual benefits for those who work until age 66. As noted earlier, years of work after age 60 can replace earlier, lower-wage years. Under our assumption that women work continuously until retirement, this effect offsets the benefits of additional wage credits for child care years.

Extensive Welfare Use Group

Figure 4.7a shows that the extensive welfare usage group is likely to rely heavily on SSI under current Social Security law. This group of women, who have more than 10 years on welfare since age 22 and lifetime wages of 0.108 of the average wage, are likely to earn only limited Social Security benefits. Those women retiring at age 62 would earn benefits equal to 30 percent of poverty, and those who can wait until age 66 will reach 42 percent of poverty. SSI would provide a substantially higher income for them at age 65 or younger if disabled. Social Security requires a substantial wage record to realize significant retirement benefits, even though the benefit formula is quite progressive.

These mothers would benefit substantially from the alternative minimum benefit, however, with their benefits reaching 85 percent of poverty for retirement at age 62 and 117 percent of poverty at age 66. Women in this high welfare use group still had many years with some earnings—sometimes combining welfare with some work at limited earnings as shown in Appendix 4.A1. The alternative providing additional credits for child care years would provide only modest gains in income, but not enough to diminish the reliance on SSI, especially for those retiring at age 62. As noted, however, this alternative would shift some of the cost of increasing retirement benefits for this group to the Social Security program and save general revenues because SSI actually pays the *difference* between the minimum benefit and the Social Security benefit.

The increased labor market participation assumption has the most dramatic effect on members of this group because they had many more zero-earnings years. As figure 4.7b shows, however, while these women would double their Social Security benefit at age 62—moving to 60 percent of poverty from 30 percent of poverty—SSI still provides greater income for them. Moreover, even those who can work until age 66 only achieve a benefit equal to what they could have realized under SSI.

The alternative minimum benefit provides significantly higher benefits for this group, while the increased wage credits for up to five child care years, again, mostly substitutes for the increment offered through SSI. The alternative minimum benefit would increase benefits to 85 percent of poverty for those retiring at age 62 and to 117 percent of poverty for those retiring at age 66. The minimum benefit under the higher work assumption provides the same benefit for this group as for the moderate welfare use group. As mentioned, we still allow both groups five years of welfare use during their lifetimes, and the higher wage assumption for the moderate welfare use group does not increase benefits above this alternative wage-indexed minimum.

Summary and Implications

Earnings in covered employment and future retirement income may be the farthest thing from a single mother's mind when she is deciding between working and caring for her children while receiving a welfare benefit. However, under current Social Security law, the number of years she works in covered employment can make a difference in achieving a decent standard of living in retirement. She can be assured that 90 percent of her average indexed monthly earnings will be replaced (provided she works at least 10 years). Annual benefit adequacy—assessed relative to the poverty threshold for an elderly person—will vary tremendously depending on the number of years she works in covered employment and also on the age at which she retires.

Considering outcomes for single mothers with wage histories similar to those we observe for women who will become eligible for benefits between 2007 and 2011, we find the following:

- Single mothers with limited welfare use (up to five years) will earn an average Social Security retirement benefit under current law of 91 percent of the poverty threshold, higher than the SSI benefit guarantee or the alternative minimum benefit considered here. The child care credit alternative would have a very modest effect (2 percent of the poverty threshold) on their retirement benefit. Women who can work until the normal retirement age of 66 will receive a benefit of 121 percent of poverty. They would not receive any additional benefits from either the minimum benefit or the child care credit alternatives.
- Single mothers with moderate welfare use (6 to 10 years) will earn substantially lower Social Security retirement benefits under current law than the limited welfare use group. Typical workers retiring at 62 would receive a benefit of 74 percent of poverty, less than the SSI benefit guarantee (available if disabled or at age 65). The alternative minimum benefit would push their annual income up to 85 percent of poverty at age 62. The child care credit alternative, however, would only increase their benefits to the SSI benefit guarantee for those with some Social Security benefits (79 percent of poverty). Women in this group who can work until the normal retirement age will do considerably better, earning a current law benefit of 100 percent of poverty.

The alternative minimum benefit would increase this to 117 percent of poverty at age 66, while the child care credit option would increase income to 104 percent of poverty.

- Single mothers with extensive welfare use (11 years or more) are the group of greatest concern. According to historical patterns of labor force participation, these women will, on average, earn a Social Security benefit of 30 percent of poverty. Even if they post-pone retirement to age 66, these women will only earn a Social Security benefit of 42 percent of poverty. On average, these women have many years with some covered earnings, although earnings are very low while on welfare. The alternative minimum benefit would substantially increase their benefit to 85 percent of poverty for retirement at age 62 and to 117 percent of poverty for retire-ment at age 66. In contrast, the child care credit option would only increase their benefit to 47 and 62 percent of poverty at ages 62 and 66, respectively.

The analyses considering outcomes for younger single mothers who retire in the future with increased work and decreased reliance on wel-fare suggest the following:

- In general, women with moderate welfare use should do better under Social Security in the future. The current-law Social Security benefit for a typical woman would be 83 percent of poverty for retirement at age 62 and 112 percent of poverty for retirement at age 66 under the assumed increase in labor force participation. While the benefit at age 62 is not much above what these women are guaranteed under SSI, it would be available to them at a younger age (if they are not disabled), and these women could avoid the burden of applying for welfare and could save for their retirement outside of Social Security without a penalty later. Of course, younger women who leave the welfare system behind them would be unlikely to want to turn back to welfare in order to increase their retirement in any case.
- Even with the increased labor force participation assumption, Social Security benefits for representative women with extensive welfare use would fall significantly short of the SSI benefit guaran-tee if they retire at age 62 (60 percent of poverty) and just meet the SSI benefit guarantee (at 79 percent of poverty) if they work until

age 66. These women would, however, fare much better under the alternative minimum benefit formula.

In general, single mothers in the limited and moderate welfare use groups will need to work until the normal retirement age to achieve a retirement benefit at or above the poverty threshold. However, it is not at all clear whether the majority of these women will be able to work until age 66. Women who use the welfare system generally have limited education and a high incidence of mental and physical health limitations. Zedlewski and Alderson (2001), for example, show that four out of ten welfare recipients had not completed high school in 1999, and almost 40 percent had significant mental or physical health problems. Moreover, as noted earlier, the majority of adults now retire before the normal retirement age for many reasons.

The current Social Security system is particularly inadequate for the most vulnerable single mothers—those who historically had more than 10 years of welfare experience, or just 2 percent of women in this age cohort. They will still need to turn back to welfare when they retire or try to live on a Social Security benefit of 30 to 60 percent of poverty (depending on the number of years they spend out of the labor force). We also show that women in this group will not achieve an adequate retirement income by working longer under the current Social Security system (even under the assumption that limits welfare use to five years). The alternative minimum benefit option, however, targets this group particularly well.

Our results also highlight current deficiencies in the SSI program. Absent the alternative minimum benefit option suggested here, many single mothers will still find that SSI is their best option in retirement despite considerable increased work effort. The option that would increase the disregarded unearned income would be particularly helpful for these women. Indexing disregarded income to the CPI since 1972 would increase the amount to $80 per month in 2000, and SSI annual income to 88 percent of poverty for those with Social Security benefits. The Social Security Administration estimates that this move would cost $20.7 billion over 10 years, and $24 billion if indexing continued after 2000 (Social Security Administration 2000b, table 1). Policymakers may also want to consider a higher disregard for those who can work until the normal retirement age to provide an incentive for working more years. Indexing the asset limits would also fit with SSI's modernization goals by creating an incentive for individuals to set aside some savings for retirement. If the asset limits were indexed to the CPI, they would be $6,000 for an individual (2000$). Social Security estimates that this feature would cost $1.8 billion over 10 years (Social Security Administration 2000b).

As noted, many of these women will qualify for disability insurance. More years in covered employment with significant earnings will increase their disability benefits and provide insurance at younger ages should they become disabled. However, only the group with significant earnings years are likely to qualify for a disability benefit in excess of that provided by SSI. Disabled workers would also benefit if SSI's unearned income disregard were indexed to inflation, because the worker could then keep a larger share of their Social Security benefits along with SSI. These single mothers will also gain benefit protection for their children in the event of their death at a young age. The value of disability and survivor's benefits should also be taken into account when considering the additional Social Security benefits from work.

Our analysis is simply illustrative. While based on historical wage profiles, it relies on many assumptions to project single mothers' earnings histories until retirement age. In addition, benefit calculations are based on synthetic wage profiles, and there are variations around these averages. However, we believe the analysis does highlight the likely retirement benefit outcomes for three relatively homogeneous groups of single mothers who have used some welfare during their adult years. These women represent 6 percent of the women in this age cohort in the PSID sample. Our historical cohort, however, may not be representative for later age cohorts, who have experienced increases in out-of-wedlock childbearing, a period of increased reliance on welfare (in the 1980s and early 1990s), and a dramatic decrease in welfare use after 1994.

Also not clear is whether our alternative work and earnings assumptions are too optimistic or too pessimistic. Our assumptions are based on the experiences observed for women leaving welfare in 1997, just at the beginning of federal welfare reform. The 0.66 probability of work after leaving welfare may not hold for women in the highest welfare use group. Some observers are worried that longer-term recipients (those more similar to individuals with more than 10 years on welfare) will not achieve the success rate of women who were among the earliest group to leave welfare.

However, it seems reasonable to conclude that single mothers will have longer work histories as a result of welfare reform. In addition, single mothers who do not qualify for spousal benefits will become an increasing share of women retiring in the future. The interplay of factors, including their wage histories, Social Security allotments, and SSI benefits, should be considered carefully to ensure that the payoff from work—now so carefully crafted to take effect in the prime-age working years—continues into retirement.

NOTES

1. Federal welfare reform also sought to increase the number of absent fathers taking responsibility for their children born out of wedlock. To the extent that state and federal reforms aimed at increasing paternity establishment and child support are successful, children's Social Security protection in case of disability or death of the noncustodial parent will increase.

2. See (Council of Economic Advisers 1999).

3. For information on recent trends in childbearing among unmarried women, see Ventura and Bachrach (2000) and Ventura et al. (2001).

4. See Rowe (2000) for a summary of the TANF work requirements across the states.

5. Under the recency of work test, a worker aged 31 or older must have worked at least 20 quarters during the 10-year period that ends with the quarter in which the disability began.

6. Workers disabled before age 47 have between zero and four dropout years.

7. The threshold for an elderly person in 1998 was $7,818. We indexed the threshold with the CPI of 2.2 percent between 1998 and 1999 and a projected CPI of 2.6 percent in 2000 (based on the first two quarters of 2000). Note that the poverty threshold for a nonelderly, single person is 8 percent higher than that for an elderly individual, based on an assumption that the elderly consume less. (The elderly threshold is used throughout this chapter.)

8. Two-thirds of aged beneficiaries also received Social Security benefits in 1998.

9. Beneficiaries may also own a home, a car with a fair market value of $4,500 or less, and a $1,500 burial policy.

10. This estimate is based on simulated eligibility relative to administrative program data for single elderly persons in the March 1999 Current Population Survey (CPS) that includes income data for 1998. See Maag (1999).

11. For a detailed overview of the PSID, see Hill (1992).

12. Becketti et al. (1988) provide one analysis of PSID representativeness over time.

13. A nationally representative sample of 2,000 Latino households was added in 1990, but this change does not affect this analysis of women in the sample since 1968.

14. The model does not impute earnings prior to age 22 (a period not observed in the PSID for this age cohort). This will bias the average lifetime earnings downward to the extent that some women will have earnings in years prior to age 22 that would substitute for zero or very low earnings years after age 22.

15. For 24 states that provided supplements to eligible aged individuals in 1999, the median monthly supplement was $31 (Committee on Ways and Means 2000, table 3-5).

16. See McGarry (2000) for a discussion of SSI program participation among the elderly.

REFERENCES

Becketti, Sean, William Gould, Lee Lillard, and Finis Welch. 1988. "The Panel Study of Income Dynamics After Fourteen Years: An Evaluation." *Journal of Labor Economics* 6 (4): 472–492.

Committee on Ways and Means, United States House of Representatives. 2000. *Overview of Entitlement Programs: 2000 Green Book Background Material and Data on Programs within the Jurisdiction of the Committee on Ways and Means.* Washington, D.C.: U.S. Government Printing Office.

Council of Economic Advisers. 1999. *The Economic Report of the President.* Washington, D.C.: U.S. Government Printing Office.

———. 2000. *The Economic Report of the President.* Washington, D.C.: U.S. Government Printing Office.

Halpern, Ariel. 1999. "Poverty Among Children Born Outside of Marriage: Preliminary Findings from the 1997 National Survey of America's Families." Washington, D.C.: The Urban Institute. *Assessing the New Federalism* Discussion Paper 99-16.

Hill, Martha S. 1992. *The Panel Study of Income Dynamics: A User's Guide.* Newbury Park: Sage Publications.

Loprest, Pamela. 1999. "Families Who Left Welfare: Who Are They and How Are They Doing?" Washington, D.C.: The Urban Institute. *Assessing the New Federalism* Discussion Paper 99-02.

———. 2001. "How are Families That Left Welfare Doing? A Comparison of Early and Recent Welfare Leaves." Washington, D.C.: The Urban Institute. *Assessing the New Federalism* Policy Brief B-36.

Maag, Elaine. 1999. "Simulated Participation in the Supplemental Security Income Program." *Transfer Income Model (TRIM3) Baseline, Internal Memorandum.* Washington, D.C.: The Urban Institute. (December).

McGarry, Kathleen. 2000. "Guaranteed Income: SSI and the Well-Being of the Elderly Poor." National Bureau of Economic Research Working Paper No. 7574. Cambridge, Massachusetts: National Bureau of Economic Research.

Meyer, Bruce, and Dan Rosenbaum. 1999. "Welfare, the Earned Income Tax Credit, and the Labor Supply of Single Mothers." National Bureau of Economic Research Working Paper no. 7363. Cambridge, Massachusetts: National Bureau of Economic Research.

Rowe, Gretchen. 2000. "State TANF Policies as of July 1999." *Assessing the New Federalism Welfare Rules Databook.* Washington, D.C.: The Urban Institute.

Social Security Administration. 2000a. *Annual Statistical Supplement, 2000.* Washington, D.C.: U.S. Government Printing Office.

————. 2000b. *Report on Supplemental Security Income, Income and Resources Exclusion and Disability Insurance Earnings-Related Provisions.* Washington, D.C.: Social Security Administration.

Toder, Eric, Cori Uccello, John O'Hare, Melissa Favreault, Caroline Ratcliffe, Karen Smith, Gary Burtless, and Barry Bosworth. 1999. *Modeling Income in the Near Term: Projections of Retirement Income through 2020 for the 1931–60 Birth Cohorts.* Final Report to the Social Security Administration. September.

U.S. Bureau of Labor Statistics. 1999. "Employment and Earnings." Washington, D.C.: U.S. Bureau of Labor Statistics.

U.S. Census Bureau. 2000. *Statistical Abstract of the United States: 2000.* 120th ed. Washington, D.C.

U.S. Department of Health and Human Services, Office of the Assistant Secretary for Planning and Evaluation. 2000. *Trends in the Well-Being of America's Children and Youth.* Washington, D.C.: U.S. Government Printing Office.

Ventura, Stephanie J. and Christine Bachrach. 2000. "Nonmarital Childbearing in the United States, 1940–1999." *National Vital Statistics Report* 48 (16).

Ventura, Stephanie J., Joyce A. Martin, Sally C. Curtin, Fay Menacker, and Brady E. Hamilton. 2001. "Births: Final Data for 1999." *National Vital Statistics Report* 49 (1).

Zedlewski, Sheila R., and Donald Alderson. 2001. "Do Families on Welfare in the Post-TANF Era Differ from Their Pre-TANF Counterparts?" Washington, D.C.: The Urban Institute. *Assessing the New Federalism* Discussion Paper No 01-03.

Appendix Table 4.A1 *Earnings Profiles for Women, Ages 47–51 in 1993*

		Group A		Group B		Group C	
		1–5 yrs on AFDC		6–10 yrs on AFDC		11+ yrs on AFDC	
Year	Age	Index	Mean Earnings	Index	Mean Earnings	Index	Mean Earnings
		Historical					
1968	22–26	0.176	982.0	0.000	0.0	0.098	545.7
1969	23–27	0.197	1158.2	0.000	0.0	0.085	500.0
1970	24–26	0.355	2196.3	0.010	59.4	0.015	90.9
1971	25–29	0.383	2490.4	0.078	505.7	0.035	228.6
1972	26–30	0.370	2642.0	0.132	943.6	0.000	0.0
1973	27–31	0.389	2946.0	0.171	1292.9	0.002	15.0
1974	28–32	0.393	3158.9	0.262	2105.0	0.021	171.4
1975	29–33	0.446	3852.6	0.179	1542.9	0.077	666.7
1976	30–34	0.386	3561.2	0.209	1928.6	0.184	1697.1
1977	31–35	0.613	5998.0	0.192	1880.7	0.116	1138.0
1978	32–36	0.577	6089.4	0.386	4076.4	0.067	711.7
1979	33–37	0.637	7308.5	0.402	4620.3	0.060	683.6
1980	34–38	0.618	7735.0	0.397	4964.3	0.079	990.9
1981	35–39	0.669	9215.0	0.477	6568.6	0.094	1295.7
1982	36–40	0.662	9618.4	0.509	7399.1	0.125	1820.0
1983	37–41	0.665	10141.2	0.560	8534.6	0.214	3267.9
1984	38–42	0.698	11269.5	0.538	8678.3	0.139	2249.7
1985	39–43	0.700	11778.5	0.675	11361.6	0.129	2162.9
1986	40–44	0.636	11020.0	0.642	11123.7	0.055	946.9

Year	Age						
1987	41–45	0.687	12660.0	0.585	10786.3	0.152	2796.4
1988	42–46	0.705	13640.0	0.729	14090.0	0.102	1978.6
1989	43–47	0.641	12887.0	0.573	11526.9	0.160	3209.0
1990	44–48	0.801	16846.5	0.580	12192.9	0.171	3602.6
1991	45–49	0.725	15821.4	0.539	11764.3	0.221	4828.6
1992	46–50	0.754	17297.5	0.545	12500.6	0.234	5376.0
1993	47–51	0.835	19318.9	0.531	12285.7	0.184	4257.1
Average		**0.566**		**0.381**		**0.108**	

Alternate Assumption about Wages

Year	Age						
1968	22–26	0.350	1948.0	0.000	0.0	0.098	545.7
1969	23–27	0.415	2446.2	0.000	0.0	0.085	500.0
1970	24–28	0.407	2518.3	0.010	59.4	0.015	90.9
1971	25–29	0.532	3456.4	0.078	505.7	0.035	228.6
1972	26–30	0.461	3286.0	0.132	943.6	0.000	0.0
1973	27–31	0.431	3268.0	0.287	2172.9	0.224	1695.0
1974	28–32	0.393	3158.9	0.536	4305.0	0.217	1746.4
1975	29–33	0.495	4275.2	0.379	3275.4	0.269	2320.5
1976	30–34	0.436	4024.1	0.346	3193.6	0.380	3508.4
1977	31–35	0.708	6923.8	0.192	1880.7	0.302	2949.3
1978	32–36	0.627	6622.7	0.455	4805.2	0.265	2798.6
1979	33–37	0.688	7892.1	0.541	6215.3	0.258	2967.3
1980	34–38	0.668	8358.9	0.533	6669.3	0.339	4245.9
1981	35–39	0.669	9215.0	0.611	8411.1	0.222	3054.5
1982	36–40	0.755	10966.8	0.509	7399.1	0.246	3578.8

(Continued)

Appendix Table 4.A1 Earnings Profiles for Women, Ages 47–51 in 1993 (Continued)

		Group A 1–5 yrs on AFDC		Group B 6–10 yrs on AFDC		Group C 11+ yrs on AFDC	
Year	Age	Index	Mean Earnings	Index	Mean Earnings	Index	Mean Earnings
1983	37–41	0.710	10815.4	0.620	9455.8	0.330	5026.6
1984	38–42	0.740	11943.7	0.652	10520.8	0.248	4008.5
1985	39–43	0.740	12452.7	0.730	12282.8	0.338	5680.4
1986	40–44	0.675	11694.2	0.695	12045.0	0.207	3585.0
1987	41–45	0.760	14008.4	0.685	12628.8	0.247	4555.2
1988	42–46	0.705	13640.0	0.824	15932.5	0.239	4616.7
1989	43–47	0.675	13561.2	0.665	13369.4	0.291	5847.1
1990	44–48	0.838	17611.3	0.729	15327.9	0.266	5597.6
1991	45–49	0.804	17532.0	0.647	14101.8	0.375	8175.5
1992	46–50	0.754	17297.5	0.596	13669.3	0.283	6491.6
1993	47–51	0.909	21029.5	0.632	14623.2	0.377	8719.6
Average		0.629		0.465		0.237	

Source: University of Michigan's Panel Study of Income Dynamics.

Notes: Analysis includes single mothers not likely to qualify for a spousal benefit who had some welfare experience since age 21.
The alternative assumes that women in Group A have no welfare experience and a probability of working of 0.66 each year with zero earnings. Group B and Group C were assigned a 0.66 probability of working for their sixth and beyond years of not working. (See text for a description of earnings assumptions.)

Table 4.A2 *Annual Social Security Benefit for Single Mothers Retiring at Age 62 and 66*

	Retirement at age 62 Wages (% poverty[1] threshold) for:			**Retirement at age 66** Wages (% poverty[1] threshold) for:		
Historical Wage Profile	*Group A*	*Group B*	*Group C*	*Group A*	*Group B*	*Group C*
Current law	$7,459 (91)	$6,105 (74)	$2,477 (30)	$9,963 (1.21)	$8,229 (1.0)	$3,458 (0.42)
Alternative I[2]	7,459 (91)	6,964 (85)	6,964 (85)	9,963 (1.21)	9,627 (1.17)	9,627 (1.17)
Alternative II[3]	7,582 (92)	6,481 (79)	3,838 (47)	10,000 (1.21)	8,529 (1.04)	5,089 (0.62)
Alternative Wage Profile	*Group A*	*Group B*	*Group C*	*Group A*	*Group B*	*Group C*
Current law	$7,879 (96)	$6,785 (83)	$4,917 (60)	$10,516 (1.28)	$9,195 (1.12)	$6,505 (0.79)
Alternative I	7,879 (96)	6,964 (85)	6,964 (85)	10,516 (1.28)	9,627 (1.17)	9,627 (1.17)
Alternative II	7,937 (97)	7,104 (86)	5,279 (64)	10,525 (1.28)	9,297 (1.13)	6,880 (0.84)

Sources: Social Security benefits calculated for synthetic wage profiles based on the University of Michigan's Panel Study of Income Dynamics, 1996–1993, using the Steuerle-Bakija-Carasso Model, Urban Institute.

[1] Social security benefit as a percentage of the poverty threshold for an elderly person living alone.

[2] Scenario I assumes a new minimum benefit (see chapter for more details).

[3] Scenario II assigns a $\frac{1}{2}$ average wage for up to 5 child caring years.

5

Social Security and the Treatment of Families

How Does the United States Compare with Other Developed Countries?

Lawrence H. Thompson
Adam Carasso

The structure of U.S. Social Security benefits has always been a compromise between two competing social goals, individual equity and social adequacy. Scaling the basic benefit to average preretirement earnings levels reflects the system's equity objective; it ensures that those who contributed more while working receive higher benefits when they retire. Its goal of social adequacy is apparent in the higher ratio of retirement benefits to preretirement earnings afforded lower-wage earners and in the provision of benefits to nonworking spouses and elderly surviving spouses without requiring additional contributions or reductions in the worker's benefit.

These two objectives often compete, creating tension. Nowhere is this tension more apparent than in Social Security's treatment of different households. Frequent criticisms of the current system include

- Certain groups, particularly widows, receive inadequate benefits. Estimates for 2000 suggest that the poverty rates of single elderly individuals are nearly double the national average and nearly five times the average rate for elderly married couples (U.S. Census Bureau 2001).[1]

- Two-earner couples often receive lower benefits than one-earner couples with the same combined preretirement earnings. The surviving spouse of the one-earner couple also typically receives a higher benefit.
- The lower earner in a two-earner couple realizes inadequate returns on his or her contributions. Because benefits are available for spouses that do not work, the lower earner's Social Security contributions in a two-earner married couple usually generate little, if any, additional benefits.
- Divorce is not adequately treated. The lower earner in a marriage that lasts fewer than 10 years derives no protection from the earnings of the former spouse during the marriage. In addition, multiple spouses may be receiving Social Security income from one person's earnings record, and the amount of the benefit depends on whether a long-ago spouse is alive or dead.
- The system does not sufficiently recognize the social value of certain nonmarket activities, particularly child rearing or caring for disabled family members. Years spent out of the workforce can significantly reduce a person's retirement benefit.

Over the years, policymakers and politicians have recommended particular program reforms to address one or more of these concerns. To date, however, few of the reform proposals have garnered significant political support. Reform has failed not because of indifference to the concerns cited, but because of the complexity of the system. More often than not, particular benefit changes that address one or more of these concerns create new equity or adequacy problems in other areas.

These issues are not unique to the United States. All developed countries have to contend with the conflict between individual equity and social adequacy in their public pension systems, and they must try to adapt their systems to the same differences in household behavior found in the United States. A review of their experiences can help us better understand our own public policy dilemmas and suggest approaches to consider in addressing them.

The purpose of this chapter is to explore how the public pension programs in other developed countries handle benefit calculations for different kinds of households. The next section reviews the structure of the public pension programs in 16 industrialized countries. No two countries examined here structure their public pension system in exactly the same way. A close review of the various approaches reveals an interesting mix of unique approaches and common threads.

After summarizing the different institutional arrangements, the chapter explores each country's structure and assesses how it performs in the areas of concern identified for the U.S. system. It first looks at benefit adequacy under the various programs, particularly for single individuals. Next, it explores how the different structures treat one- and two-earner households and reviews the impact of additional work by a lower earner on the couple's benefit entitlement. The chapter then examines the systems' treatment of divorced spouses and dependent caregivers. It closes with some summary observations.

Program Structure

Economic development, globalization, and the communications revolution have caused the structure of many social and economic institutions in different countries to become increasingly similar. Pension systems, however, appear to be an exception. Over time, almost all countries have constructed pension systems that both redistribute income to the low-income elderly and scale retirement incomes to preretirement earnings levels. However, the relative importance of the equity and social adequacy objectives, and the institutional arrangements constructed to achieve them, differ greatly. Table 5.1 describes the basic structure of the pension systems in the United States and 15 other major developed countries.

The lack of uniformity in the pension systems throughout the developed world is apparent. Of the 16 countries reviewed, 8 have a flat component in their benefit structure, 12 have an earnings-related component, and 6 have employer pension mandates. Of the eight countries with flat benefits, five also have earnings-related benefits, and three do not. Of these three, two combine the flat benefit in the public system with an employer mandate.[2] Two countries are unique: Australia relies on the combination of a means-tested program and employer mandate, and New Zealand relies only on a flat benefit.[3]

Flat benefits set an income floor for the elderly population that is available to eligible individuals without a means or income test. These benefits take one of two forms, and they vary substantially in their generosity. In four of the eight countries with a flat benefit (Canada, Denmark, New Zealand, and Sweden), the benefit is paid to all long-term residents who

Table 5.1 *Major Features of State Pension Systems in 16 OECD Countries*

Countries	Universal Benefit	Earnings-Related Benefit	Worker's Minimum Guarantee to Avg. Wage		Dependents' Benefits			Ceiling on Contributions to Avg. Wage	Employer Mandate
			Entitlement	Total[a]	Spouse[b]	Surviving Spouse	Survivor + Own Benefit?		
Australia	X	—	—	0.27	F	—	—	B	Yes
Austria		X	—	0.35	—	S	Yes	1.8	—
Belgium		X	0.41	0.41	S	S	Yes	1.8	—
Canada	X	X	0.13	0.28	—	F + S	Yes	1.0	—
Denmark	X		0.20	0.33	—	—	—	B	Yes
France		X	0.32	0.32	F	S	Yes	0.9	Yes
Germany		X	—[c]	—	—	S	Yes	1.8	—
Japan	X	X	0.23	0.23	F	F + S	Yes	2.1	—
Netherlands	X		0.33	0.33	F	—	—	B	Yes
New Zealand	X		0.40	0.40	F	—	—	B	—
Norway	X	X	0.17	0.30	F	F + S	Yes	B	—
Spain		X	0.28	0.28	—[d]	S	Yes	1.5	—
Sweden	X	X	0.14	0.22	F	—	—	1.1	Yes
Switzerland		X	0.18	0.18	—	S	No	B	Yes
United Kingdom	X	X	—	0.27	F	F + S	Yes	1.5	—
United States		X	0.24	0.24	S	S	No	2.4	—

Source: Authors' compilation based on country sources.

Notes: X = entitlement, F = flat, S = scaled to worker's average income, B = ceiling on benefit level, not on contributions. Data are for 1997, 1998, or 1999, depending on availability.

[a] Includes means-tested benefits or supplements operated as a part of the pension system.

[b] Supplemental benefit (over a single worker) for a one-earner couple.

[c] While Germany has no set minimum benefit, the wage- and salary-earner pension funds, when calculating a worker's pension, will credit career low-wage workers with the lesser of 150 percent of their actual wages or 0.75 pension points for each applicable year of low wages.

[d] Spain's minimum pension for a one-earner couple includes an 18 percent spousal bonus over the single-earner's minimum pension.

have reached the specified retirement age regardless of whether they have previously worked or contributed to the pension program.[4]

In the other four countries (Australia, France, Japan, and the Netherlands), the flat benefit is contributory and is available only to those who have paid pension contributions throughout their work life, at least in principle.[5] In practice, however, in most countries this contributory flat benefit is available to virtually everybody. In the Netherlands, benefit receipt is actually tied only to residence, since it is assumed that the required contributions were made in any year in which income is earned. In Norway, three years of contributions qualify long-term residents for a full pension. In Japan, a working spouse's contributions earn credit on both spouses' records, and individuals who are not married or employed are required to make supplemental contributions. This requirement guarantees that nearly everybody has a full career of contribution credits by retirement. The United Kingdom requires almost a full record of contributions, but its system generously fills gaps in the contribution record for individuals who provide dependent care or get divorced.

In most countries, earnings-related benefits are scaled fairly directly to average preretirement earnings covered under the program. Among the systems studied here, the United States and Switzerland are the only exceptions, and each of these country's systems has an explicitly progressive formula. The Swiss formula is far more progressive than the U.S. formula. Indeed, the Swiss system seems more like a flat benefit system supplemented by an employer mandate.

The structure and relative scope of employer mandates also vary from country to country. Most mandates evolved from collective bargaining agreements. In several countries, they still are technically just a negotiated fringe benefit. In each of the countries listed in Table 5.1, however, the mandate extends to virtually all employed workers and has been encouraged by the government (typically through formal interventions). The mandate has evolved into an explicit legal provision in Australia, France, and Switzerland, but it technically remains the product of collective bargaining in the other countries.[6]

Vertical Benefit Structure

All but one of the countries in the sample have structured their systems to provide both a minimum benefit guarantee (social adequacy) and an earnings-related benefit (individual equity); New Zealand provides only the minimum benefit. There are important country-by-country differences in how the systems are organized and financed. These variances have potentially significant implications for labor market incentives and for the interpersonal distribution of costs and benefits beyond the scope of this chapter.

Each of the countries follows one of three general approaches. Some countries provide a flat benefit along with an earnings-related supplement, either through a separate state-managed program or though an employer mandate.[7] Other countries scale benefits directly to preretirement earnings and often extend a minimum pension to workers who have more than a specified number of years of earnings credit. The United States is unique in following a third strategy that combines the equity and social adequacy objectives in one progressive benefit formula. Most countries also have some form of income- or means-tested supplement for individuals with inadequate incomes after all their other benefits have been taken into consideration.

Countries that combine a flat benefit with an earnings-related benefit exclude annual earnings below a specified level from coverage under the earnings-related component. In effect, the earnings-related component rests on top of the flat benefit. Virtually everyone starts with the same social adequacy base. Workers with very low wages receive no additional benefit from the individual equity component, but they also do not pay additional contributions. Higher-wage workers build their individual equity benefit on top of the social adequacy benefit. In these countries, the earnings-related component is invariably financed through worker and employer contributions. As noted previously, the strategy for financing the first pillar varies.

Where there is only an earnings-related component, the minimum pension overrides the normal formula.[8] In these countries, essentially all workers contribute to the earnings-related pension system. The contributions of low-wage workers, however, may produce no additional retirement benefit once enough years have been paid to qualify for the minimum pension. Higher-wage earners receive additional benefits for their additional contributions only after they have earned above the minimum guaranteed level. Often these countries use worker and employer contributions as the major source of financing for their systems, but some also add a transfer from the general budget. Countries typically consider general budget transfers as compensation for the social adequacy elements of the benefit package, although few undertake detailed analysis of the relationship between the adequacy components' actual costs and the size of the transfer.

The U.S. pattern is different. In the United States, the progressive formula redistributes income to both low-wage and short-service workers. The first few years of an average worker's career and most years of a low-wage worker's career generate fairly substantial benefits relative to contributions paid. Higher earnings and longer service yields proportionately lower returns. Also, the U.S. system finances the entire pension package from worker and employer contributions, despite the mix of social adequacy and individual equity components in that package.[9]

The U.S. system also has a minimum pension that overrides other benefits where applicable. But this minimum pension has little impact on the benefit distribution, because almost everybody eligible for the minimum gets more from the regular formula.[10] The minimum, available only to workers with at least 20 years of earnings, is scaled to the number of years of credits earned during between 20 and 30 years of service. A worker with 30 years of credited service is guaranteed a benefit equal to about 24 percent of the average manufacturing wage if drawn at the normal retirement age, and to about 19 percent if drawn at age 62.[11]

Two factors control the relationship between the benefits offered to low-wage earners and those offered to high-wage earners: (1) the relative size and structure of the social adequacy and individual equity components, and (2) the maximum benefit provisions built into all systems. Maximum provisions can be introduced either directly or indirectly. The most common indirect mechanism is a ceiling on annual earnings entered into the benefit computation. These ceilings vary substantially from one country to another. For example, earnings covered by the earnings-related portion of the French, Swedish, and Canadian systems extend to—or only slightly above—the average wage. In many of the other countries, coverage ceilings are between 1.5 and 2.0 times the average wage. The U.S. system covers earnings of up to about 2.5 times the average wage, the highest coverage ceiling of any country reviewed.

Figure 5.1 shows the net effect of these various provisions on the pensions of illustrative low, average, and high earners in each country. Here, the low earner is defined as a full-career worker who always earned 45 percent of the average wage, defined as average annual manufacturing earnings in each country. A high earner always earned 1.6 times the average.[12] The figure compares the full retirement benefit for each worker with that country's average wage and includes only the benefits paid from

Figure 5.1 *Ratio of Benefits for Low, Average, and High Earners to National Average Wage, by Country*

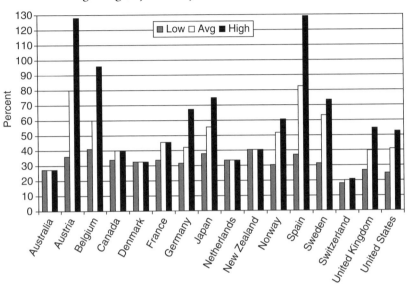

Source: Authors' calculations based on country data.
Note: Data are from 1997, 1998, or 1999, depending on availability.

the state-run systems; benefits from employer-mandated supplements are excluded from the calculations.[13.]

Two of the countries—Austria and Spain—pay benefits that are proportional to preretirement earnings (at least over the range analyzed here). In those countries, the high earner's benefit is some 3.5 times that paid to the low-wage earner, a differential that corresponds to the size of the pre-retirement earnings differential. The benefit differentials are narrower in other countries.

In the four countries that rely exclusively on flat benefits—Australia (where benefits are means tested), Denmark, the Netherlands, and New Zealand—the benefit structure of the public program is most favorable to lower-wage earners. Three of these four countries, however, also mandate supplemental benefits. In Switzerland, which employs a highly progressive structure of the formula, and in Canada and France, where the ceiling on covered earnings is fairly low, the system favors lower-wage earners almost as much. Canada and France also have mandatory supplements.

In the rest of the countries, the degree of progressivity is similar to that in the United States. U.S. benefit levels tend to be somewhat lower than those in the other countries, at least before considering the tax treatment of benefits.[14]

Dependents' Benefits

Benefits for nonworking spouses are a common feature of programs' income adequacy components, but they usually are not found in the earnings-related components. Flat grant systems, even when contributory, typically offer higher benefits to couples than to single workers. The couple's benefit, however, is often less than twice that of a single worker.[15] The United States and Belgium provide a benefit for nonworking spouses that is scaled to the worker's benefit, a feature not found in any other system. Elsewhere, earnings-related systems either have no additional benefit for a nonworking spouse or offer only an income-tested, flat supplement.

Switzerland takes yet a different approach. It requires pension contributions from working-age persons who are not employed based on the individual's income and assets. These contributions generate credits toward pension benefits. In effect, virtually all households in Switzerland are two-earner households for the purposes of calculating pension benefits.

All systems offer benefit protection for nonworking, surviving spouses. In the flat benefit schemes, the surviving spouse usually gets a benefit equal to the basic worker's benefit. In the earnings-related schemes, a surviving spouse tends to get a benefit equal to a set fraction of the worker's benefit.[16] Widows' benefits vary from a low of 40 percent of the worker's benefit under certain circumstances in Austria to a high of 100 percent in the United States. Of the countries analyzed here, the U.S. system is the only one that grants surviving spouses 100 percent of the worker benefit. More common are benefits that range from 55 to 80 percent of the worker's benefit.

Adequacy Concerns

One major concern is that U.S. benefits for single retired people are too low to prevent poverty among this group. Nonmarried elderly individuals record the second-highest poverty rates of any demographic subgroup we observed, exceeded only by children in single-parent households. How does the U.S. system's poverty protection measures for single elderly individuals compare with those in other developed countries?

Comparing international poverty rates requires poverty definitions that can be applied more or less uniformly across the different countries—a difficult task. The usual approach is to define the poverty line as a set fraction of some measure of average household income, adjusted to reflect variations in family size. Of course, the results of these comparisons vary, depending on the definitions employed and the details of each calculation.

Figures 5.2, 5.3a, and 5.3b show the results of two recent studies that examine the impact of transfers from public income support programs on the distribution of income in different countries.[17] One focuses on changes in the fraction of older households below a particular poverty line. The other looks at changes in income distribution among older households, as measured by Gini coefficients.

Figure 5.2 *Impact of Taxes and Transfers on Elderly Poverty Rate, by Country*

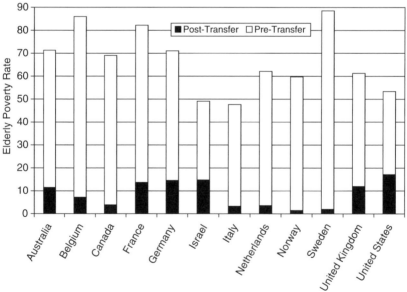

Source: Authors' calculations based on data from Awad and Israeli (1997).

Note: For each bar, the shaded and unshaded portions combined represent pre-transfer poverty levels. The shaded portion represents the poverty level after taxes and transfers.

Figure 5.3a *Income Distribution Before and After Taxes and Transfers—Elderly Couples, by Country*

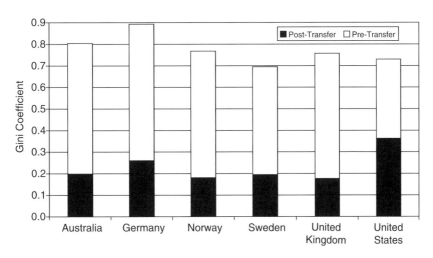

Source: Shaver (1996).

Note: For each bar, the shaded and unshaded portions combined represent pre-transfer poverty levels. The shaded portion represents the poverty level after transfers.

Figure 5.3b *Income Distribution Before and After Taxes and Transfers—Elderly Single Females, by Country*

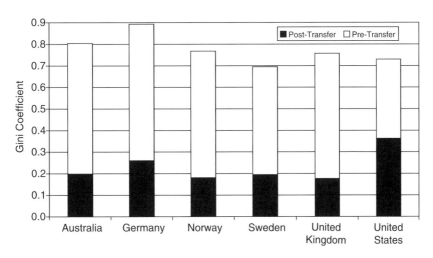

Source: Shaver (1996).

Note: For each bar, the shaded and unshaded portions combined represent pre-transfer poverty levels. The shaded portion represents the poverty level after transfers.

Although the two studies take different approaches, the general picture is the same. In all countries, older individuals' pretax and pretransfer incomes are quite low and tend to be distributed unequally. Each country's tax-transfer systems—chiefly its public pension system—reduce poverty and significantly equalize income distributions. Pretax poverty rates in the United States are actually *lower* than rates in most other countries, and market incomes are distributed *more equally*. However, the U.S. transfer system is less effective in reducing poverty and equalizing incomes than are most other developed countries' systems. As a result, after considering the impact of taxes and transfers in the United States, poverty rates tend to be *higher* and incomes tend to be distributed *less equally* than in other countries.

Figure 5.2 estimates the fraction of the elderly population falling below the poverty level before and after taxes and transfers.[18] Based on market income alone, poverty rates in the countries shown here vary from a high of 88 percent in Sweden to a low of 48 percent in Italy. The U.S. rate is just above Italy's at 53 percent. The poverty picture after taxes and transfers, however, is quite different. An assessment of net income after taxes and transfers indicates that Norway, Sweden, and Canada have the lowest elderly poverty rates, while the United States has the highest. According to this study, rates in Israel, Germany, and France are just below the U.S rates.

Figures 5.3a and 5.3b, based on Shaver (1996), examine relative poverty rates by comparing Gini coefficients for elderly couples and elderly single females in different countries. In the analysis of poverty among elderly couples, the United States had the *least unequal* distribution of market income and the *most unequal* distribution of net income (income after taxes and transfers). For single women, the United States had the second-most-equal distribution of pretransfer income, but the least-equal distribution of net income.

One major reason the U.S. Social Security system is less effective in reducing poverty among the elderly is that it provides less generous benefits to low-wage earners. Figure 5.4 compares the ratio of the social security pensions of low-wage workers in each of the 16 systems described to each country's average manufacturing wage. As before, the low-wage earner retired at the normal retirement age after a full work career spent earning 45 percent of the average manufacturing wage. For the purposes of this figure, couples consist of the low-wage worker and a spouse that never worked. The calculations focus only on benefits from the state-run system, excluding the impact of any additional, employer-mandated benefits.

Figure 5.4 *Benefit for Low-Wage Singles and Couples, by Country*

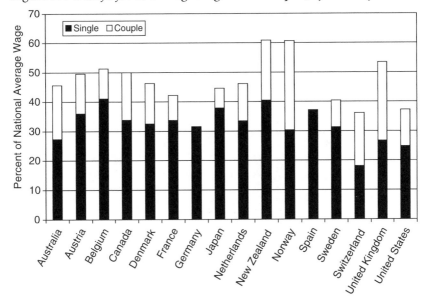

Source: Authors' calculations based on country data.
Note: Data are for 1997, 1998, or 1999, depending on availability.

Relative to prevailing wage levels, the full retirement benefit paid to the low-wage worker in the United States is lower than in every other country except Switzerland, where the public benefit is supplemented by an employer-mandated benefit. The combination of the worker's benefit and the benefit paid to a nonworking spouse is also lower than the benefit paid to a comparable couple in all other countries except Germany, according to this analysis. Moreover, this comparison may overstate the comparative generosity of the U.S. system relative to the other countries by ignoring the impact of early retirement on average actual benefit levels.[19] In the United States, more than half the nondisabled population retires at age 62, causing these individuals' benefits to be permanently reduced from 13 to 20 percent.[20]

A comparison of the benefits for the surviving spouse of a low-wage earner reveals similar results. Figure 5.5 shows benefits both for a surviving spouse who never worked and for a surviving spouse who worked at earnings averaging 75 percent of the primary worker's earnings.[21] As noted, in the United States, the benefit for a surviving spouse who never worked is usually the same as the worker's benefit, in this

Figure 5.5 *Survivors Benefits for Working and Nonworking Spouses of a Low-Wage Worker, by Country*

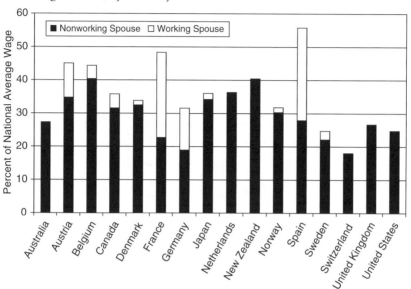

Source: Authors' calculations based on country data.
Note: Data are for 1997, 1998, or 1999, depending on availability.

case, about 25 percent of the average wage. Benefits for similar nonworking spouses are lower in Germany, France, Sweden, and Switzerland, but they are as high or higher in the other countries.

In the United States, benefits for a surviving spouse with an independent work history matching the assumptions here are no higher than benefits for a nonworking survivor. However, comparable situations produce higher benefits in France, Germany, and Sweden, the three countries that were not quite as generous for nonworking surviving spouses. They also produce higher benefits in several other countries. As a result, the surviving spouse of the two-earner, low-wage household receives lower benefits in the United States than in any other country included in this analysis.[22]

A fairly consistent picture emerges from an analysis of the structure of benefits under other countries' programs and a comparison of the treatment of low-wage earners in each country. For low-wage workers, the United States starts out with one of the lowest basic retirement benefits relative to prevailing wage levels. For couples, the gap between the

United States and other developed countries is partially closed by adding relatively generous benefits for nonworking dependents to the U.S. system. Even these benefits, however, are not enough to close the gap for surviving spouses.

Equity and Incentive Concerns

Providing additional benefits for one-earner couples creates tax-benefit differentials that can be viewed as inequitable. Couples will receive higher benefits than a single person, but may have paid no more in pension contributions or general taxes. Moreover, when extra benefits are provided to one-earner couples, the additional benefit provided to a two-earner couple is likely to be less than the additional taxes and/or pension contributions paid by the two-earner couple.

The conflict between individual equity and social adequacy cannot be avoided at lower income levels, and it is invariably resolved in favor of assuring a minimum level of income protection. At middle and higher earnings levels, however, the different approaches to providing retirement benefits can have different implications.

Figures 5.6a–d present comparisons of the benefits paid to single workers, one-earner couples, and two-earner couples in the different countries. In each case, the single (or initial) worker is assumed to earn the average wage in manufacturing; in the two-earner couple; the second worker is assumed to earn 75 percent of that average. The comparisons show that many countries provide higher benefits to one-earner couples than to single workers, but that the differential tends to be somewhat larger in the United States. Similarly (and not unrelated), they show that the incremental benefit accruing to a couple when both partners work is smaller in countries that provide extra benefits to one-earner couples than in countries that do not provide such benefits. In this case, the United States falls in the middle of the spectrum.

One-earner couples receive higher benefits than single earners in 11 of the 16 systems covered, including Belgium, the United States, and all 9 countries that have a flat component in their systems. The other five countries (Austria, France, Germany, Spain, and Switzerland) have only an earnings-related component and provide no additional benefit to a one-earner couple, except for their income-tested supplements. For one-earner couples at the average earnings level, the spouse's supplement is

Figure 5.6a *Breakdown of Benefits for an Average-Wage Couple, by Country*

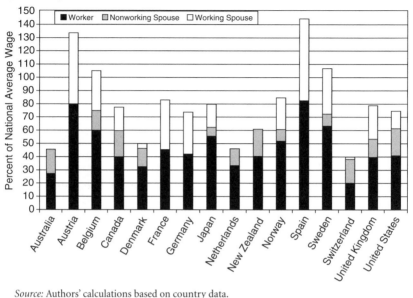

Source: Authors' calculations based on country data.
Note: Data are for 1997, 1998, or 1999, depending on availability.

Figure 5.6b *Spousal Supplement as a Percentage of an Average-Wage Worker's Benefit, by Country*

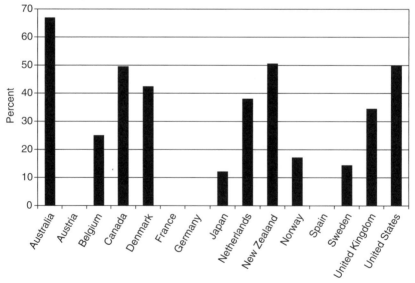

Source: Authors' calculations based on country data.
Note: Data are for 1997, 1998, or 1999, depending on availability.

Figure 5.6c *Average-Wage Worker Benefits: Ratio of One-Earner-Couple to Single-Worker Benefits*

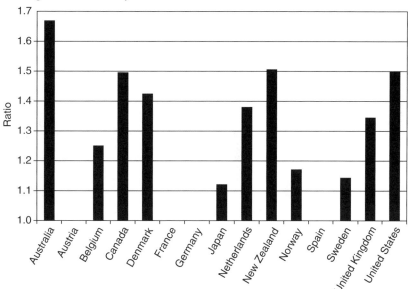

Source: Authors' calculations based on country data.
Note: Data are for 1997, 1998, or 1999, depending on availability.

higher in the United States than anywhere else (figure 5.6b). The supplement amounts to 20 percent of the average wage in the United States, but it averages only 13 percent of the average wage in the other countries with such a supplement.

The effect of the spousal supplement in the United States is to give a one-earner couple 50 percent more income than a single worker with the same preretirement earnings. For workers with average earnings, only Australia has as large a gap between one-earner couples and single workers (figure 5.6c). One consequence of paying a higher benefit to one-earner couples than to single workers is a lower return on the tax/contribution payments of a second earner. Most of the countries that rely exclusively on a flat benefit for their public pension system provide no additional retirement benefit to a two-earner couple as a result of the tax/contribution payments of the lower earner (figure 5.6d). The five countries that provide no spouse supplement are at the other end of

Figure 5.6d *Percentage Increase in Average-Wage Couple's Benefit When Other Spouse Works*

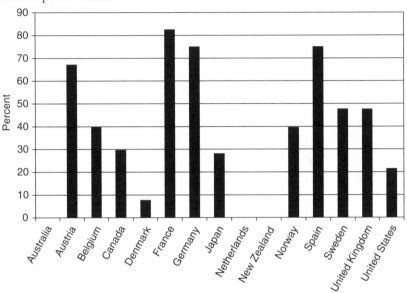

Source: Authors' calculations based on country data.
Note: Data are for 1997, 1998, or 1999, depending on availability.

the spectrum. There, the additional tax and/or contribution payments of a lower-earning spouse result in substantial increases in the couple's retirement benefits.

The rest of the countries provide the couple with some added benefit in return for the additional taxes or contributions, but the increase is not proportional to the additional contributions. Among countries that provide the supplement, the United States appears less generous than all but Denmark.

Each public pension system considered here provides benefits for a surviving nonworking spouse whose deceased husband or wife was the household' single earner. Figures 5.7a–c show the benefits payable upon the death of an average earner.

In the flat benefit systems or its components, the survivor typically reverts to the pension benefit that the worker would have received if he or she had remained single. In the earnings-related systems or its components, the survivor usually receives a benefit that is related to the benefit

Figure 5.7a *Survivors Benefits for One- and Two-Earner Average-Wage Couples, by Country*

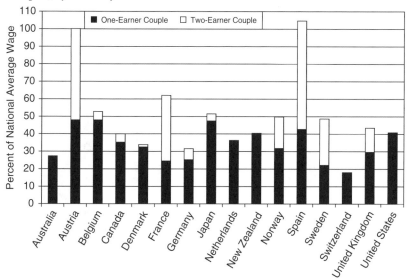

Source: Authors' calculations based on country data.
Note: Data are for 1997, 1998, or 1999, depending on availability.

the deceased worker had been receiving or would have received if he or she had lived. Sweden, however, is scheduled to phase out this kind of benefit.[23] A survivor who never worked would typically receive a benefit that ranged between 50 percent and 80 percent of the benefit the couple would have received (figure 5.7b). In this case, the benefit provided the survivor under the U.S. system would equal 67 percent of the couple's benefit, putting the United States in the middle of the range.

Countries with earnings-related benefits follow one of three approaches when the survivor is also entitled to workers benefit. Four countries—Canada, France, Spain, and the United Kingdom—allow the survivor to draw both a full survivors benefit and a full workers benefit. Another five—Austria, Belgium, Germany, Japan, and Norway—allow the survivor to combine the benefits in certain circumstances, but place limits on the size of the resulting benefit. The United States pays a working survivor the higher of the two benefits (as does Switzerland, although cases where the spouse is not entitled independently are relatively rare in that country).

Figure 5.7b *Survivors Benefit as a Percentage of One-Earner Average-Wage Couple's Benefit, by Country*

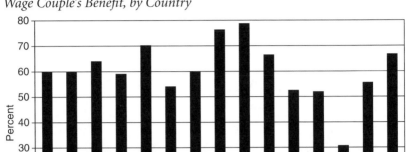

Source: Authors' calculations based on country data.
Note: Data are for 1997, 1998, or 1999, depending on availability.

Figure 5.7c shows the impact of work on the survivors' total benefit. In the examples here, the survivor of the two-earner couple receives no more than the survivor of the one-earner couple in the United States, Belgium, and four of the five countries with only flat benefits in their public systems. In Denmark, the increase in the survivor's benefit is trivial.[24] A two-earner survivor would get a higher benefit in the United States only if he or she were the higher earner. Although Belgium allows some combining of the two potential benefits, the total cannot exceed 110 percent of the survivor's pension as a worker. In practice, the increment is never very large and is available only to individuals whose own pensions are almost as high as their benefits as survivors.

Along with Sweden, which in these calculations has no earnings-related survivors' benefit, Austria, France, and Spain give substantially higher benefits to the survivor of a two-earner couple. France and Spain allow individuals to combine the full survivor and worker benefits, and France allows 40 to 60 percent of the benefit of the deceased worker to be added to the benefit of the survivor. As a result, the survivors' benefit can equal

Figure 5.7c *Percentage Increase in Benefit When Survivor of Average-Wage Couple Works, by Country*

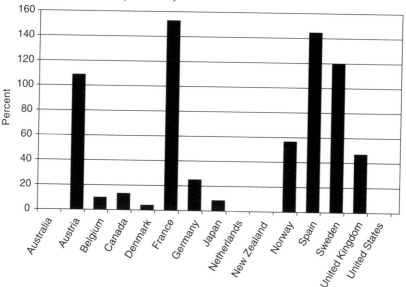

Source: Authors' calculations based on country data.
Note: Data are for 1997, 1998, or 1999, depending on availability.

or exceed the gross preretirement earnings of the higher earner in Austria and Spain, producing the third-most-generous result in France.

The increments in the other countries vary from a high of around 55 percent in Norway to a low of around 8 percent in Japan. Canada and the United Kingdom allow two-earner survivors to combine both benefits. But the impact on total retirement income is less dramatic than in some other countries, because the provision applies only to benefits in the earnings-related component of the two countries' respective systems.

The impact of work in Norway and Germany depends on the earnings level of the worker and spouse. Germany has complex rules that allot larger benefit increments to survivors with higher preretirement earnings levels, whereas Norway gives the biggest increments to households with lower preretirement earnings. Japan is similar to the United States—the survivor of a two-earner couple can qualify as a worker or a survivor, whichever is more advantageous. Japan, however, offers a third option equal to 50 percent of each benefit. This option produces a modest increase in the total benefit paid to many survivors from two-earner couples. In the United States, however, such a provision would not be as helpful as in Japan, because the U.S. survivor benefit for a nonworking spouse is set at a higher percentage of the worker's benefit.

In summary, supplemental benefits for nonworking spouses are a common feature of the social adequacy-oriented, flat benefit systems (or its flat components), whether the system is contributory or not. Such supplemental benefits are relatively rare in the individual equity-oriented, earnings-related systems (or its earnings-related components). Not surprisingly, since the U.S. system combines the social-adequacy orientation and the individual-equity orientation in one benefit formula, a spouses' supplement can be found in the U.S. benefit package. The structure of the U.S. supplement, however, does differ from that in other countries. Along with Belgium, it is the only country that grants higher supplements for the spouses of higher-wage workers. All countries that offer a spousal supplement are subject to the same criticism: the benefit provides little or no return for the taxes of the lower-earning spouse of a two-earner household.

All systems provide benefits to nonworking surviving spouses, but only the U.S. plan offers a benefit of 100 percent of the worker's basic benefit. All other countries set the survivor's benefit at a smaller fraction of the worker's benefit. By setting the survivor's benefit at 100 percent of the worker's benefit, the United States is able to pay the survivor of a one-earner couple a benefit equal to two-thirds the benefit that the couple had been receiving. This percentage is fairly typical of the difference between the benefit offered a one-earner couple and the benefit offered the survivor across the sample of countries, even if the method used to arrive at this result is not typical.

The U.S. system's treatment of the survivor from a two-earner couple is not typical, however. Most other countries that have earnings-related components allow survivors from two-earner couples to combine all or a portion of their workers' and survivors' benefits. The result can either be a modest or a major increase in the benefit offered such survivors, depending on the details of the computation rules.

Survivors from two-earner couples tend to get the same benefit as survivors from one-earner couples under the flat benefit systems. These systems also offer no benefit in return for the taxes and or pension contributions paid by the lower-earning spouse.

Treatment of Divorce

Table 5.2 describes system strategies for handling divorce. The countries appear to fall into three basic groups. Systems in the first group contain no special provisions for dealing with divorced couples. The second group grants some form of division of credits at the time of divorce. The third group contains special benefits for qualified divorced individuals.

Divorce has no material impact on benefit rights under most flat benefit plans or components; accordingly, they contain no special provisions dealing with divorce. In effect, a divorce converts a couple into two single individuals under a flat system, leaving each individual with the same benefit as his or her never-married counterpart.

In other cases, a system contains no provision dealing with divorce, even though the end of the marriage might cause the lower earner to lose income. For example, Sweden has no special provisions for handling divorce under its earnings-related component. Although divorce does not cause a reduction in aggregate benefit payments in Sweden, it can leave a lower earner without an equitable claim on the couple's previous income. Japan also has no provisions for providing income protection to divorced persons with no earnings credits of their own under the earnings-related portion of its pension system.

Five countries divide credits at divorce, three according to a formula and two under court-supervised agreements between the divorcing parties. Switzerland and Canada divide credits acquired during the marriage equally under their respective earnings-related components.[25] Germany's more ambitious system attempts to divide all pension entitlements acquired during the marriage through a relatively complicated methodology. In most cases, the net result is that rights under the public pension are adjusted to achieve the net transfer that is necessary to equalize all public and private pension entitlements generated during the marriage. Appendix 5.A describes Germany's approach in greater detail.

Canada has had difficulty fully implementing its credit-splitting arrangement. In that country, as in the United States, provincial (equivalent to state) courts handle divorces, while the federal government runs the national pension plan. The federal government does not have the authority (or at least chooses not to exercise it) to order the provincial courts to inform the pension agency when a divorce is granted. Instead, the pension agency must rely on the lower-earning spouse to report the divorce. Early

Table 5.2 *Divorce Benefits Provided by OECD State Pension Systems*

Countries	Divorce Benefit
Australia	Means-tested A$178.65 per week and A$9,289.80 per year for single women age 50 without kids if separated or divorced at age 40.
Belgium	37.5% of former spouse's earnings while married, less own pension rights during same period. Divorced widow only entitled to a benefit from her former husband (80% of husband's full benefit) if not entitled to benefit on her own record. Must not have remarried. No benefits for divorced widower.
Canada	Universal: None. Contributory: pension credits accumulated by couples with marriages of one or more years are split equally.
Denmark	None.
France	If income is under Fr83,658 per year and is not remarried, receives 54 percent of insured's pension, proportionately divided among all eligible former spouses.
Germany	Pension rights are summed and the spouse with fewer pension rights is granted half the difference at the expense of the spouse with more pension rights.
Japan	National pension program: Any combination of one's own years of contributions and years simply married to a person who has contributed that adds to 25 produces a full pension of ¥804,200 per year. Employee's Pension Insurance: None.
Netherlands	None.
New Zealand	Only if single parent with children. Covered under family allowances.
Norway	Transitional grant to divorced, separated, or unwed parent, plus child care benefit, if applicable. Full, ongoing survivor's benefits available if (a) marriage lasted 25 years (15 years if had children) and (b) spouse has not remarried.
Spain	Spouses resolve pension divisions subject to court guidance and approval.
Sweden	None
Switzerland	All earnings while married are split evenly between both spouses and included in their individual pension determinations.
United Kingdom	State pension: Higher-earning spouse's earnings record is substituted either for (a) all tax years until the last year of the marriage or (b) only those tax years spanning the marriage, whichever is more favorable. Earnings-related: (legislation effective April, 2000) pension sharing between spouses negotiated by agreement or court order.
United States	50% of former spouse's benefit if marriage lasted 10 years or more.

Note: Countries often provide for pension division in their mandatory occupational or private pension schemes.

Source: Social Security Programs throughout the World, 1999; various country publications.

in the system's existence, only a relatively small fraction of all divorces were reported. As described in Appendix 5.A, the Canadian system has been amended several times over the years to improve reporting mechanisms, and further changes are likely in the near future. In the 1980s, Canadian legislation extended credit splitting to common-law marriages, and a recent Supreme Court decision interpreted the legislation to include same-sex partners.

Spain allows divorcing spouses to reach an accommodation about pension rights under the general supervision of the court granting the divorce. The United Kingdom recently instituted a similar arrangement concerning benefits in its earnings-related component. We have no information on the effectiveness of the arrangement in Spain, and it is too early to know how well the provision will work in the United Kingdom.

Five of the countries have chosen to deal with divorce through special benefit provisions: the United States, Norway, Belgium, the United Kingdom (with respect to the flat benefit), and France. All the countries except France use a strategy that increases total benefit outlays.

In the United States, marriages lasting 10 years can create a situation where more than one divorced spouse or surviving spouse is collecting benefits based on a former spouse's earnings record. Belgium's and Norway's approaches to this potential duplication are similar. In both countries, divorced surviving spouses (but only former wives in Belgium) can draw a full benefit so long as they do not have a higher benefit on their own record and do not remarry. These two countries differ, however, in their treatment of divorces in which each former spouse is still alive. In Belgium, the spouse's benefit is, in effect, prorated to reflect the fraction of the worker's career pursued during the marriage. Norway has no spousal benefit in its earnings-related component, and the system provides no additional protection to a divorced spouse whose former partner is still alive. Most individuals, however, would qualify for the flat benefit. In the event of divorce, the U.K. system allows a one-earner couple to apply credits toward its flat benefit twice, once for the working spouse and once for the nonworking spouse.

France has no spousal or divorced-spouse benefits. It provides for divorced surviving spouses using the same principle that Belgium applies when the higher earner is still alive—it divides the existing benefit for surviving spouses among all eligible survivors according to the length of each respective marriage.

Divorce presents relatively few problems in the countries that have flat benefit systems or components; under most circumstances, the former spouses of a marriage will retain his or her own entitlement to the basic benefit. In the flat system, the major impact of divorce is likely to be a slight increase in the total cost of providing benefits, given that two single benefits usually amount to more than a couple's benefit.

In earnings-related components or systems, divorce creates a unique set of equity and adequacy conflicts, particularly in countries without a separate, flat-rate adequacy component. When a couple has only one earner and is sharing the pension credits, divorce can produce two inadequate pensions. In Germany, for example, equal division of an average earner's pension would leave each partner of a one-earner marriage with a benefit equal to 21 percent of the average wage. In France, apportioning the surviving spouse's benefit is likely to produce similar consequences.

Divorce is less likely to create serious adequacy problems in Canada and Switzerland, where nonworking spouses receive an independent entitlement to a retirement benefit. In Canada, credit splitting applies only to the earnings-related component. Each party retains his or her full entitlement to the flat benefit. Similarly, Switzerland's mandatory participation of nonworking spouses and the very progressive benefit formula mute the impact of credit splitting in the public pension system. In most situations, sharing will likely have minimal impact on each partner's public pension benefit.

Adequacy problems can be avoided by adding benefits to the system. But this measure can mean that the pension contributions of a divorced person will produce more benefits than the contributions of an individual who stays married or single. Each of the countries that uses this approach creates the same benefit anomalies found in the United States, where the amount of the benefit depends on whether the worker is dead or alive. The situation is actually worse in Norway and France, where there are no continuing spousal benefits, and in Belgium, where the continuing spousal benefit is lower than that available in the United States.

Dependent Care Credits

Most countries that base either eligibility or benefit amounts on earnings histories grant credit for time spent out of the labor force caring for children. Several countries also provide credit for time out of the labor force spent supplying unpaid care to sick or disabled persons. Of the countries reviewed here, only the United States and Spain have no specific provisions covering child care.[26]

Table 5.3 describes the dependent care provisions by country. Under the U.S. system, benefits are based on the average of the individual's highest 35 years of indexed earnings. Labor market activity exceeding 35 years—labeled "dropout years"—is ignored. Under the U.S. approach, people who temporarily leave the labor force to care for a young child or other dependents are penalized if the amount they would have earned by staying in the labor force is higher than the lowest year included in their average earnings calculation. The odds of avoiding this penalty are probably rather small.

Three countries use the principle of dropout years to recognize child care responsibilities, Canada, France, and the United Kingdom. For example, in Canada any year in which an individual had a child under the age of seven can be dropped from the benefit calculation if it would improve the result. In effect, persons with young children are credited with the higher of their actual earnings and the average of their earnings in all the other years of their career. In the United Kingdom, as long as people have at least 20 years of contributions, years spent raising a child under 16 and without earnings are ignored in calculating the flat benefit.

The rest of the countries studied here incorporate child credits by adding a specific credit to the earnings record. Belgium and Japan credit the individual with the same amount as was earned in the year before leaving the labor force. Germany, Norway, and Switzerland give individuals caring for children a credit equal to a specified fraction of the average wage, ranging from 54 percent of the average wage in Switzerland to 75 percent of the average wage in Germany. Sweden offers individuals a choice between their prior earnings or 75 percent of the average wage.

Age limits on the child being cared for vary widely. Japan's credit only applies for the caretaking of children under two years old; Germany and Belgium set the age limit at four, and Sweden's age limit is five. At the other extreme, child care credits are available in the United Kingdom and Switzerland until the child turns 16 and 17, respectively. Germany, Norway, and the United Kingdom also allow credits for years spent caring for a sick or disabled person.

Table 5.3 *Contribution Credits and Dropout Years in 16 OECD State Pension Systems*

Countries	Pension Contribution Credits or Allowed Drop-Out[a] Years
Australia	Not applicable*
Austria	(Credits) Full-time education; Military service; Maternity and child-raising; Sickness benefit or unemployment benefit receipt.
Belgium	(Credits) Raising children age 3 or under. Credited each year with earnings equal to earnings in year prior to child's birth.
Canada	(Drop-outs) Years of zero or low earnings while raising children under age 7.
Denmark	Not applicable*
France	(Drop-outs) Zero years not averaged in.
Germany	(Credits) Raising children age 3 or under; Military service; Full-time education; Unpaid home nursing care for 14 or more hours per week. Value of credit is 0.75 pension points for each applicable year.
Japan	(Credits) Raising children age 1 or under (post-maternal leave). Credited with earnings equal to prior year's earnings.
Netherlands	Not applicable*
New Zealand	Not applicable*
Norway	(Credits) Persons taking unpaid, home care of children under age 7, the disabled, sick, or elderly are credited with 3.00 pension points for each applicable year.
Spain	None
Sweden	(Credits) Full-time education; Military service; Raising children 4 or under. For child care, the credit awarded the parent each year is the most favorable of (1) earnings level before the child birth, (2) difference between own earnings and 75% of average covered earnings, (3) a wage-adjusted amount of 36,300 SEK in 1999.
Switzerland	(Credits) Combined child-raising and education credit for children 16 and under. The credit, equal to having earned a salary 3 times the minimum pension (28,944 CH in 1999 or 43% of the average wage), is awarded to single spouse or divided equally between two spouses.

Table 5.3 *Contribution Credits and Dropout Years in 16 OECD State Pension Systems (Continued)*

United Kingdom	(Drop-outs) Years of earnings below the contribution floor while (1) in receipt of child care benefits for a child under 16, (2) spending 35 or more hours a week caring for someone receiving an attendance or disability allowance, and (3) in receipt of income support and also caring for a sick or disabled person at home are dropped out of the average wage determination for SERPS. No limit on dropped-out years allowed but at least 20 qualifying years are necessary to receive full basic pension.
United States	None

* Country's system either awards pension amounts linked to years of residence or otherwise is insensitive to amount of annual contributions.

ᵃ Years excluded from calculations of years of pension contributions and pension eligibility generally because individual, while not in the labor force, was making a contribution deemed socially valuable (e.g., raising children, caring for elderly dependents, on income assistance, etc.).

Source: Social Security Programs thoughout the World, 1999; various country publications.

Summary of Major Findings

Comparative studies, such as the one presented here, are not likely to prescribe specific features of a reform proposal. Each country's public pension system reflects its own unique social preferences and institutional history, and no two countries have structured their systems in exactly the same way. Nonetheless, this review does suggest some approaches that U.S. reformers may wish to adapt. It also reveals some of the challenges that these reformers will likely face. We review several major findings that shed light on the U.S. system and suggest areas that might benefit from reform.

First, almost all the countries have constructed systems that mix adequacy and equity objectives. A common strategy is to combine a public program heavily oriented toward ensuring social adequacy with a supplemental program heavily oriented to supplying individual equity. The second program may also be public, or it may come out of an employer mandate.

Among the countries examined, the United States is unique in offering a single public program with no employer mandate complementing it. Instead, the U.S. system uses a progressive benefit formula to balance adequacy and equity concerns. In evaluating the reforms of other countries, this fundamental structural difference between the United

States and the other countries must be taken into account. Particular reforms may have different consequences in the United States.

Second, the U.S. system is generally less generous than the other systems, particularly for low and average earners. Because U.S. earners start out with a less generous worker's benefit, the supplemental benefit for nonworking spouses plays an important role in assuring a minimum level of protection relative to prevailing national wage levels. Limiting the size of the spousal supplement, at least for those with earnings less than or roughly equal to the average, could seriously erode the protection offered lower-income families.

Third, spousal supplements are a fairly common part of the adequacy component of national systems, although they often take the form of an additional flat benefit and are occasionally income tested. The common criticism that a working spouse in the United States receives a lower return on additional tax or contribution payments applies equally to most of the other countries. This appears inevitable in systems that incorporate social adequacy elements into the benefit structure. As a possible alternative, the United States might follow other countries practice of placing a flat dollar cap on the size of the spousal benefit. For example, the spouse's supplement might be limited to 50 percent of the retirement benefit of a worker who always earned the average wage. This change would preserve the benefit for lower-wage households, while minimizing any negative impact on individuals at higher earnings levels.[27]

Fourth, benefits for surviving spouses are common. In contrast to spousal benefits, however, they tend to be earnings related in countries with earnings-related systems. Relative to the worker's benefit, the survivor's benefit is higher in the United States than in any other country. However, under the U.S. system, the difference between the benefit paid to a survivor and the benefit paid to a one-earner couple is fairly typical. As with spousal benefits, the United States offers a relatively generous survivor benefit to offset the impact of its relatively modest worker benefits.

Like spousal benefits, survivor benefits reduce the working spouse's return on additional tax or contribution payments to a pension system. The impact is strongest in the United States as well as in flat benefit countries that give both a survivor who worked and a survivor who did not work the same benefit. The more common approach in countries with earnings-related components is to allow a survivor to combine credits. Depending on the specifics of the proposals, the survivor's combined credits can result in a very modest increase in benefits, such as in

Japan, or in a very generous increase, such as in Spain or Austria. The more modest approaches are obviously more affordable.

Several countries split earnings credits at divorce, while several others deal with divorce through more ad hoc approaches similar to the U.S. approach. When used, credit splitting is determined through a standard formula in some countries and through court supervision of divorce proceedings in others. Although some detail on credit splitting is presented in Appendix 5.A, conclusions on its effectiveness and reform potential would require more in-depth analysis.

The countries that deal with divorce through supplemental benefits all contain the same equity and return-on-contributions concerns as those found in the U.S. system. In fact, the U.S. system offers more adequate benefits while the divorced worker is alive than do the three other countries that use a supplemental approach. In countries that use credit splitting without a flat-benefit floor, serious adequacy problems can arise.

Finally, the United Stands stands virtually alone in not compensating people who leave the labor force temporarily to care for young children. The other countries' different approaches suggest ways to add such protection, although each type of program would increase the total cost of the social security benefit package.

NOTES

1. The U.S. average poverty rate for single individuals over age 65 was estimated to be 20.8 percent in 2000. By comparison, the rate for couples where the head was over age 65 was 4.4 percent, and the rate for the population as a whole was 11.3 percent (U.S. Census Bureau 2001).

2. Japan and the United Kingdom allow employers to contract out of the earnings-related benefit if they provide an occupational pension that is as good as the state pension. The United Kingdom also allows individuals to contract out of either the state system or their employers' pension system.

3. Ireland, which is not part of this analysis, also relies exclusively on a flat benefit, although its benefit is contributory.

4. In principle, a demogrant provides a more effective floor of protection since it covers all elderly people, with the possible exception of recent immigrants. Concerns have been expressed, however, that in our political and social context a demogrant would eventually be means-tested if it were paid to all elderly individuals without regard to prior contributions (see, for example, Advisory Council on Social Security 1979). Experience abroad supports this concern. In Canada, the flat benefit is now "clawed back" from higher-income elderly individuals through a special surtax on the personal income tax. Until recently, New Zealand's flat benefit was paid only to those with incomes below a specified level; in the future, Sweden's flat benefit will gradually be converted into a

minimum pension guarantee whose size will fall as the pension from the rest of the state system rises. Within the last decade, Finland also converted a universal flat benefit into an income-tested supplement complementing its pension program.

5. Denmark actually has two flat benefits, one is universal and the other is contributory. The universal benefit is by far the larger of the two.

6. Of the countries listed here, all but France has an advance-funded system. The French and Dutch systems are defined benefit systems. Sweden is shifting from a defined benefit to a defined contribution system. Australia and Switzerland mostly use defined contribution systems, and Denmark has a defined contribution system.

7. Switzerland and Australia largely follow this model as well.

8. One major exception is Germany, where extra protection for long-service, low-wage workers is provided by increasing individuals' earnings credits rather than providing an explicit minimum benefit. For German workers with at least 35 years of service, the earnings entered into the benefit calculation (technically, the calculation of the number of pension points) are increased to the lower of 1.5 times the actual amount earned or 75 percent of the national average wage that year.

9. A few trivial exceptions to this principle apply; for example, general revenue was transferred to offset the cost of special wage credits awarded to certain Japanese-Americans interred during World War II.

10. This benefit is referred to as the "special minimum pension," a name it earned when a regular minimum pension benefit was still available. Only years with earnings above a certain floor figure in this benefit's computation. The 1999 earnings floor was just over $8,000. The earnings floor is indexed to average earnings levels. Of the 44.2 million beneficiaries at the end of 1998, only about 150,000 received benefits based on this minimum pension. For many years, the United States also had a minimum pension payable to all individuals eligible for benefits, without regard to the number of years of earnings or earnings levels. That provision was repealed in 1981, however, owing to concerns that it was poorly targeted.

11. As the retirement-age increase phases in, the Social Security benefit guaranteed to those retiring at age 62 with 30 years of service will drift down to just over 17 percent of the average wage. A worker with few assets who claims the special minimum benefit prior to reaching the normal retirement age is likely to become eligible for a Social Security Insurance (SSI) supplement at 65. The SSI program guarantees a single worker who also receives Social Security a benefit equal to about 23 percent of the average wage.

12. The definition of low and high earners is modeled after that used in the annual Board of Trustees reports. The calculations for each country use the benefit rules in effect in 1999, but apply the rules to earnings at the levels prevailing in 1996–97. In the United States, the average annual manufacturing wage is within a few hundred dollars of the average earnings used to index earnings under the Social Security program. Analyses of the adequacy of a pension system frequently focus on the replacement rate awarded a hypothetical worker who always earned the average wage, even though such a worker rarely exists. At least in the United States, actual wage histories are quite heterogeneous, with some workers exhibiting rising relative wages over their careers, others exhibiting declining relative wages, and many others showing gaps of several years with no earnings at all (Bosworth, Burtless, and Steuerle 1999). Despite the heterogeneity, the hypothetical average worker may not be a bad proxy for the general level of benefits for regular, full-career workers. In the United States, the benefit for such a worker retiring at age 65

in 1999 would have been $11,454 (Board of Trustees 1999), whereas the actual average full rate benefit ("primary insurance amount") for men retiring in 1999 was $12,278 (Social Security Administration 2000). The average full rate benefit for women retiring in 1999 was $10,008.

13. The calculations shown for Sweden here and elsewhere in this chapter apply to the Swedish system as it was structured in 1997. Sweden is slowly phasing in a new mechanism for calculating the earnings-related benefit. The new mechanism will produce minor changes in some of the benefit levels, but will not change the basic outline presented here. Additional details are available in Scherman (1999).

14. The United States differs from many other developed countries in that, at least for moderate-income households, Social Security benefits are exempt from income tax. The effect of payroll and income taxes on replacement rates is explored for a subset of these countries in Appendix 5.B. Since the thresholds governing the exemption are not indexed, inflation will gradually eliminate the tax advantage.

15. Two notable exceptions are Canada, where a couple's benefit under the flat grant portion is twice the single worker's benefit, and Japan, which allows couples to combine credits for the purpose of establishing their entitlement under its flat grant, but offers no additional benefit if the nonworking spouse has no credits whatsoever.

16. Sweden has scheduled a phaseout of its earnings-related benefit for surviving spouses. The benefit, which is 40 percent of the workers benefit, is not offered to those born after 1944. The treatment of survivors is being reexamined in Sweden as part of its broader reform effort.

17. For further explanation, see Shaver (1996) and Awad and Israeli (1997). Other closely related studies include Smeeding (1997); Bradshaw and Chen (1996); and Hauser (1997).

18. Figure 5.2 shows data for two countries not contained in table 5.1, Israel (IL) and Italy (IT). In the figure, the poverty level is defined as one-half of each country's after-tax median household income, adjusted for family size. This definition is increasingly used by the Organization for Economic Cooperation and Development and the member countries of the European Union. Although the U.S. poverty level was approximately one-half of median household income when the term was first defined in the mid-1960s, it is currently closer to 40 percent of median household income.

19. Of the persons filing for a retirement benefit in the United States in 1998, 57 percent of the men and 58 percent of the women were 62 years old. Their benefits would be permanently reduced 13 to 20 percent below the rate shown here. Reduced benefits for early retirement are also available in Canada, Denmark, Japan (flat portion only), Spain, and Sweden. The other countries do not offer the option of taking a lower benefit at an earlier age.

20. Only three other countries allow early retirement with reduced benefits, Canada, Germany, and Japan. In Canada, early retirement is available only in the earnings-related portion of the program; in Japan it is available only in the flat portion of the program. Germany reduces benefits by only 0.3 percent per month, whereas the reduction factor in the United States is 0.56 percent per month. As noted previously, United States' income tax treatment is more favorable than that in many other countries, but this better treatment does not benefit low-income workers much since they typically do not pay income taxes on their benefits in any country.

21. The 75 percent figure is arbitrary. It roughly equals the ratio of the average lifetime earnings for female retired workers to average lifetime earnings for male retired workers in the U.S. Social Security program.

22. This comparison focuses on benefit rates at the normal retirement age and probably understates the adequacy of benefits in Austria, Denmark, the Netherlands, and Switzerland. Each of these countries indexes benefits after retirement to wage growth (or, in the case of Switzerland, the average of wage and price growth). In most cases, wage indexing will produce more rapid post-retirement adjustments than will price indexing, leading to more adequate benefits for those who have been retired for a number of years.

23. Sweden previously provided a benefit to elderly surviving spouses equal to 40 percent of the worker's earnings-related pension. Starting with the 1945 birth cohort, however, the benefit will become progressively less generous until it is converted entirely to a temporary transition benefit. The survivor will continue to be eligible for a base benefit and an income-tested supplement.

24. The increase in Denmark occurs only in a very modest contributory portion of its public pension program. In the example used here, the increase amounts to about 3 percent of the benefit.

25. Switzerland, Denmark, and the Netherlands also require credit splitting in the employer-mandated portion of the benefit package.

26. Spain bases retirement benefits on a replacement factor that depends on the individual's years of contributions multiplied by a measure of earnings just before retirement. Dropping out of the labor force to care for young children is not likely to affect the measure of average earnings, but it would reduce the replacement rate somewhat. Dropping out of the labor force late in life to care for elderly parents, however, could have a serious impact on pension benefits.

27. The U.S. Congress introduced a flat dollar limit on the spouse's benefit in 1967, but repealed the limit in 1969.

REFERENCES

Advisory Council on Social Security. 1979. *Report of the 1979 Advisory Council on Social Security.* Washington, D.C.: U.S. Department of Health, Education and Welfare.

Austrian Documentation. 1994. *Social Security In Austria.* Vienna, Austria: The Federal Press Service.

Awad, Yaser and Nirit Israeli. 1997. "Poverty and Income Inequality: An International Comparison, 1980s and 1990s." Luxembourg Income Study Working Paper No. 166. Luxembourg: Luxembourg Income Study. July.

Board of Trustees of the Old-Age, Survivors and Disability Insurance Trust Fund. 1999. *1999 Annual Report.* Http://www.ssa.gov/OACT/TR. (Accessed August 2001).

Bosworth, Barry, Gary Burtless, and Eugene Steuerle. 1999. "Lifetime Earnings Patterns, the Distribution of Future Social Security Benefits, and the Impact of Pension Reform." Center for Retirement Research at Boston College Working Paper No. 1999-06. Boston: Center for Retirement Research at Boston College.

Bradshaw, Jonathan and Jun-Rong Chen. 1996. "Poverty in the U.K.: A Comparison with Nineteen Other Countries." Luxembourg Income Study Working Paper No. 147. Luxembourg: Luxembourg Income Study.

Canada Pension Plan. 1997. *Credit Splitting: Canada Pension Plan.* Human Resources Development Canada. Http://www.hrdc-drhc.gc.ca/isp/cpp/credit_e.shtml# pantage. (Accessed August, 2001).

Clubinfos. 1996. "Pension Rights for Divorced Spouses." Geneva, Switzerland. April. No. 5.

The Danish Labor Market Supplementary Pension Fund (ATP). 1998. *Annual Report and Accounts, 1998.* Denmark: The Danish Labor Market Supplementary Pension Fund.

Department of Social Security, Benefits Agency. 1999. *A Guide to Widow's Benefits.* London, England. September.

Federal Ministry of Labor and Social Affairs (Bundesministerium für Arbeit und Sozialordnung). 1999. *Social Security at a Glance.* Berlin, Germany. April.

Hauser, Richard. 1997. "Adequacy and Poverty Among the Retired." Paper presented at OECD-ILO Joint Workshop on Development and Reform of Pension Schemes, Paris, December 15–17.

Human Resources Development Canada. 2000. Fact Sheets on *Old Age Security* and *The Canada Pension Plan.* Http://www.hrdc-drhc.gc.ca/isp/common/oastoc_e. shtml. (Accessed August, 2001).

Internal Revenue Service, U.S. Department of the Treasury. 1999. "1999 1040 Instructions." Http://www.irs.gov. (Accessed August, 2001).

Max Planck Institut für Ausländisches und Internationales Sozialrecht. 1998. *Comparative Study on Credit-Splitting in the Federal Republic of Germany and Canada and Arrangements in Selected Other Countries.* Munich, West Germany. December. Volume IV.

Ministry of Health and Social Affairs. 1999. *The Norwegian Social Insurance Scheme: A Survey.* Http://www.dep.no/shd/engelsk/publ/veiledninger/030041-120007/ index-dok000-b-n-a.html. (Accessed August, 2001).

Scherman, Karl Gustaf. 1999. *The Swedish Pension Reform.* Geneva, Switzerland: Social Security Department, International Labour Office. *Issues in Social Protection,* Discussion Paper no. 7.

Shaver, Sheila. 1996. "Universality and Selectivity in Income Support: An Assessment of the Issues." Luxembourg Income Study Working Paper No. 145. Luxembourg: Luxembourg Income Study.

Smeeding, Timothy. 1997. "Reshuffling Responsibilities in Old Age: The United States in a Comparative Perspective." Luxembourg Income Study Working Paper No. 153. Luxembourg: Luxembourg Income Study.

Social Security Administration. 1999. *Annual Statistical Supplement to the Social Security Bulletin, 1998.* SSA Publication No. 13-11700. Washington, D.C: Government Printing Office. August.

———. 1999. *Social Security Programs throughout the World, 1999.* SSA Publication No. 13-11805. Washington, D.C.: Government Printing Office. August.

———. 2000. *Annual Statistical Supplement to the Social Security Bulletin, 2000.* Http://www.ssa.gov/statistics/Supplement/2000/. (Accessed August, 2001.)

The Social Insurance Bank (SVB). 1997. *Dutch National Old Age Pensions (AOW) Brochure.* Netherlands. February.

U.S. Census Bureau. 2001. "Poverty, 2000." March Current Population Survey. Http://www.census.gov. (Accessed August, 2001).

Credit Splitting of Public Pension Benefits on Divorce in Canada and Germany

Credit splitting recognizes that both spouses share in the building of their assets and entitlements regardless of salary level, employment status, or duration of the marriage (beyond some minimum qualifying period). Several countries have established "credit-splitting" provisions that allow their national pension systems to equally divide a one-earner or two-earner couple's accumulated wage credits between both spouses in the event of divorce.

Canada

Canada enacted credit splitting in 1978. Arguments in favor of the policy were that it recognized homemakers' contributions to household assets and to the economy and that it targeted benefits to women at greatest risk of poverty. The mechanisms set for realizing these goals were equal division of pension credits accumulated over the length of the marriage and independent entitlement to benefits. Arguments against the 1978 law were that it would add administrative burdens, lead to unwarranted intervention by the government in the financial affairs of private citizens, and create an equity dilemma by dividing single pensions among two people. The provision enacted represented a compromise between the two camps. The legislation deemed that earnings splitting would apply only at the time of divorce and only if one of the spouses (presumably the lower earner) applied to the Human Resources Department in Ottawa within two years of the divorce date.

Experience with this initial arrangement was that very few people applied for credit splitting (2.2 percent of divorce cases in the year after the bill was passed). Officials hypothesized that the low take-up rate reflected insufficient publicity as well as a reluctance on the part of the lower-earning spouse to complicate the divorce process.

The credit-splitting arrangement was modified in 1987, after a decade of debate. At that time, credit splitting at divorce was made mandatory, the time limit for informing the Human Resources Department was eliminated, and credit splitting was extended (on an optional basis) to the dissolution of common-law marriages. Forcing couples to split credits was still controversial, however, and the Provinces were given the authority to override the provision for divorces occurring within their territory, providing that explicit mention of the override was made in the divorce agreement. Three provinces, British Columbia, Saskatchewan, and Quebec, have opted out of the mandatory system.

To boost take-up rates, the Canadian government undertook a special outreach project in 1993 to better publicize credit splitting to the public. A full-time outreach team used a range of media and publicity techniques to disseminate information, including presentations targeted to senior women, the disabled, and various ethnic groups; videos (in six languages) for distribution to libraries and cable TV outlets; posters sent to companies for display in the workplace; and news articles published in major papers. In addition, special booklets were distributed to lawyers, and advertisements were targeted to various law publications. This special outreach project was folded into ongoing publicity efforts by the Canadian Pension Plan and, while there has been some increase in credit splitting take-up rates (16.3 percent of divorce cases as of 1996), the number of applications are still well below the expected level.

Germany

The German system applies credit splitting to all the public social insurance and private pension benefits that a divorcing couple is eligible to receive. Credit splitting is mandatory[1] and covers all old-age pension systems. In contrast to Canadian arrangements, the German family court system, which tries divorces, automatically carries out credit splitting as soon as the couple files for divorce. The family court judge gathers the necessary information from the divorcing parties and the relevant pension agency, makes the credit-splitting calculation, and sends the verdict to the pension agency. Hence, Germany has nearly a 100 percent take-up rate in its credit-splitting program, and credit splitting applies to about 90 percent of all divorces tried. However, such efficiency is not without its burdens. A 1987 report[2] estimated that family court judges spent fully 17 percent of their time just rendering credit-splitting decisions for divorce cases, on a volume of more than 100,000 cases per year. No insurance experts are assigned to assist these judges.

Different credit-splitting approaches apply to different benefit types but all approaches seek to equalize credit balances between spouses at the point the marriage ends. The law intends these methods be pursued hierarchically: if the normal means of credit splitting used in the public pension scheme was not applicable, then quasi-credit-splitting would be tried, and so on down the list. The overall method is to determine the equivalent value of these diverse pension rights under the public pension system and, in some cases, transfer the higher-earning spouse's forfeited credits to the lower-earning spouse's "account" under the public system. The credit-splitting approaches are listed below, along with their most common area of application.

Splitting	public pension scheme
Quasi-splitting	public pension + civil servant pension schemes
Real splitting	private pension
Extended quasi-splitting	public professional pension and civil servant supplementary pension schemes
Splitting on a wait-and-see basis	private pensions (where credits can lapse and/or their amounts are not pre-defined)

In splitting public retirement benefits, the German approach differs from the Canadian method. Rather than simply sum and halve all pension credits accumulated during a marriage, the German system calculates the pension right of each spouse at the time of divorce, based on all past credits earned, then prorates this pension entitlement by the number of credits the spouse has accumulated during the marriage. The goal is the same as the Canadian method: to provide divorcing individuals with equivalent pension rights at the point of separation.

The German formula is fairly simple and is applied to the pension rights of each spouse. A "fictitious" pension is calculated for the individual using credits and earnings from all prior years of work up to the present. Then the pension credits are summed for the period that corresponded to the marriage. The amount of pension credits earned during the marriage is divided by the amount of credits earned during the worker's whole career; this becomes the fraction of the worker's career pension subject to division. A nonworking spouse would have claim to half the working spouse's pension rights. As in Canada, the higher-earning spouse forfeits pension rights to the lower- or nonearning spouse.

The 1987 Max Planck Institute report cited earlier suggested that the annual pension right amount transferred to the average woman was $2,130 between 1979 and 1985. In 1997 wage-indexed terms, that amounts to $3,550.

Generally, the same approach is applied to other categories of pension and social insurance, but the valuation of the credits becomes more complicated. In splitting credits from private pension plans, for example, vesting issues and decisions about whether individuals who subsequently change jobs retain claims to earned credits arise. According to rulings by the German courts, pension credits can only be considered for splitting purposes if they have not lapsed and as long as they represent a predefined amount of the pension benefit at the time of divorce. If the private pension is flat or indexed to prices, then its value must be converted using the wage-indexing formula for the public pension. Thereafter, the process already described is followed (although other complexities must be remedied along the way). If credits have not lapsed and represent defined amounts at the time of divorce, the splitting method employed is called "real splitting." Otherwise, the "splitting on a wait-and-see basis" takes effect, meaning the lower-earning spouse is granted a claim on the higher-earning spouse's pension, but the valuation cannot be resolved until both spouses have reached pensionable age, even if credits lapse before that time. Private insurance (a life annuity with supplementary disability insurance) is treated similarly when determining whether to apply real splitting or splitting on a wait-and-see basis.

A P P E N D I X   5B

Impact of Tax Treatment on Replacement Rates

The comparisons in the body of the chapter ignore the impact of both payroll and income taxes. At present, U.S. Social Security benefits are excluded from the income tax base for middle- and low-income households, whereas they are taxable in many other industrialized countries. U.S. employee payroll tax rates are lower, however, than in many other countries. The difference in income tax treatment causes the United

States to appear somewhat more generous in its net replacement rates than in its gross replacement rates. The difference in payroll tax rates partially offsets the lower gross rates.

The table below compares gross and net replacement rates for illustrative workers in six countries. The workers are assumed to have always earned the average manufacturing wage in the respective countries; in two-earner couples, the second worker is assumed to have earned 75 percent of the average wage. Gross replacement rates are simply the calculated gross benefit divided by the average manufacturing wage. Net replacement rates are the benefit net of any income taxes divided by the national average wage net of all income taxes and employee payroll taxes. The calculations assume that the households have no other source of income and use standard deductions.

Appendix Table 5B.1 *Gross and Net Replacement Rates (Percent)*

	Single Worker		One-Earner Couple		Two-Earner Couple	
Country	Gross	Net	Gross	Net	Gross	Net
Australia	27	33	46	51	42	25
Canada	40	45	60	65	44	46
France	45	60	45	56	47	59
Germany	42	57	42	59	42	57
Sweden	63	66	72	76	61	58
United States	41	55	61	78	43	57

Note: "Replacement rate" is defined as the ratio of the retirement benefit accrued by a person earning the national average wage to the national average wage in the year before he or she retires. "Gross" and "net" are the replacement rate before and after payroll, and income taxes are applied to the benefit and the national average wage.

For the illustrative U.S. workers, net replacement rates exceed gross replacement rates by 14 percentage points for the single worker and the two-earner couple and by 17 percentage points for the one-earner couple. Most of the difference reflects favorable income tax treatment— wages are taxable while benefits for average earners with no other income are not. Deducting the employee payroll tax from earnings effectively raises the replacement rate by only 3 to 4 percentage points.

Germany's relatively high employee social insurance contributions lead to a similar difference between gross and net replacement rates for the illustrative German workers. The differences between the two rates are less pronounced in the other countries.

Under current U.S. law, the thresholds that determine whether Social Security benefits are tax exempt are not adjusted according to wage and price increases. Thus, over time, as general wage and price levels rise, nominal benefit levels will also rise, and an increasing fraction of U.S. Social Security benefits will be subject to income taxation. The wider taxability of benefits will narrow the gap between net replacement rates and gross replacement rates.

APPENDIX 5C

Survivors Benefits, Divorce Benefits, and Child Care Credits in 16 Countries

Australia

Public Pension Benefits. Universal, means-tested benefit.

Workers Benefit Calculation. None, pension benefit is universal.

Survivors Benefits. No provision.

Divorce. No provision because of universal benefit.

Child Care Credit. No provision.

Austria

Public Pension Benefits. Earnings-related benefit and minimum benefit.

Workers Benefit Calculation. Worker receives 1.83 percentage points for each of his or her first 30 years worked plus 1.675 points for working years 31–45. The resulting percentage is multiplied by the average of the worker's best 15 years of earnings. The pension benefit replaces 80 percent of the national average wage for an average wage worker.

Survivors Benefits. A nonworking surviving spouse receives 60 percent of the deceased's pension. A minimum benefit that replaces 35 percent of the average wage is available if it is larger. Working surviving spouses receive survivors pensions plus their own pensions. The survivor pension is calculated as follows. First, the surviving spouse's best 15 years of average wages are divided by the deceased spouse's average wages. This fraction is multiplied by 24 percent, and the result is subtracted from 76 percent. This figure (with a maximum set at 60 percent and a minimum at 40 percent) represents the fraction of the deceased's pension to which the surviving spouse is entitled.[3] The survivor's pension entitlement is then added to the full amount of the surviving spouse's own pension. Working widow(er)s who earned 75 percent of the average wage receive a benefit replacing 100 percent of their wages.

Belgium

Public Pension Benefits. Earnings-related benefit and minimum benefit.

Workers Benefit Calculation. Equals 60 percent of career average earnings, assuming 45 years of contributions; 75 percent for one-earner couples. Pension benefit replaces 60 percent of national average wage for a single average-wage worker.

Survivors Benefits. A nonworking surviving spouse receives a survivor's pension equal to 80 percent of deceased's pension and replacing 60 percent of the average wage. A minimum benefit that replaces 41 percent of the average wage is available. Surviving spouses who work are entitled to a survivor's pension plus a pension based on their own work record, but the combined amount cannot sum to more than 110 percent of the survivor's pension. For example, if the deceased earned average wages of 100, while the widow(er) earned more than 88, the widow(er)'s own benefit would actually exceed 110 percent of the survivor's benefit, making it the better option.[4] In our simulation, however, 110 percent of the survivor's benefit is the better option. The widow(er)'s combined benefit replaces 53 percent of the average wage.

Divorce. The individual receives 37.5 percent of a former spouse's average earnings over the duration of marriage, less his or her own pension rights accrued during the same period. (This percentage rate was designed to be half the 75 percent rate one-earner couples receive.) If a former spouse has average earnings of 100, the divorced spouse receives no benefit if his or her own average earnings exceed 62.5. Again, a minimum benefit applies.

Child Care. A spouse raising a child age three or under is credited for pension purposes with the earnings in his or her most recent year of work, for each applicable year.

Canada

Public Pension Benefits. Universal benefit, income supplement, and earnings-related benefit.

Workers Benefit Calculation. Equals 25 percent of career average earnings (dropping out the 15 percent of years with lowest earnings, and replaces 24 percent of national average wage for the average wage worker.

Survivors Benefits. A nonworking widow(er) receives (1) 60 percent of deceased's earnings-related pension (capped at roughly 14 percent of average wage), (2) his or her own universal benefit (fixed at 13 percent of average wage), and (3) an income-tested supplement. This sums to a total benefit of 35 percent of the average wage. The minimum benefit the widow(er) can receive, equal to the universal pension plus the full income-tested supplement, produces a benefit of 28 percent of the average wage.

   A working widow(er) may receive four pension benefits: (1) 60 percent of the deceased's earnings-related pension (capped as above), (2) his or her own earnings-related pension, (3) his or her own universal benefit, and (4) an income-tested supplement, if the phase-out range has not been exceeded. In our simulation, the widow(er) receives a total benefit amounting to 46 percent of the average wage and no income-tested supplement.

Divorce. Under the earnings-related tier, both spouses are credited with accruing equal pension rights during the span of their marriage. The credits earned by one or both spouses over the duration of the marriage are simply summed and then split in half. The result is the higher-earning spouse forfeits pension rights to the lower-earning spouse.

Child Care. A spouse raising a child age seven or under has the option of dropping these low or zero years of earnings from his or her career average if it improves the benefit.

Denmark

Public Pension Benefits. Universal benefit, income-tested benefit, and flat contributory benefit. The universal benefit replaces 15 percent of average wage; the universal supplement replaces 13 percent if the worker is eligible for flat contributory benefit, 14 percent if not; and the flat contributory benefit replaces five percent of the average wage.

Workers Benefit Calculation. None, benefits are not related to earnings or contributions.

Survivors Benefits. A nonworking widow(er) receives a survivor's lump-sum benefit equal to 35 percent of the capital value of the deceased's flat, contributory benefit.[5] For the purposes of this chapter, however, we assume no-cost annuitization of the survivor benefit, which works out to 2 percent of the average wage. In addition, the widow(er) receives the universal benefit, or 15 percent of the average wage, and an income-tested supplement that replaces an additional 16 percent of the average wage, for a total replacement rate of 33 percent. Note that the amount of the widow(er)'s benefit receipt is insensitive to the deceased's career earnings.

A working widow(er) would receive (1) a universal benefit, (2) a flat contributory benefit, (3) an annuitized survivor benefit of the same amount as the nonworking widow(er)'s above, and (4) an income-tested supplement. While working widow(er)s receive a flat contributory benefit compared with their nonworking counterparts, this additional amount reduces their income-tested benefit almost dollar for dollar so that they effectively receive the same replacement rate as nonworking widow(er)s—34 percent of the average wage. Again, benefit receipt in Denmark is not tied to earnings but to years of contributions or residence by couples and survivors.

Child Care. No provision.

France

Public Pension Benefits. Earnings-related benefit and means-tested minimum benefit.

Workers Benefit Calculation. Equal to 50 percent of career average earnings, assuming 40 years of contributions, and replaces 45 percent of national average wage for an average wage worker.

Survivors Benefits. The nonworking widow(er)'s benefit equals 54 percent of the deceased's pension and replaces 25 percent of the average wage. The minimum benefit replaces 22 percent.

Working widow(er)s receive the survivor benefit plus their own pension, without any reduction for the combination. The combined benefit replaces 62 percent of the average wage.

Divorce. Same as survivor's benefits, but means-tested if income exceeds 44 percent of the French average wage. In addition, the divorced spouse cannot have remarried, and if other former spouses of the insured exist, this benefit amount is proportionally divided among these individuals according to the length of the respective marriages.

Child Care. Years of low or zero earnings while raising a child are not averaged in for benefit calculation purposes.

Germany

Public Pension Benefits. Earnings-related benefit.

Workers Benefit Calculation. Workers accumulate pension points for each year they work, equal to the ratio of their own wages to average covered wages. A worker earning the average wage in a given year receives one pension point. The sum of these pension points is multiplied by the monthly pension amount of 47.65 (representing one year of earnings at the average wage) and equals the worker's monthly pension. The pension for the average wage earner replaces about 42 percent of the national average wage.

Survivors Benefits. A nonworking widow(er)'s benefit equals 60 percent of the deceased's pension and replaces 25 percent of the average wage. Germany is one of the few industrialized countries to provide no minimum benefit for dependents through its social security system, although welfare benefits are available.

A working widow also receives 60 percent of the deceased's pension in theory, the system uses a complex formula for calculating the reduction when this pension is added to the widow's own earnings-related pension. In summing the widow(er)'s survivor and retirement pensions, the "offset" 47.65 multiplied by 12×26.4^6 is subtracted from the full survivor's pension; then, an additional 40 percent of the remaining survivor's pension is subtracted. The formula favors surviving spouses of higher-wage workers.[7] Indeed, for the working survivor of an average wage worker, the offset exceeds the possible survivor's benefit so the widow(er) just receives the retirement pension. If the widow(er) earned 75 percent of the average wage, the benefit would replace 32 percent of earnings.

Divorce. The German system calculates the pension right of a spouse at the time of divorce, based on all past credits earned, then prorates this pension right by the number of credits the spouse accumulated during the span of marriage. This calculation is done for both spouses, and the prorated amounts are then summed and divided in half. As in Canada, the higher-earning spouse forfeits pension rights to the lower-earning spouse.

Child Care. A spouse raising a child age three or under receives a credit of 0.75 pension points per applicable year.

Japan

Public Pension Benefits. Flat contributory and earnings-related.

Workers Benefit Calculation. Applicable only to the earnings-related tier. The worker benefit equals 0.75 percent multiplied by the number of months of contributions multiplied by indexed monthly wages, assuming 25 years of contributions. The earnings-related benefit replaces 32 percent of the national average wage for an average wage worker.

Survivors Benefits. There are no widower benefits in Japan. A nonworking widow receives 75 percent of the deceased's earnings-related benefit (second tier) plus a full, flat contributory benefit.[8] The former replaces 26 percent and the latter replaces 24 percent, for a total of 50 percent of the average wage.

A working widow has several options for collecting survivor's benefits. She may receive the maximum of the full flat contributory benefit plus (1) 75 percent of her husband's earnings-related benefit, (2) 50 percent of her own earnings-related benefit plus 50 percent of her husband's, or (3) 100 percent of her own earnings-related benefit. In our simulation, the widow would choose option 2, the first tier of which would give her 23 percent of the average wage, while the 50/50 split between her husband and her own earnings-related benefit would give her 28 percent, for a total of 51 percent of the average wage.[9]

Divorce. No provision. (A credit-splitting regime is under consideration.)

Child Care. The mother is credited for pension purposes for one year of maternity leave at the level of her most recent wages.

The Netherlands

Public Pension Benefits. Flat quasi-contributory benefit.[10]

Workers Benefit Calculation. None, as pension benefit is virtually universal.

Survivors Benefits. Nonworking widow(er)s receive the survivor's benefit as it is larger than the old-age benefit for a single person. The benefit replaces 36 percent of the Dutch average wage, while the old-age benefit would replace 33 percent.

Working widow(er)s effectively receive the larger of the survivor's benefit or their own benefit, as the former is reduced by the amount of all additional income. In our simulation, the survivor's benefit is always more, and as above, this benefit replaces 36 percent of the average wage. The widow(er)'s retirement benefit would replace 33 percent.

Divorce. No provision.

New Zealand

Public Pension Benefits. Universal benefit.

Workers Benefit Calculation. No calculation, benefit is flat and automatic, replacing 40 percent of the average wage.

Survivors Benefits. Provision only for young widows (not for widowers).

Divorce. No provision because of universal benefit.

Child Care. No provision because of universal benefit.

Norway

Public Pension Benefits. Flat contributory benefit and earnings-related benefit.

Workers Benefit Calculation. Workers are credited with pension points each year, calculated as the ratio of a year's wages minus the base amount, all over the base amount, with a maximum of 7 pension points per year. A retirement pension equals the average of the 20 best years of pension points times 0.42 times the base amount. A worker who earns the average wage all his or her life will have about a 5 pension point average, the base amount replaces 17 percent of the average wage.

Survivors Benefits. Nonworking widow(er) receives only a survivor's benefit, composed of two parts. The first part is the base amount which replaces 17 percent of the average wage. The second part is 55 percent of the deceased's earnings-related benefit. The combination is income-tested as follows: the full survivor's pension is reduced by 40 percent of the excess over one-half of the base amount. The resulting sum replaces 32 percent of the average wage. As a result of the income-test, the surviving spouse of a high-wage earner only receives a 35 percent replacement rate, which is not significantly higher, while the low-wage analog receives 30 percent. If the deceased did not have sufficient earnings to qualify for a pension under the earnings-related scheme, the widow(er) may receive a supplement to the base amount, equal to another 79.33 percent of it. This supplement is reduced one for one against any other income.

Working widow(er)s receive the following pension components: their retirement benefit made up of (1) the base amount, (2) an earnings-related benefit plus their survivor's benefit made up of the base amount again, and (3) 55 percent of the deceased's earnings-related benefit. All four components are summed and the total pension amount is reduced by 40 percent of the excess over one-half the base amount. The adjusted sum replaces 50 percent of the average wage. High-wage survivors of high-wage spouses see little increase because of the income test (improvement to a 55 percent replacement rate) while the low-wage analog gets 32 percent. If neither the widow(er) nor the deceased had participated in the earnings-related scheme, the widow(er) would be eligible for the same supplement as described in the previous paragraph.

Divorce. Transitional grant (lasting six months) equal to survivor benefit plus child care benefit, if applicable, is given to divorced, separated, or unwed parent. Full, ongoing survivors' benefits for divorced survivor are available if the marriage lasted 25 years (15 years if the couple had children) and the divorced widow(er) has not remarried.

Child Care. Persons taking unpaid home care of children under age seven are credited for pension purposes with 3.00 pension points for each applicable year, or 73 percent of the average wage.[11]

Spain

Public Pension Benefits. Earnings-related benefit.

Workers Benefit Calculation. Workers benefit equals 96/112 times average of last eight years' earnings times 100 percent.[12] Benefit replaces about 83 percent of the national average wage for an average wage worker.

Survivors' Benefits. Nonworking widow(er)s receive 45 percent of the deceased's benefit, replacing 43 percent of the average wage. The minimum benefit replaces 28 percent.

Working widow(er)s also receive 45 percent of the deceased's benefit plus their own benefit, without reduction. The survivors benefit replaces 43 percent while the retirement benefit replaces 62 percent, for a total of 105 percent of the average wage.

Divorce. Spouses resolve public pension divisions with court guidance and subject to court approval.

Child Care. No provision.

Sweden

Public Pension Benefits. Universal benefit and earnings-related benefit.

Workers Benefit Calculation. As with Norway, workers are credited with pension points each year, calculated as the ratio of a year's wages minus the base amount, all over the base amount. A retirement pension equals the average of the 15 best years of pension points times 0.6 times the base amount. An average wage worker would get about 5.4 points and the base amount replaces 15 percent of the average wage.

Survivors' Benefits. No benefits for widowers (without dependent children). Widows do not receive survivors' benefits except for a transitional period lasting six months after their husbands' deaths. A nonworking widow without any other income would receive the universal benefit plus an income-tested supplement equal to 55.5 percent of the universal benefit, the sum of which (1.555 times the universal benefit) replaces 22 percent of the average wage.

Working widows would receive the universal benefit plus their own earnings-related benefit. The former replaces 15 percent of the average wage, while the latter replaces 34 percent, for a total of 49 percent.

Divorce. No provision.

Child Care. A spouse raising a child age four or under is credited for pension purposes with the most favorable of (1) her earnings level prior to child birth, (2) the difference between her own earnings and 75 percent of average covered earnings, or (3) a wage-adjusted amount equal to the base amount (15 percent of the average wage).

Switzerland

Public Pension Benefits. Earnings-related benefit.

Workers Benefit Calculation. Thirteen percent of the average wage plus 13/600 of average annual income; if annual income is above 47 percent of average wage, then 19 percent of average wage plus 8/600 of average annual income. Note that all persons, whether working or not, are responsible for contributing to the social security system, even if contributions must be made on assets rather than income. Hence, all retired persons are eligible for at least the minimum "earnings-related" benefit, even dependent spouses. The pension benefit replaces about 20 percent of the national average wage for the average wage worker.

Survivors Benefits. No benefits for widowers (without dependent children). Nonworking widows receive the larger of 80 percent of the deceased's benefit, or the minimum work benefit. In the simulation, the nonworking widow always receives the minimum work benefit, replacing 18 percent of the average wage. The survivor benefit replaces 16 percent.

Working widows receive the larger of the survivor benefit or their own benefit. Actually, a widow married to an average-wage worker would always opt for her own retirement benefit owing to (1) the very progressive Swiss benefit formula, and (2) the relatively generous minimum benefit for workers, which exceeds 80 percent of an average-wage earner's pension. The widow's own retirement benefit replaces 20 percent of the average wage, the minimum benefit replaces 18 percent, and her survivor's benefit would only replace 16 percent. Even if the widow were married to the high-wage earner, her own benefit and the minimum benefit would each continue to exceed the survivor's benefit.

Divorce. All earnings accrued during a couple's marriage are split evenly between both spouses for pension calculation purposes.

Child Care. A credit for raising children age 16 or under is worth 3 times the minimum pension (54 percent of the average wage) and is either awarded to a single spouse or divided equally between two spouses.

United Kingdom

Public Pension Benefits. Flat contributory benefit and earnings-related benefit.

Workers Benefit Calculation. Note that workers in the United Kingdom can and often do opt out of the state system to participate in employer, professional, or wholly private pension schemes. The state pension formula is a combination of a flat contributory benefit and an earnings-related benefit. The flat contributory benefit requires workers to contribute 44 out of 49 years to receive 20 percent of the national average wage (for all wage earners). The state earnings-related scheme awards 1.25 percentage points against the amount of earnings in each year exceeding a floor (set at about 20 percent of the national average wage), for a maximum of 25 percentage points (equal to 20 years credited wages). The amount of wages above the floor in each year is wage-indexed to the level of wages in the year the worker retires; all amounts are averaged and this average is multiplied by 25 percent, producing a benefit that replaces about 20 percent of the national average wage for the average wage earner. When added to the flat contributory benefit, this results in a 40 percent replacement rate for the average-wage worker.

Survivors' Benefits. No benefits for widowers. Nonworking widows receive the maximum basic pension plus 50 percent of their deceased husband's pension (25 percent of earnings).[13] The two pension benefits replace 20 percent each, or 40 percent together. The minimum benefit, which is means-tested, replaces 27 percent of income.

A working widow receives the sum of the following pension components without reductions: (1) her own flat contributory benefit (replaces 20 percent of average wage), (2) her own earnings-related benefit (replaces 13 percent), and (3) survivor benefit equal to 50 percent of deceased's earnings-related pension (replaces 10 percent), for a total replacement rate of 43 percent of the average wage. The same minimum benefit above applies.

Divorce. Flat contributory: Higher-earning spouse's earnings record is substituted either for (a) all tax years until the last year of the marriage or (b) only those tax years spanning the marriage, whichever is more favorable. Earnings-related: Legislation effective April 2000 calls for pension sharing between spouses negotiated by agreement or court order.

Child Care. Years of earnings below the contribution floor while receiving child care benefits for a child under age 16 are dropped out of contribution years requirements and average wage determinations for both the flat contributory benefit and the earnings-related benefit. No limit on dropped-out years is allowed, but at least 20 qualifying years are necessary to receive a full benefit for either tier.

United States

Public Pension Benefits. Earnings-related benefit.

Workers Benefit Calculation. The pension formula in the United States is more complex than that for the other countries studied here, but essentially, all of a worker's past wages are wage-indexed to the national average wage the year the worker turns 60, and the 35 highest years of earnings are selected and averaged. A *kinked, redistributive* benefit formula with rates of 90 percent, 32 percent, and 15 percent is applied to this career average, producing a benefit that replaces 41 percent of the national average wage for the average-wage worker.

Survivors Benefits. A nonworking widow receives 100 percent of her deceased husband's pension, replacing 41 percent of the average wage.

Working widows receive the larger of the survivor benefit or their own retirement benefit. A widow earning 75 percent of the average wage would clearly opt for the survivor benefit because her average-wage husband earned more. This benefit replaces 41 percent.

Divorce. Women married at least 10 years who have not subsequently remarried receive 50 percent of their former spouse's retirement benefit.

Child Care. No provision.

Assumptions of the Simulation

1. We model benefits for the U.S. Social Security Administration's three prototypical workers, classified as "Low," "Average," and "High," who earn 45 percent, 100 percent, and 160 percent of the average wage in the countries considered, respectively.
2. Widows were married to husbands who were the same age and became widowed at the normal retirement age.
3. Our analysis ignores death benefits and lump-sum grants that do not represent the capital value of the pension.
4. In the following examples, unless stated otherwise, the deceased worker is assumed to earn the average wage while the surviving spouse is either a non-worker or earns 75 percent of the average wage.
5. For minimum-benefit purposes, workers contributed to the pension system for 35 years. For regular retirement benefits, workers entered the labor force at age 22 and worked until the normal retirement age. In some countries, the minimum and retirement benefits calculated may be proportionately reduced if the work years requirement is not met in full (e.g., 40 years of work may be required to receive a full benefit). Those reductions have been incorportaed where applicable.
6. Generally, the benefit numbers and formulas we use pertain to the 1997–99 period and the country average wages are from 1996 or 1997, depending on the latest data available. However, in cases where current or about-to-be legislated reforms would substantially alter benefits, we have employed the new rules in the benefit calculations. Sweden is one example. That country is phasing out survivors' benefits even though persons retiring at present would still be eligible to receive them.

NOTES TO APPENDIXES

1. However, marriage contracts and judicially approved agreements can exclude credit-splitting. Data suggest that credit-splitting is excluded in between 10 and 15 percent of all tried cases.

2. Max Planck Institut für Ausländisches und Internationales Sozialrecht, *Comparative Study on Credit-Splitting in the Federal Republic of Germany and Canada and Arrangements in Selected Other Countries*, Munich, West Germany, December 1987, Volume IV.

3. In effect, the larger the gap in earnings between the spouses, the larger the survivor's benefit provided by this formula, assuming the survivor here had the lower earnings.

4. Example: Survivor's benefit of 100×60 percent $\times 80$ percent $\times 110$ percent = own pension of 88×60 percent. The retirement pensions of widow(er)s earning over 88 exceed 110 percent of their survivors' pensions.

5. For workers who have contributed in all years since 1964, regardless of income or level of contributions, the full contributory benefit is worth 18,000 DKK ($2,663) or 5 percent of the average wage.

6. The offset equals the monthly pension, times 12, times the sum of the average woman's career pension points, i.e. 26.4. These numbers change slightly each year based on wages and life expectancy.

7. The working widow(er) of a high earner, i.e. one that earned 160 percent of the average wage, receives slightly less than a third of the full survivor's benefit after reductions, plus own benefit. The replacement rate of the combined benefit equals 64 percent of the average wage, the survivor's benefit contributing 13 percentage points of that level.

8. The first tier benefit is awarded to a household rather than an individual (i.e. two or more persons would receive the same absolute amount as an individual) and years of marriage to a contributor can substitute for one's own missing years of contributions. In any case, a widow always receives the full value of the benefit whether the number of contributions are sufficient or not.

9. Options 1 and 3 are always less than option 2 and equal to one another for any income level since we require the widow earn 75 percent of the deceased's wage; the linear benefit formula means the benefit she earns on her own record will always be 75 percent of his.

10. Wage earners must pay social security contributions but those who do not work can qualify for the full benefit by accumulating 50 years of residence. All residents received the full benefit.

11. Norwegian pension points are calculated as the ratio of a year's wages minus the base amount all over the base amount, e.g. 3.00 pension points represents four times the base amount which was 167,260 NOK ($22,331) in 1997 or 73 percent of the average wage.

12. Technically, workers receive 50 percent for the first 15 years of contributions, 3 percent for each year of contributions between 15 and 26 years exclusive, and 2 percent for each year thereafter, up to a maximum of 100 percent. Workers in our simulation contributed for 43 years, so they receive the maximum.

13. The applicable survivor's percentage just changed for April 2000. Formerly, the widow received 100 percent of the deceased's pension, but we are applying the new rules to the 1997 numbers to remain current.

6

Social Security Benefits for Spouses and Survivors

Options for Change

Melissa M. Favreault
Frank J. Sammartino
C. Eugene Steuerle

Because Social Security promises more benefits than current tax rates can support, some changes to the system are inevitable. Most recent reform efforts have focused mainly on one of two goals: restoring balance within the Social Security trust funds while maintaining as much of the current benefit structure as possible, or providing smaller public benefits supplemented by private benefits from individual accounts. Both approaches largely ignore the vital question of how the public system would and should distribute benefits among different types of families.

No matter how the Social Security system evolves, issues surrounding how to apportion benefits across families will remain. In addition to benefits for retired and disabled workers, the current structure provides benefits for the nonworking spouses and survivors of those workers at no cost to the family in terms of either reduced worker benefits or additional contributions. These added family benefits are an important part of the social insurance role of the program, providing needed support for many older retirees. Yet some modification to the current structure of family benefits might better fulfill that role and also better serve other program objectives. Social, demographic, and economic forces have all dramatically changed the structure of the modern family and its relationship to the economy since the inception of the program. As a consequence, a system designed to meet the needs of the U.S. population in 1940 may not meet the needs of U.S. families in 2040.

The Evolution of Family Benefits

Social Security's family benefit structure evolved, as do all programs, within the context of its own time. Three conditions seem especially important when considering how family benefits in Social Security formed.[1] First, the combination of high unemployment rates, low pension coverage rates, the failure of many pension plans, and significant poverty rates in old age created demand for a system that would focus initially on adequacy and poverty relief. Legislators adopted spousal and survivor benefits mainly to provide higher benefits in retirement to couples than to single individuals for the simple reason that two elderly adults have greater income needs than one adult. The central issue was need, not whether any additional work-related contributions justified the additional transfer.

Second, the typical household that policymakers so often pointed to in Social Security's early days was a male worker with a wife who was not working in the formal marketplace. This stereotypical household provided the basis for many aspects of Social Security's design. Even as the system gradually began to address other needs, extensions were largely confined to gaps in coverage related to a married-couple household. Young widows first became eligible for survivors benefits in 1950, while divorced spouses first became eligible for benefits in 1965. Again, Social Security did not require extra contributions for this added insurance protection for widows or for the additional benefits of the divorced spouse.[2]

Third, following the model of defined benefit private pension plans then prevalent, Social Security designers structured worker benefits in part on the basis of earnings replacement rates, and set spousal and survivor benefits in relationship to that replacement rate. If Social Security were to replace 40 percent of a single worker's wages, for instance, then a worker and spouse might require 60 percent of those wages to come closer to maintaining their standard of living while working. Hence, spousal benefits were set at one-half the primary worker's benefit. Similarly, debates over the size of survivors benefits mainly focused on what percentage of the worker's benefit should be replaced.

Because in the 1940s most unmarried individuals with children were widows, the system largely ignored the needs of those individuals who raised children but never married, or who were married for only a few years. One rationalization for this apparent omission was that Social Security was intended as a program to replace lost earnings because of a worker's retirement, death, or, in later years, disability. During Social Security's early years, women raising children were not expected to work (even though they were increasingly working during World War II, the first years when benefits were paid). This attitude was apparent in the design of Aid to Families with Dependent Children (AFDC), a social assistance program enacted as part of the Social Security Act of 1935 that was structured around the notion that unpartnered women would stay home with their children.

Time and attitudes change. The single-earner married couple household is no longer typical. Married-couple families account for slightly over half of all households, and in most working-age married couples (70 percent) both spouses work. More and more children are now raised outside the traditional two-parent family. About a third of children currently live in single-parent households, usually with a single mother. Work is the norm among single-parent families. Labor force participation rates for single mothers with young children reached 67 percent by 1998 and 81 percent for single mothers with older children.[3] Public policy today not only accepts but also encourages work among single parents. In 1997, Congress replaced AFDC with a program that required beneficiaries to work as a condition of receiving assistance (i.e., Temporary Assistance to Needy Families).

Principles and Criteria

In approaching an issue such as changes to Social Security's spousal and survivor benefits, it is best to start with some basic principles by which we can fully assess the current structure and possible modifications to that structure. (See box 6.A for a description of Social Security benefit calculations.) Four elements characterize the objectives of most tax and expenditure programs, including Social Security.[4]

The first is *income adequacy,* or the extent to which the program distributes more resources to those who are worse off than to those who are better off, typically measured by annual income. Social Security attempts to meet this objective by providing higher replacement rates for lower-wage workers and benefits for nonworking spouses and survivors, although, as we shall see, those payments may not in fact enhance progressivity.[5] One important measure of the program's success in meeting this objective is its antipoverty effectiveness.

Box 6.A. Social Security Benefit Calculations under Current Law: A Brief Summary

Social Security benefits are intended to replace, in part, earnings lost because of retirement, disability, or death of a wage earner. To be eligible for benefits, a worker must be fully insured. Those eligible to retire in 1991 or later require 40 quarters of coverage to be fully insured. Those born earlier and those who become disabled or die before retirement need fewer quarters. Workers can gain up to four quarters of coverage a year if they have earnings from employment covered by the Social Security program. The amount of earnings required to gain a quarter of coverage grows each year by the growth in the average level of wages. In 2000, a worker who earned more than $3,120 would receive credit for four quarters of coverage.

The size of a worker's cash benefit is determined by his or her average lifetime earnings. Beginning with those born after 1928, retirement benefits are based on earnings averaged over the highest 35 years of earnings. Past earnings are indexed to reflect economywide wage growth during the worker's career. The worker's average indexed monthly earnings (AIME) is then used to compute benefits. The benefit formula is weighted in favor of workers with low AIMEs, providing workers with low lifetime earnings benefits that are a higher fraction of preretirement earnings.

Workers may claim their retirement benefits when they turn 62. If workers accept benefits before the full retirement age (which ranges from age 65 to age 67, depending on one's year of birth), benefits are reduced for each month of early retirement. Workers who retire after the full retirement age receive delayed retirement credits (through age 70).

Social Security also provides benefits for aged spouses of retired or disabled workers and aged survivors of deceased workers. The system provides additional benefits for younger spouses or survivors who are raising children and for younger disabled survivors. The spousal benefit is equal to 50 percent of the retired or disabled worker's full benefit amount, while aged widow(er)s of deceased workers can receive up to 100 percent of the deceased's retirement benefit. Spousal and survivor benefits are payable only to the extent that they exceed the recipient's own benefit as a worker. Beneficiaries receiving their own retirement benefit and a partial spousal or survivor benefit are termed dually entitled. This dual entitlement provision effectively limits total benefit payments to the higher of a person's own worker benefit or any dependent benefit to which he or she is entitled. Spousal benefits are available at age 62 and survivor benefits at age 60; both are reduced if accepted before the full retirement age.

The program provides divorced persons whose marriage lasted at least 10 years the same spousal and survivor benefits as spouses and survivors of intact marriages. Unlike under private pension systems, payment of additional spousal, survivor, or divorced spousal benefits does not affect the worker's basic benefit.

A second objective is *individual equity,* based on the idea that individuals should get what they pay for. In a government program, this criterion generally means that participants should receive benefits in return for the taxes they pay. Analysts of Social Security often measure the extent to which the program achieves this standard by calculating the rate of return for various groups. In the case of current spousal and survivor benefits, however, the system is more or less a pure transfer—no additional contributions are required to get the benefit—which means that other taxpayers must subsidize those transfers. The worker benefit may not provide a return equal to the full amount of taxes paid, but it does provide something at the margin. Many working spouses get nothing back at all at the margin.

A third objective is *horizontal equity,* or equal treatment of individuals in equal circumstances. When applied to Social Security, the goal here is to provide families of the same cohort with the same total earnings with roughly equal amounts of benefits, regardless of how much each spouse contributed to the family's total income. This goal is often not met under the current system. The principle of horizontal equity is also violated in the case of households with different marital histories; for example, even for couples with the same level of contributions and earnings, the current system generates differences in benefits for those with long marriages, short marriages, or no marriage at all, and creates benefit differences between divorced persons with a living or a deceased former spouse.

A measure of horizontal equity is the treatment of single heads of household. Single heads of household and their children are at high risk of poverty throughout their lifetimes. Under the current Social Security system, single parents often have access to *fewer* benefits, even if they work steadily for many years, than do persons in long-term marriages who have not worked, made payroll contributions, or raised any children. At the same time that Social Security has offered these families less support than their married counterparts, other components of the U.S. social safety net that once served this population have shrunk, imposing more limitations on and conditions for support.[6]

A fourth objective is *efficiency,* which translates into trying to achieve the greatest good for the lowest cost. A standard source of inefficiency in a government program is the amount of distortion that it causes in individual behavior, for example, by creating incentives for people to work or save less than they would otherwise. Applying this principle to Social Security suggests that the system should distribute benefits in a way that has the least effect on work incentives and that the marginal returns to payroll tax contributions should not vary according to family circumstances. One measure of efficiency is whether the effect of additional earnings on lifetime benefits of a couple is the same when only one spouse works and when both spouses work.[7]

Evaluating the Current Structure

The Social Security program has a mixed record in trying to balance its sometimes conflicting objectives. Despite a progressive benefit structure and additional benefits for dependents and survivors, poverty rates remain high for some older Americans, particularly single women. Although benefits are based on past lifetime earnings and thus are higher for those who have contributed more, one-earner couples receive much higher lifetime benefits than two-earner couples with the same lifetime earnings. Depending upon the timing and circumstances of marriage and divorce, lifetime benefits can also vary a great deal, despite equivalent past contributions, Although additional earnings can increase a worker's expected lifetime benefits, the returns to a second earner in a married couple are much less than the returns to additional earnings by the primary earner. Finally, although the system provides benefits for dependents and survivors, it fails to provide the same benefits for single heads of household.

Antipoverty Effectiveness

Although Social Security has had great success in reducing poverty among the elderly, almost one-fifth of all women age 85 and over still have income below the poverty level. Most couples enter retirement with reasonably adequate financial resources. Only about 5 percent of couples with heads age 62 to 64 have income below the poverty level, and even by the time the head reaches age 85, just 6 percent of older couples are in poverty (see table 6.1). Poverty among older survivors, however, remains relatively high. Between 16 and 18 percent of widows over 65, for instance, have incomes below poverty, and more than 27 percent of these widows have incomes below 125 percent of poverty. According to Smith (this volume), women and older survivors are likely to continue to fare poorly in future decades when poverty levels are measured relative to average wages.

Table 6.1 *Poverty Rates by Age, Sex, and Marital Status, 1998*

	Married Couples	Women				Unmarried Men
		Total	Widowed	Never Married	Divorced	
Percentage with Income Below the Poverty Threshold						
Age						
62–64	4.9	22.1	21.2	26.9	19.6	18.6
65–74	4.6	18.2	15.6	21.0	22.7	15.5
75–84	5.7	19.0	17.7	30.1	19.9	12.5
85+	6.0	18.7	17.3	21.4	a	9.1
Percentage with Income Below 125 percent of the Poverty Threshold						
Age						
62–64	7.3	29.2	27.9	31.9	29.2	18.6
65–74	7.5	29.1	27.2	32.9	30.8	25.1
75–84	9.2	29.4	27.8	41.3	34.0	21.3
85+	11.8	30.3	28.9	30.1	a	14.1

Source: Social Security Administration (2001).
Note: "a" denotes too few cases to permit reliable estimation.

The death of a spouse can drastically worsen a survivor's financial situation (Holden and Zick 1997; Burkhauser, Butler, and Holden 1991). Significant costs and income losses often accompany a spouse's death. A survivor may lose full or partial pension benefits[8] and possibly earnings, if the deceased spouse had been working. Social Security contributes to a widow or widower's income loss because survivor benefits are between one-half to two-thirds of the total benefits paid to a couple. Because Social Security benefits on average make up more than 80 percent of the total income of low-income couples, this loss can be particularly harmful to the surviving spouse of these couples.

Widowhood is not the only reason that those who enter retirement without a spouse have inadequate income. In fact, those who never married, on average, appear to be less well off than those facing retirement widowed, or even those who are divorced. Almost one third of never-married women ages 65 to 74 have incomes below 125 percent of the poverty threshold, compared with 27 percent of widows and 31 percent of divorcées. Further, the discrepancy between never-married women and widows, in particular, may increase with age.

As a consequence, altering spousal and/or survivor benefits alone cannot eliminate poverty among retirement-age women because a significant fraction of the poorest women never marry. The same point holds for divorced women and young survivors: changes to spouse and survivor benefits will not necessarily affect them in the near term, and these changes are less likely to help this vulnerable group in the far future.

Although the Supplemental Security Income (SSI) program is designed to help the neediest elderly, it is important to understand that Social Security already pays out several hundred billion dollars in benefits each year—enough to supply every current beneficiary with a benefit above the poverty level. Therefore, provisions that pay more benefits to higher-income workers than to lower-income workers detract from the system's ability to redistribute support more equally.

Higher benefits per se are not necessarily the culprit, however. To the extent that these higher payments reflect some return on individuals' additional contributions, they are consistent with the objective of individual equity outlined earlier. They are also important in maintaining broad support for the program. By contrast, spousal and survivor benefits are both unrelated to additional contributions and provide the largest transfers to individuals who are married to the richest workers. The U.S. system differs from some other countries', which tend to grant more equal spousal or survivor benefits regardless of how much a person's spouse earns (see Thompson and Carasso, this volume).

Equal Treatment of Families with the Same Lifetime Earnings

The objective of horizontal equity, or the equal treatment of equals, raises complex questions because people enter retirement with such varied marital, child bearing, and work histories. One issue is how to treat workers with equal earnings if their household sizes differ. The private pension system generally accords equal benefits to workers with equal earnings. For example, a married worker receives the same annual benefits as a single worker unless he or she elects to accept a lower benefit in return for survivor protection for his or her spouse. In a social insurance system, such an approach may not be adequate if the spouse's additional needs leave a couple with meager or below-poverty-level income.

When income adequacy is not an issue, however, it is not clear why a single earner should receive less in total benefits than a one-earner couple with the same earnings level. Presumably, both members of the couple could have worked. One justification for the different treatment would be that society wanted to offset some of the costs of child care. Even so, the current legal standard of paying more to a high earner's spouse (who might raise children) than to a lower-earner's spouse remains problematic. The gap implies that child rearing by the higher-earning couple is more valuable. Moreover, this approach fails to provide unmarried persons *any* compensation for raising children, while it provides substantial additional compensation to married persons who do not raise children.

Under the current system, never-married persons, two-earner married couples whose spouses' relative lifetime earnings are unequal, and married couples with just one earner all can receive widely different benefits, even when their lifetime earnings are the same. Because Social Security payroll taxes are proportional to earnings, these differences in benefits do not reflect any differences in past contributions to the system.

The variation in Social Security benefits for households with the same lifetime earnings stems from several factors: the progressive benefit formula, the presence of spousal and survivor benefits, and a benefit formula based on individual earnings rather than on a couple's combined earnings. For example, a one-earner couple receives more than a two-earner couple with the same lifetime earnings because, in addition to

Table 6.2 Comparison of Benefits among Households with the Same Lifetime Earnings

	Average Indexed Monthly Earnings ($)	Couple's Retirement Benefit			Survivor Benefit		Total Lifetime Benefit ($)
		Worker Benefit ($)	Spouse Benefit ($)	Total ($)	Survivor Benefit ($)	% of Couple's Benefit	
One-Earner Couple							
Couple	2,525	1,101	550	1,651	na	na	272,594
Spouse 1	2,525	1,101	0	1,101	1,101	67	
Spouse 2	0	0	550	550	1,101	67	
Two-Earner Couple (85/15 split)							
Couple	2,525	1,321	149	1,470	na	na	243,354
Spouse 1	2,146	980	0	980	980	67	
Spouse 2	379	341	149	490	980	67	
Two-Earner Couple (60/40 split)							
Couple	2,525	1,394	0	1,394	na	na	194,497
Spouse 1	1,515	778	0	778	778	56	
Spouse 2	1,010	616	0	616	778	56	
Two-Earner Couple (50/50 split)							
Couple	2,525	1,394	0	1,394	na	na	177,384
Spouse 1	1,263	697	0	697	697	50	
Spouse 2	1,263	697	0	697	697	50	
Single Individual	2,525	1,101	0	1,101	na	na	156,512

Source: Author's calculations.
Notes: Average indexed monthly earnings are equal to one-twelfth of projected average annual earnings in 1999. Example assumes no reduction for early retirement and that retirement occurs in 1999.
NA = Not applicable.

the worker's retirement benefit, the nonworking homemaker receives a spousal benefit (see table 6.2). Even when a partial spousal benefit is payable to a two-earner couple, a one-earner couple still does better; in the example, the two-earner couple receives no additional aggregate benefits because spousal benefits are reduced by the amount of benefits derived from the earnings of the lower-earning spouse.

When one member of a married two-earner couple dies, the survivor continues to receive lower benefits than the survivor of a one-earner couple with the same lifetime family earnings. This relative distinction emerges because the survivor benefit, equal to 100 percent of the deceased worker's retirement benefit, is payable only to the extent that it exceeds the survivor's own retirement benefit. Relative to the couple's combined benefit, a survivor benefit can decline by a maximum of one-half (for a two-earner couple with equal earnings) to a minimum of one-third (for a one-earner couple). For two-earner couples, the more equal the spouses' lifetime earnings, the greater is the reduction.

In general, a couple that has a highly unequal split in spousal earnings will receive higher lifetime benefits than a couple whose earnings are more equal. The differences in lifetime benefits are not small. Counting expected retired worker, spousal, and survivor benefits, a one-earner average-wage couple retiring today can expect to receive more than 150 percent of the expected lifetime benefits granted a comparable two-earner couple in which each spouse had the same lifetime earnings. Significantly, black couples—because their earnings tend to be split more equally than white couples'—benefit less from spousal and survivor benefits (Ozawa and Kim 2001).

During Social Security's early years, the inequity between couples with the same lifetime earnings may not have been as glaring because a relatively large fraction of couples had only one earner. Today, one-earner couples represent a minority of retired couples, and their number will dwindle further in the future. Most women now qualify for some retirement benefits based on their own earnings. At present, 65 percent of female Social Security beneficiaries age 65 and older qualify for benefits as either a retired worker or a dual beneficiary (Social Security Administration, Office of Research, Evaluation, and Statistics 2000). The remainder receive benefits solely as a spouse (13 percent) or solely as a survivor (22 percent).

The percentage of women qualifying for retirement benefits based on their own earnings will continue to increase rapidly. By 2000, 88 percent of women born in the 1946–50 period had already acquired sufficient coverage from Social Security to be fully insured. Insurance rates for women in later birth cohorts were equally high or higher, reaching 91 percent for those born in 1971–75 (Social Security Administration, Office of Research, Evaluation, and Statistics 2000). It is not surprising, then, that projections for future retirees suggest that more than 90 percent of all women will receive at least some benefit based on their own earnings.

Even though more women will qualify for benefits based on their own earnings, spousal benefits will not disappear anytime soon. Sandell and Iams (1997) estimate that the percentage of wives receiving benefits based solely on their own earnings will rise from 33 percent of individuals retiring in 1995 to 59 percent of those retiring in 2015. Still, 41 percent of wives will be either dually entitled or receiving only a spousal benefit in 2015. The percentage of widows receiving a full or partial survivor benefit will be even higher, in small part because women in older cohorts participated in the labor force at lower rates. More important, however, a women's own retirement benefit must exceed her deceased spouse's benefit for her not to be dually entitled. Projections from the Social Security Administration's MINT model suggest that the percentage of women whose retired worker benefits are higher than their husbands' should rise from about 12 percent for the 1931–35 cohort to about 26 percent for the 1955–60 cohort. Thus, even for cohorts retiring around 2020, about three-quarters of widows can expect to receive total worker and survivor benefits no higher than if they had not worked at all.

Another equity consideration is how the system treats couples who have been married for different numbers of years. In particular, marriage length differences because of divorce can significantly affect benefits (see box 6.B, which describes how assets are split). Under current law, divorced persons need to have been married for 10 years in order to receive a spousal or survivor's benefit, while workers need to have been married for only one year before their spouses qualify. Whereas private systems generally allocate assets upon divorce according to the length of the marriage, the Social Security system either grants the benefits or does not, and the divorced worker is not required to contribute in either case.

Several stylized examples illustrate some of the horizontal equity implications arising from the current law's treatment of divorce (see box 6.C). The examples also underscore the importance of Social Security's marriage duration requirements in our increasingly individualistic society. Demographers estimate that about 43 percent of recent marriages

Box 6.B. How Social Security "Shares" Assets upon Divorce

Divorce poses especially complex problems for the principle of equal treatment of equals in Social Security. When a marriage dissolves, Social Security allocates accrued entitlement to spouses in a complex way. We can define Social Security's method for allocating accruals according to four aspects: the *asset* that is split, the *interval* over which entitlements are split, the *fraction* of the entitlements that each spouse receives, and *conditions that invalidate* a person's entitlement to these shared assets.

Asset to split. In principle, the Social Security accruals that spouses split could take many forms, for example, their total earnings credits or their eventual total benefits. In the case of need, the benefit or earnings pie that the spouses split could further be supplemented by a transfer from other persons in the system. In practice, Social Security requires an earner to give nothing up to share benefits with a divorced spouse. Instead, it provides divorced spouses with the same additional benefits it allows the spouse of a married worker. If the earner marries again, a double benefit is allowed. Essentially other taxpayers must pay for the benefits received by the divorced spouse. Note also that a higher earner does not receive any benefits from the lower earner's earnings during the marriage.

Interval to split assets over. The most obvious interval for allotting shared accrued entitlement to couples who divorce is the course of their marriage. This period could, however, be too narrow a remedy in some cases. For example, if one spouse helped the other obtain an expensive higher education, then he or she might have a legitimate claim on part of his or her spouse's future earnings. In Social Security, the interval over which an individual has potential entitlement to his or her spouse's Social Security earnings is the entire career regardless of years of marriage (as long as the marriage lasts 10 years or more).

(Continued)

Fraction to each spouse. Drawing from the spirit of community property rules, half of accrued benefits over the period of marriage could be granted to each spouse. An alternative would be to let the fraction vary with the fraction of household responsibilities that each spouse undertook during or after the marriage or to vary according to relative needs. Another alternative would be to let the couples decide the fraction directly or through the court system. The fraction of assets Social Security attributes to each partner is difficult to classify neatly. A divorced spouse of an eligible worker is entitled to one-half of his or her former spouse's benefit before his or her death and 100 percent of his or her former spouse's benefit after he or she dies. Consider the simple case where a single-earner couple divorces and the nonearning spouse does not work after the divorce. Effectively, the divorced spouse receives one-third the total benefit when the former spouse is alive and 100 percent of a smaller total benefit when the former spouse is dead. But cases vary widely.

Conditions that might invalidate entitlement or allocation. At one extreme, the decision to remarry could be considered irrelevant when allocating marital retirement assets at the time of divorce. At the opposite extreme, remarriage could invalidate entitlement to a prior benefit. Social Security currently falls close to the latter pole. A divorced spouse gives up a claim to benefits based on the former spouse's earnings if he or she remarries before age 60. Note that both spouses also retain the right to entitle a new spouse to an additional benefit after a divorce.

will end in divorce (Schoen and Weinick 1993),[9] and data reveal that about 63 percent of those couples who divorced in recent years did so before the 10-year entitlement point specified in the Social Security regulations (see table 6.3). Combined, these figures imply that Social Security denies a spouse *any* credit for his or her partner's Social Security earnings in about one-quarter (63 percent of 43 percent) of all recent marriages. However, because divorced persons tend to remarry at fairly high rates, a significant fraction of those persons who divorce will enter retirement eligible for a Social Security spousal benefit of some sort.

If Social Security did not award or revoke benefits based on whether one married, there would be no incentive to marry—or not marry—to

Box 6.C. Examples of Inequities Arising from the Treatment of Divorce

- A divorced woman with low earnings married to a high-earning male for 11 years would receive about $237,000 (2000 dollars) in lifetime Social Security benefits in 2040. In fact, she would receive the same amount even if she never worked or paid taxes to Social Security. On the other hand, a woman with low earnings who divorced after only five years would net only $95,000 in lifetime benefits based upon her own work, and she would have paid more than $50,000 of taxes along the way.
- If a high-wage male worker had three former spouses, all from marriages that lasted 10 years or more, the spousal and survivor benefits payable on his earnings record would be $710,000. Spousal and survivor benefits would be only $237,000 if he had had only one spouse. In both cases, he would not be required to share any portion of his own benefit.
- A woman divorced from a high-wage male after more than 10 years of marriage would receive about $237,000 in spousal and survivor benefits. However, if she happened to remarry and her new husband was a low earner, her benefits would fall to about $101,000—a steep penalty for remarrying.
- Finally, a divorced spouse entitled to a benefit under a former marriage is put in the strange situation of being much better off if her former husband dies rather than lives. A divorced woman whose high-wage spouse has died before she reaches normal retirement age would receive $373,000 in benefits; if her husband had outlived her, she could expect only $186,000.

The examples, of course, are highly stylized and represent extreme cases,[10] but they demonstrate that the current system imposes *both* penalties and bonuses for remarrying.

Table 6.3 *Duration of Marriages at Time of Divorce, 1990 Divorce Registration Area*

Years of Marriage	Percentage of All Divorces
Less than 1	3.3
1 to 4	31.7
5 to 9	28.3
10 to 14	15.0
15 to 19	9.2
20 to 24	6.2
25 or more	6.2
Less than 10	63.3
Median (7.2 years)	
Mean (9.8 years)	

Source: Clarke (1995, p. 19–20).

gain or retain Social Security benefits. In addition, people with more equal experiences would be treated more equally. A recent study (Brien, Dickert-Conlin, and Weaver 2000) suggests that survivors who would receive a larger benefit based on their former spouses' earnings records either do not marry, or postpone marriage, because of Social Security's remarriage penalty. Discouraging marriage is problematic not only because it raises equity concerns, but also because marriage provides a form of insurance protection. Johnson and Favreault (2001), for example, show that spouses often adjust their work effort near retirement when their spouses need to leave the labor force for some involuntary reason, such as a health problem or a layoff.

Treatment of Single Parents

Child bearing and marital status have become increasingly decoupled in our society. Nearly one-third of all children are now born to unmarried women (Ventura et al. 2001). In most instances, however, Social Security treats single parents the same as it treats other unmarried workers.[11] Single mothers have strikingly low Social Security benefits, even relative to other divorced and never-married women. Projections of benefits for Social Security recipients age 62 and over in 2040 suggest that annual Social Security benefits will be 30 percent higher for unmarried women without children than for unmarried women who have had children (see table 6.4). As a consequence, the potential for future poverty

Table 6.4 *Estimated Social Security Benefits for Never-Married Women Age 62 and Older, 2040*

	Mean Benefit (1998 $)	Benefits Less Than Poverty Threshold (%)
With children	10,636	34
Without children	13,908	11

Source: Authors' calculations using the Urban Institute's DYNASIM3.

among never-married women with children remains quite high. More than one-third (34 percent) of these women's Social Security benefits will fail to put them above the poverty level.

As noted, single individuals and people with less than 10 years of marriage to a particular spouse do not benefit from spousal and survivors benefits, among the most important social adequacy features of the system. The inequities of this particular structure, however, are most pronounced for single heads of household. Under current law, for instance, the nonworking spouse of a high-wage male, regardless of child-raising decisions, can expect to receive about $237,000 in Social Security benefits. By contrast, a single female head of household who earns a low wage and contributes taxes to Social Security can currently expect only about $95,000 in benefits. In effect, a person who pays more taxes, raises children, and has fewer economic resources may receive only about two-fifths the benefit of someone who does not pay additional taxes, may not have raised children, and has a more favorable economic situation.

Marginal Returns to Payroll Tax Contributions

Spousal and survivor benefits, as currently designed, discourage work by a lower-earning spouse much more than they discourage additional work by a higher-earning spouse (see, for example, Feldstein and Samwick 1992). Although the lower-earning spouse's earnings are subject to payroll tax, a couple's or a survivor's Social Security benefit is likely to increase little, if at all, as a result of the additional earnings. A spouse or survivor is entitled only to the higher of his or her own benefit or the spousal or survivor benefit. Hence, additional contributions by a working spouse of a beneficiary often yield no additional benefit—although even the highest-income workers' additional contributions yield additional benefits. For example, a hypothetical one-earner couple earning the average wage and retiring in 2040 would receive lifetime benefits of about $427,000. If a second spouse also worked and earned the average wage, lifetime benefits for the couple would increase by 11 percent to $473,000. However, if the first spouse earned twice the average wage and the second spouse did not work, benefits for the couple would increase by 33 percent to $565,000. In either case, the additional payroll tax contributions by the couples would be the same.

Evaluating Reform Proposals

Using the principles described, we evaluate several recent proposals relating to Social Security's family benefit structure. Some of these proposals deal more successfully with some problems in the current system than others. No single change can simultaneously address vertical equity, horizontal equity, and benefit adequacy. To make improvements in all areas, then, reformers must craft a package of reforms. For example, a change might improve horizontal equity but reduce progressivity. A package approach would allow policymakers to add other reforms, such as changes in minimum benefits or the benefit rate structure, to restore, or even increase, progressivity. Thus, overall, the package might improve both horizontal equity and progressivity, although neither piece by itself could have achieved as optimal a result. At the same time, some proposals do so poorly according to almost every standard that the case for them is weak.

Four Options to Increase Adequacy

We begin by comparing four proposals that attempt to address income adequacy by providing additional benefits to older survivors and workers with low lifetime earnings, particularly those who have spent time out of the labor force caring for children. These proposals would increase benefits without increasing taxes or imposing offsetting benefit cuts on other recipients.

OPTION 1: INCREASE SURVIVOR BENEFITS TO 75 PERCENT OF A COUPLE'S COMBINED BENEFIT.

Increasing survivor benefits to 75 percent of a couple's combined benefit would remove some of the current disparity in survivors benefits among couples with the same lifetime earnings but a different share of earnings from each spouse. It would raise benefits for all survivors, but particularly survivors of couples who did not receive spousal benefits, for whom the current survivor benefits can be as low as 50 percent of the couple's benefit when both were alive. It would raise survivor benefits by a maximum of 50 percent for a two-earner couple with equal lifetime earnings and a minimum of 12.5 percent for a one-earner couple.[12] The version of this option we consider here would not change the survivor benefits received by a divorced surviving spouse.

OPTION 2: INTRODUCE CHILD CARE CREDITS.

This option would provide up to five years of earnings credits to parents who have children under the age of six in their care. The credits would raise countable annual earnings for purposes of computing Social Security benefits to one-half the average wage in each child care year. Child care credits with a cap on the amount of credit provide a somewhat more even subsidy to workers who are raising children than alternative proposals that would exclude child care years from the averaging period for calculating benefits. The effect of this closely related alternative—child care dropout years—is to replace periods of zero or low earnings with a worker's average earnings from his or her own remaining work years, thus providing more generous credits for child care to workers with higher lifetime earnings.[13]

OPTION 3: CREATE A NEW MINIMUM BENEFIT.

The minimum-benefit option would provide a benefit equal to 60 percent of a wage-indexed poverty threshold for workers with at least 20 years of qualified earnings (earnings that meet the current law threshold for four covered quarters).[14, 15] The benefit would increase by 2 percentage points for each additional year of qualified earnings, and reach 100 percent of the wage-indexed poverty threshold for workers with 40 or more years of earnings. Because the minimum benefit would increase with average wages in the economy, this option would allow recipients to maintain their relative economic standing in the population. The benefit would grow faster than the official poverty level, which is indexed to prices. The option that we examine would continue to index the benefit guarantee to wages after retirement as well. Thus, it would provide the greatest benefits to older workers; in some cases, retirees whose initial retirement benefits exceed the minimum would later switch to the minimum benefit when their price-indexed benefit fell below the requisite amount. We also examine an alternative minimum-benefit option that would provide a benefit equal to the wage-indexed poverty threshold to all covered workers and eligible spouses/survivors regardless of the number of years worked.

OPTION 4: REDUCE LENGTH OF MARRIAGE REQUIREMENT FOR SPOUSAL AND SURVIVOR BENEFITS.
A fourth option specifically targets divorced men and women whose marriages are of relatively short duration. Under this option, a person would be eligible for divorced spousal/survivor benefits if his or her marriage lasted at least seven years (rather than the current minimum of ten years).[16]

Analysis of Benefit Adequacy Options

We analyze the effects of these four options (or five options in those cases where both minimum benefits are examined) for a simulated population of Social Security recipients in the year 2040 and for some representative workers. The representative, or individual, worker analysis highlights benefit differences between workers with certain stylized earnings histories, and reveals some of the horizontal equity and efficiency issues. The overall simulation analysis provides a measure of the overall distribution of a particular reform's effects across the entire beneficiary population.[17] Because Social Security pays an overwhelming fraction of spousal and survivor benefits to women, we present results from the simulation analysis for women only.

These proposals vary considerably in size. The 75 percent survivor benefit option is the most expensive (a 4.5 percent increase in total benefits), followed by the minimum benefit (a 1.8 percent increase), the child care credit (a 0.3 percent increase), and the reduction in the length of marriage requirement (a 0.2 percent increase).[18] We take this variation in the options' sizes into account by focusing on the shares of benefits that individuals in different income groups receive under a reform, rather than on differences in the absolute amounts of benefits that each proposal awards. If a lower-cost proposal does better per dollar spent, then it would be preferable to increase spending on that type of option rather than on an option with inferior benefits relative to costs.

ANTIPOVERTY EFFECTIVENESS. For our first measure of the four proposals' antipoverty effectiveness, we compare the percentage of the additional benefits that go to women in the lowest lifetime earnings quintiles. We take the ratio of measured lifetime earnings to the Social Security average wage, averaged over all years from ages 25 through 62. For a married woman, lifetime earnings is the average of her own and her husband's lifetime earnings; for a widow, it is the average of her own and her deceased husband's lifetime earnings. We obtain the thresholds for the earnings quintiles using the lifetime earnings of all Social Security beneficiaries (men and women) age 62 or older in 2040.

All four options would raise benefits for lower-income women. The minimum benefit, child care credits, and the reduction in the length of marriage requirement would each provide at least two-thirds of the additional benefits to women in the two lowest lifetime earnings quintiles (see table 6.5). Those women receive less than three-tenths of all current law benefits paid to women. The distribution of gains under the survivor benefit increase option is about the same as the distribution of benefits under current law. Under this option, only 25 percent of the gains would go to the women in the two lowest lifetime earnings quintiles. The most progressive option of all is the minimum benefit with no work requirement.

Another measure of the proposals' progressivity is the percent of women in different income quintiles who would gain as a result of the reform. At least one-quarter of women in the lowest lifetime income group would gain from child care credits, work-related minimum benefits, and increased survivor benefits (see table 6.6). The survivor benefit increase option would, by design, supplement benefits for all survivors, and not help currently married, divorced, or never-married women.[19] While the proposal would help many poor widows, it would also increase benefits for higher-income survivors, with the highest dollar increases going to women with the highest lifetime earnings. As a result, even among widows, it would not be very cost-effective in terms of efficiently targeting additional resources toward poverty alleviation. Clearly, the unrestricted minimum benefit would increase benefits for the greatest number of low-lifetime-income women, more than three-quarters of whom would see higher benefits.

Even though the work-related minimum-benefit option would target a greater percentage of the additional benefit to widows in the lowest

(*text continues on page 200*)

Table 6.5 *Distribution of Gains for Various Benefit Increase Options (Female Beneficiaries Age 62 and Over in 2040)*

			Percentage Distribution of Gains under Each Option			
					Minimum Benefit	
	Percentage Distribution of Current Law Benefits	*75 Percent Survivor Benefit*	*Child Care Credits*	*Work Requirement*	*No Work Requirement*	*Seven-Year Marriage Requirement*
Lifetime Earnings Quintile	*(1)*	*(2)*	*(3)*	*(4)*	*(5)*	*(6)*
All Women						
Lowest	12	9	45	58	63	41
Second	17	16	25	27	23	27
Middle	20	20	15	9	9	16
Fourth	25	28	12	5	4	10
Highest	26	27	4	1	1	6
All	100	100	100	100	100	100

Source: DYNASIM3, The Urban Institute.
Note: Example assumes no reduction for early retirement and that retirement occurs in 1999.

Table 6.6 *Percentage of Women with Higher Benefits for Various Benefit Increase Options (Female Beneficiaries Age 62 and Over in 2040)*

Lifetime Earnings Quintile	75 Percent Survivor Benefit	Child Care Credits	Minimum Benefit		Seven-Year Marriage Requirement
			Work Requirement	No Work Requirement	
	(2)	(3)	(4)	(5)	(6)
All Women					
Lowest	29	30	42	80	2
Second	36	25	29	54	2
Middle	38	17	13	28	1
Fourth	40	11	6	13	1
Highest	29	5	1	3	a
All	34	18	19	36	1
Married Women					
Lowest	a	45	61	98	1
Second	a	38	50	87	2
Middle	a	29	29	58	1
Fourth	a	21	13	31	1
Highest	a	10	3	6	1
All Married Women	a	28	29	53	1
Widows					
Lowest	100	15	23	64	1
Second	100	7	6	19	1
Middle	100	3	2	6	a
Fourth	100	2	1	2	a
Highest	100	0	a	0	0
All Widows	100	5	6	17	1
Divorced Women					
Lowest	a	26	36	71	4
Second	a	30	28	49	3
Middle	a	17	3	12	2

(*Continued*)

Table 6.6 *Percentage of Women with Higher Benefits for Various Benefit Increase Options (Female Beneficiaries Age 62 and Over in 2040) (Continued)*

	75 Percent Survivor Benefit	Child Care Credits	Minimum Benefit		Seven-Year Marriage Requirement
			Work Requirement	No Work Requirement	
Lifetime Earnings Quintile	(2)	(3)	(4)	(5)	(6)
Fourth	na	7	0	a	1
Highest	na	5	0	0	1
All Divorced Women	a	19	18	35	3
Never-Married Women					
Lowest	na	42	59	96	na
Second	na	31	235	62	na
Middle	na	16	2	16	na
Fourth	na	5	0	0	na
Highest	na	2	0	0	na
All Never-Married Women	na	21	24	42	na

NA = Not applicable.
a = A small fraction (less than 1 percent) receive a benefit increase.
Source: DYNASIM3, The Urban Institute.
Note: Example assumes no reduction for early retirement and that retirement occurs in 1999.

lifetime earnings quintile, most low-income widows would not receive additional benefits. Two factors explain this lack of coverage: many would not meet the years-of-work requirement and most would still qualify for higher benefits as a survivor. Only 6 percent of widows overall benefit from the proposal, including 23 percent of widows in the lowest income quintile. Beneficiaries would need to have worked for at least 20 years to qualify for any benefits and at least 40 years to qualify for full benefits. Low-income never-married and divorced women are more likely to qualify for higher benefits than widows. In the lowest income quintile, about three-fifths (59 percent) of the never-married group and over a third (36 percent) of the divorced group would receive benefit increases.

Under an alternative minimum-benefit option that does not require beneficiaries to have worked at all, 64 percent of widows, 71 percent of divorced women, and virtually all never-married women in the lowest lifetime income quintile would see gains. The unrestricted minimum benefit would be far more costly, however, increasing overall benefits by 5.2 percent compared with a 1.8 percent increase under the more limited minimum-benefit option.

The child care credit proposal would increase benefits for almost one-fifth (18 percent) of all women. Never-married, married, and divorced women are the most likely to gain, while widows are the least likely. Fewer widows gain because even with the boost to their own earnings records, the benefits they can receive as a survivor typically exceed the benefits they can receive based on their own earnings.

The reduction in the number of years of marriage required for a person to gain eligibility for spousal and survivor benefits has more skewed effects than the other three proposals. It does not affect many women, but those whom it does affect see a very large change in benefit. Our estimates suggest that only about 3 percent of divorced women—about 8 percent of the women who were married for less than 10 years—would gain.

Our third indicator of the four proposals' antipoverty effectiveness is a comparison of post-reform benefits to the poverty threshold. Aside from the minimum-benefit options, none of the other proposals would reduce the overall percentage of women who receive benefits that are below poverty levels by more than a percentage point (see table 6.7). The proposal to increase survivor benefits would, however, cut the already low percentage of widows with benefits below poverty by over two-fifths. The reduction occurs partly because this option concentrates all its effect on survivors, and thus offers this group a bigger benefit increase than the other two options, and partly because many widows only need small increases to move their benefits above this line. The work-related minimum-benefit option would reduce the percentage of women whose benefit is less than the poverty level by well over one-third. The unrestricted minimum, of course, would eliminate poverty for all groups.

Just as today, divorced and never-married women of the future are far more likely than their married and widowed counterparts to have benefits that do not exceed the poverty threshold. Our simulation suggests that under current law, 17 percent of the divorced women will have projected benefits below the poverty line. That percentage is virtually unchanged by the child care credit and reduced marriage length requirement options.

Table 6.7 Benefits Relative to the Poverty Threshold, Benefit Increase Options (Female Beneficiaries Age 62 and Over in 2040)

				Minimum Benefit		
	Current Law	75 Percent Survivor Benefit	Child Care Credits	Work Requirement	No Work Requirement	Seven-Year Marriage Requirement
	(1)	(2)	(3)	(4)	(5)	(6)
All Women	**7.8**	6.9	7.4	4.8	0.0	7.7
Married Women	**0.5**	0.5	0.4	0.2	0.0	0.5
Widows	**5.8**	3.2	5.7	4.2	0.0	5.8
Divorced Women	**16.5**	16.5	15.6	9.9	0.0	15.8
Never-Married Women	**22.8**	22.8	21.7	13.0	0.0	22.8

Source: DYNASIM3, The Urban Institute.

The percentage is projected to fall to 10 percent with the work-related minimum benefit. For never-married women, the corresponding figure for the proportion with benefits that fail to exceed poverty under current law is a significantly higher 23 percent. That percentage barely changes with the child care credit option, but it falls to 13 percent with the work-related minimum benefit. By definition, the proposal to change marriage durations has no effect on those who never married.

Bear in mind that the simulations simply compare Social Security benefits with the appropriate poverty threshold. Because we are not measuring income from other sources, such as SSI, pensions, earnings, or assets, we cannot assess the percentage of beneficiaries that would be poor.[20]

HORIZONTAL EQUITY.   None of the options would effectively address the unequal treatment of average-wage one- and two-earner couples with the same lifetime earnings. Under current law, a one-earner couple in which the worker earned twice the average wage over his or her lifetime could expect to receive about $96,000 more in lifetime benefits—including spousal and survivor benefits—than a comparable two-earner couple (see table 6.8). Although the option to increase survivor benefits and the work-related minimum-benefit option would reduce the difference in lifetime benefits between these hypothetical one- and two-earner couples, the change would be modest. For example, the survivor benefit option would increase the ratio of lifetime benefits for a two-earner couple from 79 percent to 85 percent of the benefits for a one-earner couple with the same lifetime earnings. The child care credit option would not increase benefits for either a one- or two-earner couple with combined earnings equal to twice the average wage. The work-tested minimum benefit makes a slight improvement, while the unrestricted minimum-benefit option would slightly worsen the difference in lifetime benefits. The poor performance occurs because the large increase in benefits for a nonworking spouse in the one-earner couple would more than offset the small gains for each spouse in the two-earner couple.

Compared with current law, all options would boost lifetime benefits for low-wage two-earner couples relative to one-earner couples with the same lifetime earnings (see table 6.8). The child care credit would close most of the gap because it would attribute much higher earnings to each working spouse during child care years than during other years of work. A minimum benefit pushes the system for low earners more in the direction of an individual rather than a family benefit. The version that rewards years of work per se can create greater benefits for the two-earner couple than the

Table 6.8 *Comparison of Lifetime Benefits for Hypothetical One- and Two-Earner Couples*

	Current Law	75 Percent Survivor Benefit	Child Care Credits	Minimum Benefit	
				Work Requirement	No Work Requirement
	(1)	(2)	(3)	(4)	(5)
A: One-earner couple: Earns twice average wage	$450,111	$465,942	$450,111	$450,111	$479,737
B: Two-earner couple: Both earn average wage	$354,481	$396,438	$356,030	$369,924	$369,924
Difference (B–A)	$95,630	$69,504	$94,082	$80,187	$109,812
Ratio (B/A)	79%	85%	79%	82%	77%
A: One-Earner couple: Earns twice low wage	$232,436	$249,072	$240,610	$294,805	$363,529
B: Two-Earner couple: Both earn low wage	$192,587	$265,216	$238,183	$363,529	$363,529
Difference (B–A)	$39,849	–$16,144	$2,427	–$68,724	$0
Ratio (B/A)	83%	106%	99%	123%	100%

Source: DYNASIM3, The Urban Institute.

one-earner couple with equal levels of earnings. Both the one-earner and two-earner couple would gain from an earnings-based minimum benefit, but the two-earner couple would gain much more in this low-wage case. Indeed, their total lifetime benefits would exceed the benefits of the one-earner couple, reversing the situation under current law. On the other hand, when the minimum is not based on years of work, the two couples come out with the same lifetime benefits, suggesting complete neutrality with respect to the fraction of earnings each spouse contributes because everyone in this example qualifies for the same minimum.

MARGINAL RETURNS TO PAYROLL TAX CONTRIBUTIONS. Only the option to increase survivor benefits would effectively increase the marginal returns to a second earner, although even then, the change would be modest. Couples with and without a wife working would both receive even higher lifetime benefits under this proposal. For example, under current law a hypothetical one-earner couple in which the husband earned the average wage could expect an 11 percent increase in lifetime benefits if the wife also worked and earned the average wage. With the option to increase survivor benefits, the increase in expected lifetime earnings from the wife working would rise to only 15 percent, still well below the 33 percent increase in benefits if the additional earnings had come from the husband (see table 6.9). That is, the couple is still better off if the husband increases his earnings rather than if the wife goes to work. (The results are similar if we assume that the husband is the second earner in the couple, but the figures would change slightly because of the different life expectancies of males and females.)

The child care credit option would have no effect on marginal returns for workers with average wages. During eligible child care years, however, low-wage workers could receive the same credits toward future benefits whether they worked (and paid taxes on earnings) or did not work. Hence, that option could create a short-term work disincentive if people recognize and are influenced by the effect of current earnings on future retirement benefits. The trade-off would be, of course, that workers choosing to reduce their hours of work would be engaged in the socially valuable work of caring for children. The credit could conceivably encourage work over a person's lifetime if the credits make it more likely that by working a few more years a person with a sporadic work history could become fully insured. However, the credits are unlikely to result in many married workers qualifying for benefits solely on the basis of their own earnings and thus would do little to address the system's current disincentives.

Table 6.9 Comparison of the Increase in Lifetime Benefits from Additional Earnings for Hypothetical One- and Two-Earner Couples

| | Current Law | 75 Percent Survivor Benefit | Child Care Credits | Minimum Benefit | |
				Work Requirement	No Work Requirement
	(1)	(2)	(3)	(4)	(5)
A: One-earner couple: average wage male	$426,759	$441,769	$426,759	$426,759	$461,979
B: Two-earner couple: average wage male and female	$473,249	$508,736	$473,249	$473,877	$473,877
C: One-earner couple: male earns sum of male and female average wage	$568,126	$588,107	$568,126	$568,126	$572,072
Percentage increase if wife works at average wage (A to B)	10.9%	15.2%	10.9%	11.0%	2.6%
Percentage increase if husband increases his work effort by the female average wage (A to C)	33.1%	33.1%	33.1%	33.1%	23.8%

Source: DYNASIM3, The Urban Institute.

MINIMIZING ANOMALIES WITH REGARD TO MARRIAGE AND DIVORCE. The survivor benefit increase, child care credit, and two minimum-benefit options differentially reduce some horizontal inequities among individuals with different marital histories. For example, compare two divorced women who each earned low wages over their lifetimes: assume one was married to a high-wage spouse for 11 years, and the other was married to a high-wage spouse for 5 years (see table 6.10). As described earlier, current law treats these women very differently. The first woman, who has the advantage of being entitled to spousal and survivor benefits, receives a lifetime benefit of about $237,000. The second woman receives a benefit of less than half that amount, or just under $95,000, for a gap of $142,000.

Under the child care credit option, the gap between the two women's lifetime benefits decreases to about $112,000. The two minimum-benefit options reduce the difference in lifetime benefits much further to about $50,000. While both child credits and minimum benefits, then, reduce this particular horizontal inequity in the Social Security system, the minimum-benefit proposals offer a more substantial improvement. They would not eliminate the difference because the woman married for more than 10 years would still qualify for a survivor benefit that exceeded the minimum benefit, while the other woman would not. By contrast, the survivor benefit increase actually widens the gap between these two women; the lifetime benefits to the woman married for more than 10 years increase, while the benefits for the woman married just 5 years remain the same.

A second example in table 6.10 illustrates the proposals' respective impact on Social Security's current "remarriage penalty." A low-wage divorced woman formerly married to a high-wage worker receives a significant reduction in lifetime benefits—a difference of more than $135,000—if she remarries a low-wage male. With the survivor benefit increase and child care credit options she loses somewhat less—between $106,000 and $111,000 in benefits—if she remarries. Under the minimum-benefit options, her remarriage penalty is smaller still at around $43,000 in the restricted case and $47,000 in the unrestricted case.

A third example in table 6.10 reveals that none of the options essentially improves the differences that arise because of variations in the timing of beneficiaries' husbands' deaths.

TREATMENT OF SINGLE HEAD OF HOUSEHOLD. Finally, we examine how these benefit increase proposals affect one of our key target groups: unmarried heads of households. We compare the benefits of a nonworking

Table 6.10 *Benefit Options and Marriage Neutrality ($)*

| | | Lifetime Benefits | | Minimum Benefit | |
	Current Law	75 Percent Survivor Benefit	Child Care Credits	Work Requirement	No Work Requirement
Marriage Duration					
Low-wage divorced woman married for 11 years to high-wage male	$236,565	$249,137	$236,565	$236,565	$240,559
Low-wage divorced woman married for 5 years to high-wage male	94,521	94,521	124,624	181,863	193,471
Difference	142,044	154,616	111,942	54,703	47,088
Remarriage					
Low-wage divorced woman married more than 10 years to high-wage male	236,565	249,137	236,565	236,565	240,559
Low-wage divorced woman remarries low-wage male	101,494	142,497	126,026	193,471	193,471
Difference	135,071	106,640	110,539	43,095	47,088
Timing of ex-Spouse's Death					
Low-wage divorced woman, high-wage ex-husband dies at Normal Retirement Age	372,558	372,886	372,558	372,558	372,558
Low-wage divorced woman, high-wage ex-husband outlives her	186,279	186,279	186,279	186,279	196,099
Difference	186,272	186,272	186,272	184,934	179,689

Source: Steuerle-Bakija-Carasso model, The Urban Institute.

spouse of a high-wage worker with no children with those for a low-wage single mother.[21] Under current law, we find that a woman who marries a high-wage worker receives a significant lifetime transfer from Social Security, almost $237,000 (see table 6.11). A single mother, in contrast, receives a benefit of just $95,000 and a net lifetime transfer of about one-fifth as much as the other woman's (or $42,000) because she also paid taxes during her working career. These calculations yield an overall lifetime difference in total benefits of $142,000 and net benefits of $194,000. With a child care credit, the single mother's lifetime benefits increase moderately, by just over $30,000, while the married woman without children maintains the same level of benefits. The gap between the two women's lifetime benefits thus narrows to about $112,000. Under both minimum-benefit proposals, the single woman's benefit increases even more, by just over $93,000, and this differential between the two women declines further, to around $50,000 on a lifetime basis. The survivor benefit increase actually widens the gap between these two women to almost $155,000, due to the increased lifetime value of the survivor benefit.

If the concern is allocating benefits to women with children,[22] then by definition, the reduction in poverty for child care credits is almost exclusively distributed among them.[23] Microsimulation results (not shown) also demonstrate that both minimum-benefit options give proportionately more to never-married women with children than to their counterparts without children, likely because of the role that child rearing played in their low lifetime incomes.

Three Reform Package Options

We also consider three expenditure-neutral packages that would balance benefit increases for some retirees with benefit cuts for others. These packages are a more realistic way to explore the distributional consequences of Social Security reform. Given that the system is so far out of long-term fiscal balance, Congress is not likely to enact options that create only winners.

The first two options would shift some benefits from the first years of retirement to the later years of retirement. The rationale for such a shift is that most retirees have more outside resources and capabilities early in retirement than later. (For example, they are more likely to be able to work, and they are more likely to have savings and income from pension benefits.) The third option would generally shift benefits from higher to lower lifetime earnings beneficiaries.

Table 6.11 *Lifetime Benefits for Single Head of Household and a Nonworking Spouse ($)*

| | | | Lifetime Benefits | | | |
| | | | | | Minimum Benefit | |
	Current Law	*75 Percent Survivor Benefit*	*Child Care Credits*	*Work Requirement*	*No Work Requirement*
Benefits for nonworking spouse of high-wage male	**$236,565**	$249,137	$236,565	$236,565	$240,559
Net Transfer	**236,565**	249,137	236,565	236,565	240,559
Benefits for low-wage single female head of household	**94,521**	94,521	124,624	181,863	193,471
Net Transfer	**42,412**	42,412	54,762	129,755	141,364
Difference between nonworking spouse and single mother	**142,044**	154,616	111,942	54,703	47,088
Net Transfer	**194,153**	206,725	181,803	106,810	99,195

Source: Steuerle-Bakija-Carasso model, The Urban Institute.

OPTION 5: INCREASE SURVIVOR BENEFITS BUT REDUCE SPOUSAL BENEFITS.
A majority of the 1994–96 Advisory Council on Social Security (1997) endorsed a 75 percent survivor benefit in combination with a reduction in the spousal benefit to 33 percent. Although the reduction in the spousal benefit would offset some of the cost of the increased survivor benefit, the combination would not be revenue neutral. The Social Security Actuaries estimated at that time that the combined proposal would increase long-term costs by 0.32 percent of taxable payroll. We therefore simulate this option, but to achieve revenue neutrality, we simultaneously reduce Social Security benefits for higher lifetime earnings recipients by reducing the top two rates in the primary insurance (PIA) formula by 5 percent—that is from a rate of 32 percent to 30.4 percent and from 15 percent to 14.3 percent.[24]

OPTION 6: WAGE-INDEX BENEFITS, BUT REDUCE INITIAL BENEFITS.
We also consider an option that indexes benefits to wages rather than prices but reduces initial benefits by a sufficient amount to keep total expenditures constant. In our simulations, an across-the-board cut in benefits of 12 percent for beneficiaries age 62 and over fully offsets the increase in benefits in the simulation year from wage indexing. Under this option, wage indexing would increase benefits for most widows and other older recipients, but at the expense of lowering benefits for all recipients at younger ages.

OPTION 7: A MINIMUM BENEFIT WITH A CAP ON SPOUSAL BENEFITS.
The final option would combine the work-related minimum benefit that we described earlier with a cap on spousal benefits. The cap would equal the spousal benefit payable based on the earnings of a worker who had always earned the average wage. We balance the net additional outlays in 2040 by shaving the top two rates in the PIA formula by 1 percent (e.g., the top rate was reduced from 32 percent to 31.68 percent).

Package Options Analysis

Our simulation results demonstrate how the three combination options affect the distribution of Social Security benefits in 2040 (see table 6.12). At a single point in time, both the decrease in spousal benefits to finance an increased survivor benefit(s) (option 5) and the exchange of lower

Table 6.12 *Gainers and Losers by Age and Lifetime Income Class, Balance Options (Female Beneficiaries Age 62 and Over in 2040) ($)*

		75 Percent Survivor Benefit with 33 Percent Spouse Benefit			
		Lower Benefits under Option		Higher Benefits under Option	
	Average Current Law Benefits (1998$)	*Percentage of Units*	*Average Loss*	*Percentage of Units*	*Average Gain*
	(1)	(2)	(3)	(4)	(5)
All Women by Lifetime Earnings Quintile					
Lowest	$10,744	65	−$621	12	$1,976
Second	15,806	64	−774	21	2,310
Middle	19,065	62	−930	25	2,775
Fourth	22,225	60	−1,169	27	3,425
Highest	25,384	71	−1,045	24	4,724
Total	18,533	64	−904	22	3,171
All Women by Age					
62–64	18,963	80	−922	5	2,904
65–69	21,146	82	−989	10	3,628
70–74	20,240	76	−946	15	3,713
75–79	18,343	67	−844	22	3,177
80+	16,185	44	−814	35	2,976
Total	18,533	64	−904	22	3,171

a = A small fraction (less than 1 percent) receive a benefit increase.
Source: DYNASIM3, The Urban Institute.

up-front benefits for higher later benefits through wage indexing, (option 6) effectively transfer benefits from married women to widows. The option to increase survivor benefits but reduce spousal benefits would also transfer lifetime benefits between married couples, depending upon the mix of husband and wife earnings. Relative to current law, the option to wage index benefits but reduce initial benefits would affect the lifetime benefits of couples only to the extent that the length of the husband's and wife's lifetimes differ from average outcomes. The minimum benefit with a cap on spousal benefits (option 7) would also trans-

Wage Indexed Benefit With Initial Benefit Reduction				Minimum Benefit With Cap on Spousal Benefits			
Lower Benefits under Option		Higher Benefits under Option		Lower Benefits under Option		Higher Benefits under Option	
Percentage of Units	Average Loss	Percentage of Units	Average Gain	Percentage of Units	Average Loss	Percentage of Units	Average Gain
(6)	(7)	(8)	(9)	(6)	(7)	(8)	(9)
41	−$707	57	$903	43	−$118	42	$1,936
45	−998	53	1,205	70	−135	29	1,328
50	−1,257	50	1,448	87	−191	12	1,121
52	−1,490	48	1,580	93	−263	6	1,158
59	−1,819	41	1,555	98	−222	2	1,072
49	−1,293	50	1,309	78	−198	19	1,572
95	−1,782	5	861	73	−240	21	1,827
94	−1,714	6	1,023	78	−250	18	1,525
84	−1,087	15	809	81	−225	16	1,509
39	−605	59	739	76	−184	22	1,502
4	−604	96	1,578	78	−154	18	1,604
49	−1,293	50	1,309	78	−198	19	1,572

fer benefits from married people to widows, but would further redistribute benefits to certain never-married and divorced women.

ANTIPOVERTY EFFECTIVENESS. In addition to distributional effects arising from differences in marital status, other differences can be observed among the three packages. About two-thirds of women at a single point in time in 2040 lose (often temporarily) under the option to increase survivor benefits but reduce spousal benefits, while one-fifth gain (see table 6.12). Many women who lose do so because of the cut in benefits for higher lifetime earnings recipients. Among women who do gain (almost all widows by definition), benefit increases are higher for those women with higher lifetime earnings. The percentage of women who lose is roughly the same in all lifetime earnings quintiles (except the highest), but the percentage with gains is smallest in the lowest quintile.

Under the proposal to reduce initial benefits but index subsequent benefits, gains and losses in a single year are fairly equally distributed among women. Losers from the reform make up 49 percent of the group, compared with 50 percent who gain. (For a very small fraction, benefit changes are only a few dollars a month.) A higher percentage of women in the lowest lifetime earnings quintile (57 percent) gain under the proposal than in other quintiles.

The third package, which allows a work-related minimum benefit while capping spousal benefits and slightly trimming benefits for higher lifetime-earnings recipients, is the most obviously progressive of the three. While far more women lose than gain under the reform (78 percent compared with 19 percent), the sizes of losses are fairly small (an average of $198), with greater losses at the top of the income distribution than at the bottom. Gains are far more significant, averaging almost $1,600 annually, and are concentrated in the lower two lifetime earnings quintiles.

The wage-indexing proposal redistributes benefits from earlier in retirement to later, as intended (see table 6.12). Ninety-five percent of women younger than age 65 have lower benefits, while 96 percent of women age 80 and over have higher benefits. The percentage of women with increased benefits rises with age. In the 75 to 79 age group, nearly three-fifths of the women are gainers.

The package containing a minimum benefit with a cap on spousal benefits is the only one of the three that has a large effect in reducing the percentage of women whose benefits are less than the poverty threshold (see table 6.13). The biggest effects are for divorced and never-married women, for whom the percentage with below poverty benefits falls by about 6 and 10 percentage points, respectively.

The option to increase survivor benefits and reduce spousal benefits and benefits for higher-income workers results in a small increase in the overall percentage of married women with benefits below the poverty threshold—although the rate remains below 1 percent—and increases in the percentage for divorced and never-married women (see table 6.13).

For both divorced and never-married women, the wage-indexing package has a very small impact on the number of women whose Social

Table 6.13 *Benefits Relative to the Poverty Threshold by Age and Marital Status, Option Packages (Female Beneficiaries Age 62 and Over in 2040)*

| | Percentage with Benefits Below Poverty Threshold | | | |
| | Current Law | 75 Percent Survivor Benefit with 33 Percent Spousal Benefit | Wage Index Benefit With Initial Benefit Reduction | Minimum Benefit with Cap on Spousal Benefits |
Lifetime Earnings Quintile	(1)	(2)	(3)	(4)
All Women				
62–64	**9.9**	10.3	12.7	7.6
65–69	**5.6**	6.2	7.0	4.3
70–74	**5.8**	6.3	6.5	4.1
75–79	**6.7**	6.8	6.4	3.3
80 +	**10.4**	10.0	7.5	6.2
All	**7.8**	7.9	7.3	4.9
Married Women				
62–64	**0.8**	1.0	1.0	0.5
65–69	**0.3**	0.6	0.4	0.2
70–74	**0.3**	0.4	0.3	0.0
75–79	**0.1**	0.1	0.1	0.0
80 +	**0.9**	0.9	0.6	0.2
All Married Women	**0.5**	0.6	0.5	0.2
Widows				
62–64	**6.4**	5.0	7.8	4.3
65–69	**3.3**	2.3	3.3	2.8
70–74	**2.8**	2.4	2.8	2.2
75–79	**3.8**	2.6	2.8	2.8
80 +	**7.7**	5.8	4.6	5.5
All Widows	**5.8**	4.4	4.0	4.2
Divorced Women				
62–64	**23.8**	26.5	30.6	22.5
65–69	**11.1**	13.6	14.4	10.0

(*Continued*)

Table 6.13 *Benefits Relative to the Poverty Threshold by Age and Marital Status, Option Packages (Female Beneficiaries Age 62 and Over in 2040) (Continued)*

	Percentage with Benefits Below Poverty Threshold			
Lifetime Earnings Quintile	Current Law	75 Percent Survivor Benefit with 33 Percent Spousal Benefit	Wage Index Benefit With Initial Benefit Reduction	Minimum Benefit with Cap on Spousal Benefits
	(1)	(2)	(3)	(4)
70–74	**14.1**	16.3	15.9	10.0
75–79	**14.0**	15.9	13.8	6.1
80 +	**21.3**	24.2	16.5	11.4
All Divorced Women	**16.5**	18.9	16.2	10.3
Never-Married Women				
62–64	**24.3**	24.3	31.1	15.5
65–69	**19.1**	20.3	24.4	12.7
70–74	**16.6**	17.1	19.3	11.7
75–79	**25.7**	26.7	25.7	11.6
80 +	**29.1**	30.7	24.7	14.7
All Never-Married Women	**22.8**	23.8	24.2	13.0

NC = no change from current law.
Source: DYNASIM3, The Urban Institute.

Security benefits alone fail to put them over the poverty line in 2040. For divorced women, the overall rate falls slightly, although the rate among those aged 62 to 64 increases from 24 percent to 31 percent. For never-married women, the rate increases slightly overall, but the rise is fairly substantial for women age 62 to 69.

It's important to keep in mind the limitations of our simulations. We are comparing the Social Security benefit with a poverty threshold— not the total income of the individual or the household with the poverty threshold. Because we do *not* include non–Social Security income in our calculations, we miss important trends in other forms of family income. We also miss the tendency for other income (for example, earnings and defined benefits pension income) to decrease with advancing age. In expenditure-neutral exchanges, there are both losers and winners. Options that provide a greater share of benefits later in life when other sources of income, such as pensions or own earnings, tend to be lower would look more favorable with a more comprehensive measure of antipoverty effectiveness. They would also look more favorable if we were to take into account the inducement to work a little longer at younger ages.

These microsimulation estimates provide a cross-sectional look at women at one point in time, 2040, rather than a view that is based on individuals' entire lifetimes. Different survival probabilities between men and women, across birth cohorts, and across racial and socioeconomic groups will affect how these cross-sectional changes develop over beneficiaries' lifetimes.

HORIZONTAL EQUITY. The proposal to provide a 75 percent combined survivor benefit, while limiting the spousal benefit to 33 percent, does significantly reduce the disparate treatment under current law of two-earner and one-earner couples with equal incomes. In the hypothetical example comparing a one-earner couple where one spouse earns twice the average wage with a two-earner couple in which each spouse earns the average wage, the difference in benefits drops from about $95,500 under current law to about $29,000 (see table 6.14). More than half this shift comes from a reduction in the lifetime benefits of the one-earner couple. In the case of low-wage couples, the option nearly eliminates the difference between a one- and two-earner couple.

The option to provide a minimum benefit but to cap spousal benefits also significantly reduces the disparity in benefits between a one- and a two-earner couple. For the low-wage couples in the example, the difference between the couples actually shifts, so that the two-earner couple receives more in lifetime benefits from Social Security than the one-earner couple at the same total earnings level. The option to wage index benefits but to reduce initial retirement benefits, by design, does not change expected lifetime benefits for either couple.

MARGINAL RETURNS. The combination of a higher survivor benefit and a lower spousal benefit improves the marginal returns to earnings by a second earner, although not to the point where the marginal contribu-

Table 6.14 *Comparison of Lifetime Benefits for Hypothetical*
One- and Two-Earner Couples ($)

Lifetime Benefits for	Current Law	75% of Combined Benefit and 33% Spousal	PIA Reduction and Wage-Indexing	Minimum Benefit with Cap on Spousal Benefit
A: One-earner couple: Earns twice average wage	**$450,111**	$416,792	NA	$412,819
B: Two-earner couple: Both earn average wage	**354,481**	388,040	NA	369,344
Difference	**95,630**	28,752		43,475
Percentage Difference (B/A)	**79**	93		89
A: One-earner couple: Earns twice low wage	**$232,436**	$219,611	NA	$294,221
B: Two-earner couple: Both earn low wage	**192,587**	214,446	NA	363,529
Difference	**39,849**	5,166		−69,307
Percentage Difference (B/A)	**83**	98		124

PIA = Primary Insurance Amount.
NA = Not applicable.
Source: Steuerle-Bakija-Carasso model, The Urban Institute.

tion to lifetime benefits is equivalent to a one-earner couple's in which
the sole earner had the same additional earnings (see table 6.15). The
minimum benefit with a cap on spousal benefits also improves the
returns from earnings by a secondary earner, but again, not to the point
where benefits are equal to the returns for the primary earner.

Other Combinations

As we have seen, it is possible to combine Social Security reform options
that together help address the problems of inadequate benefits for some
recipients, unequal treatment of couples with different combinations of
lifetime earnings, and inadequate returns on the contributions of a
lower-earning spouse. This combination approach to correcting problems

Table 6.15 *Comparison of the Increase in Lifetime Benefits from Additional Earnings for Hypothetical One- and Two-Earner Couples ($)*

Lifetime Benefits for	Current Law	75% of Combined Benefit and 33% Spousal	PIA Reduction and Wage-Indexing	Minimum Benefit with Cap on Spousal Benefit
A: One-earner couple: average wage male	$426,759	$395,635	NA	$395,189
B: Two-earner couple: average wage male and female	473,249	496,301	NA	471,508
C: One-earner couple: Male earns sum of male and female average wage	568,126	523,779	NA	501,676
Percentage Increase, A to B	10.9	25.4		19.3
Percentage Increase, A to C	33.1	32.4		26.9

PIA = Primary Insurance Amount.
NA = Not applicable.
Source: Steuerle-Bakija-Carasso model, The Urban Institute.

also allows consideration of other substantial changes to the system. Here we briefly discuss two approaches—individual accounts and earnings sharing—that could be incorporated into more comprehensive plans.

INDIVIDUAL ACCOUNTS. One such substantial change is the adoption of individually based saving plans, either as a partial replacement or an add-on to the current system. Penner and Cove (this volume) analyze the impact of this type of change on family benefits. In addition to the replacement or add-on approach, reformers have proposed a "double-decker" system. This type of system combines a pure minimum benefit with an individual account feature. However, under any reform, even one containing an individual account, some Social Security transfer base will likely remain. Within that base, all the issues we raise here again need to be addressed.

EARNINGS SHARING. In the past, analysts have also proposed earnings sharing as a more comprehensive way to treat different types of married couples similarly.[25] Earnings sharing proposals equally divide a husband and a wife's combined earnings during the years of their marriage to determine Social Security benefits. This approach is based on the principle that marriage is an equal partnership and that both members of the couple should accrue individual claims to future retirement benefits. (See Perun, this volume, for further discussion of property rights associated with marriage.)

Earnings sharing, in combination with the phase-out of spousal benefits, would equalize the treatment of married couples with the same lifetime earnings. Because past earnings would be split equally between spouses, different couples with the same earnings would receive the same benefits regardless of the share of earnings from each spouse. This parity would achieve the goal of horizontal equity.

Earnings sharing by itself, however, would be somewhat less successful in targeting benefits to elderly widows, and could reduce benefits for many of these widows. For this reason, most earnings-sharing proposals have included provisions that allow a spouse to inherit earnings credits when his or her spouse dies. Even with this provision, some elderly widows would be worse off than under current law. Combining earnings sharing with other provisions, such as the minimum-benefit option described earlier, could better target benefits to those in need. To hold everyone harmless in any reform is essentially one way to create a standard for no reform. After all, someone always has to pay for others' increased benefits.

No One Reform Enough

The results presented in this chapter suggest that reforms can help the Social Security system better meet its sometimes conflicting objectives. Of course, trade-offs remain unavoidable in any proposal. When it comes to family benefits, one general conclusion is that how well a proposal adheres to all principles is how it affects single heads of household, a growing segment of the population that is particularly vulnerable to poverty.

The proposal to increase survivors benefits to 75 percent of a couple's combined benefit does little to change the distribution of benefits among widows. Thus, it is not very efficient in targeting benefits to low-income survivors. A child care credit proposal, by contrast, would distribute more than half the additional benefits to women in the two lowest lifetime earnings quintiles. The proposals to provide minimum benefits tend to distribute more benefits to those with lower lifetime earnings (for example, more than 85 percent of the additional benefits for widows and more than 95 percent of the additional benefits for divorced and never-married women go to individuals in the two lowest lifetime earnings quintiles) and distribute the largest share of gains to those with less income. However, a minimum benefit based on years of coverage would still have trouble providing much assistance to many women with few years of coverage.

When it comes to horizontal equity comparisons between two- and one-earner couples, all proposals tend to have mixed effects, although some combination of a higher survivor's benefit and a lower spousal benefit appears to provide greater equality at different income levels. Similarly, this combination provides a higher return for additional work by the spouse, at least at the income levels examined here.

Research is needed on a variety of other fronts. One area is in establishing alternative measures of poverty effectiveness. For instance, when we redistribute benefits from early in retirement to later in retirement, we favor those years where earnings, pensions, and other income sources tend to be lower. Such proposals would fare better under an income measure that included all sources of income and took into account possible labor market effects. Further work is needed on alternative designs of minimum-benefit proposals.

Proposals often considered in isolation—for example, earnings/benefit sharing and carve-out or add-on individual accounts—need to be examined as part of more comprehensive packages. Combined with minimum-benefit-type proposals, in particular, such reforms might avoid some of the potential problems that emerge when such changes are considered in isolation.

NOTES

1. This section draws heavily from Berkowitz (this volume).

2. A typical private insurance company, for example, would reduce a worker's benefit by enough to pay for any additional spousal or survivor benefit that he or she elected to take.

3. See Zedlewski and Saha (this volume).

4. In a social insurance context, a fifth type of objective/principle is the broad sharing of the risks of long-term pension commitments (see, for example, Aaron and Reischauer 1998). We do not discuss risk-sharing outside of our first principle (ensuring income adequacy), but we recognize its importance in discussions of other aspects of Social Security reform.

5. Because some portion of Social Security benefits are subject to federal income taxes for beneficiaries with incomes above certain thresholds, the distribution of benefits after taxes is more progressive than the pretax distribution.

6. See, for example, Zedlewski and Saha (this volume), on programs such as Temporary Assistance to Needy Families and Supplemental Security Income (SSI).

7. We measure only the increase in benefits—and not the increase in benefits as a percentage of the increase in contributions—because we assume that taxes will increase by the same amount in either case.

8. This is less frequently the case since the Retirement Equity Act of 1984 (REA) amended the Employee Retirement Income Act of 1974 (ERISA) to provide rights to private pensions for spouses. (See Perun, this volume, for details on ERISA and REA.)

9. This estimate relies on 1988 marital status lifetables. Bramlett and Mosher (2001) provide slightly higher estimates using data that are more recent, but less complete (survey data rather than registration records).

10. For example, only about one in seven individuals projected to reach retirement age (62 to 69) in 2020 with either an ongoing marriage or a prior marriage that lasted at least ten years will entitle more than one spouse/former spouse to Social Security spousal benefits. Almost none will entitle more than two former spouses to benefits.

11. One provision that affects some single parents is the child care dropout years that Social Security grants in some disability cases (see Social Security Administration 2001, table 2.A10).

12. In a recent paper, FitzPatrick and Entmacher (2000) provide a detailed analysis for representative couples of the effects of changing the survivor benefit to either 67 percent or 75 percent of a couple's combined benefit.

13. Iams and Sandell (1994) compare a child care dropout year proposal with a proposal for child care credits.

14. Social Security currently provides for a minimum benefit for some rare cases of low-wage workers who have worked at least 10 years in covered employment. The number of years of creditable earnings are equal to years in which earnings exceed 15 percent of the adjusted maximum taxable earnings in that year. In 2000, workers needed to earn at least $8,505 to meet this requirement. In December 1999, the minimum benefit was equal to $29 per month for each year in excess of 10, up to a maximum of $581 per month for workers who had worked 30 or more years. Very few workers receive the special minimum benefit. In 1999, only 131,000 retired workers out of a total of 27.8 million received benefits based on the special minimum primary insurance amount. Their average PIA was $503.

15. The poverty threshold would be wage-indexed starting in 2010.

16. Analysts who have expressed concern about the 10-year marriage duration requirement for divorced spousal benefits have also proposed considering both work and marriage history when determining eligibility for spousal benefits (see, for example, Hartmann, Hill, and Witter 1999).

17. The hypothetical examples use the Steuerle-Bakija-Carasso model, which we describe in the appendix. We simulate the distribution of benefits and the effects of the proposals in 2040 using the latest version of the Urban Institute's Dynamic Microsimulation Model, DYNASIM3, described in Smith (this volume, appendix 3.A).

18. The minimum-benefit option without a work test would raise total projected benefits in 2040 by 5.2 percent, making it more than twice as costly as the next most expensive option (the 75 percent survivor benefit option).

19. A small number of currently married women would gain because they were receiving survivor benefits from a previous marriage.

20. In forthcoming work (Favreault and Sammartino 2002), we take additional income sources into account.

21. Note that the estimates for this second worker are the same as for one of the workers in the prior table, though the two cases demonstrate different concerns with Social Security.

22. We do not consider the proposal to decrease required marriage lengths for divorced spouse benefits here. Generally, it is difficult to measure total gain under a reform that is directed toward women with children, as classification of these women is complicated by custody and timing of divorce issues.

23. In our projections, a small number of divorced women who never had children did benefit from the credit. This result occurs because the women could benefit from a credit that was awarded to a former spouse who had had children with another woman.

24. For research examining similar options, see Burkhauser and Smeeding (1994) and Sandell and Iams (1997).

25. See U.S. Department of Health and Human Services (1985) and the Congressional Budget Office (1986).

REFERENCES

Aaron, Henry J., and Robert D. Reischauer. 1998. *Countdown to Reform: The Great Social Security Debate.* New York: Century Foundation.

Advisory Council on Social Security. 1997. *Report of the 1994–1996 Advisory Council on Social Security. Volume 1: Findings and Recommendations. Volume 2: Reports of the Technical Panel on Trends and Issues in Retirement Savings Technical Panel on Assumptions and Methods and Presentations to the Council.* Washington, D.C.: Advisory Council on Social Security.

Bramlett, Matthew D., and William D. Mosher. 2001. "First Marriage Dissolution, Divorce, and Remarriage: United States." *Advance Data* 323. Washington, D.C.: Department of Health and Human Services, Centers for Disease Control and Prevention, National Center for Health Statistics.

Brien, Michael J., Stacy Dickert-Conlin, and David Weaver. 2000. "Widows Waiting to Wed? (Re)Marriage and Economic Incentives in Social Security Widow Benefits." Http://www.maxwell.syr.edu/maxpages/faculty/sdickert/papers/widow.pdf. (Accessed September 28, 2001).

Burkhauser, Richard V., J. S. Butler, and Karen C. Holden. 1991. "How the Death of a Spouse Affects Economic Well-Being After Retirement: A Hazard Model Approach." *Social Sciences Quarterly* 72 (3): 504–519.

Burkhauser, Richard V., and Timothy M. Smeeding. 1994. *Social Security Reform: A Budget-Neutral Approach to Older Women's Disproportionate Risk of Poverty.* Syracuse, N.Y.: Syracuse University, Center for Policy Research, Maxwell School.

Clarke, Sally C. 1995. "Advance Report of Final Divorce Statistics, 1989 and 1990." Monthly Vital Statistics Report 43 (9, March supplement). National Center for Health Statistics.

Congressional Budget Office. 1986. *Earnings Sharing Options for the Social Security System.* January. Washington, D.C.: Congressional Budget Office.

Favreault, Melissa M., and Frank J. Sammartino. Forthcoming 2002. Impact of Social Security Reform on Low-Income and Older Women. Paper prepared for AARP. Washington, D.C.: The Urban Institute.

Feldstein, Martin, and Andrew Samwick. 1992. "Social Security and Marginal Tax Rates." *National Tax Journal* 45 (1): 1–22.

FitzPatrick, Christina Smith, and Joan Entmacher. 2000. "Increasing Economic Security for Elderly Women by Improving Social Security Survivor Benefits." Paper presented at annual conference of the National Academy of Social Insurance, Washington, D.C., January 27.

Hartmann, Heidi, and Catherine Hill, with Lisa Witter. 1999. *Strengthening Social Security for Women: A Report from the Working Conference on Women and Social Security, July 19–22, 1999, Airlie House, Warrenton Virginia.* Washington, D.C.: Task Force on Women and Social Security, National Council of Women's Organizations in Collaboration with the Institute for Women's Policy Research.

Holden, Karen C., and Cathleen D. Zick. 1997. "The Economic Impact of Widowhood in the 1990s: Evidence from the Survey of Income and Program Participation." Paper presented at the 1997 Population Association of America Annual Meeting, Washington, D.C. March.

Iams, Howard M., and Steven H. Sandell. 1994. "Changing Social Security Benefits to Reflect Child-Care Years: A Policy Proposal Whose Time Has Passed?" *Social Security Bulletin* 57 (4): 10–23.

Johnson, Richard W. and Melissa M. Favreault. 2001. "Retiring Together or Working Alone: The Impact of Spousal Employment and Disability on Retirement Decisions." Center for Retirement Research at Boston College Working Paper #2001-01. Chestnut Hill: Center for Retirement Research at Boston College.

Ozawa, Martha N., and Hak-Ju Kim. 2001. "Money's Worth in Social Security Benefits: Black-White Differences." *Social Work Research* 25: 5–14.

Sandell, Steven H., and Howard M. Iams. 1997. "Reducing Women's Poverty by Shifting Social Security Benefits from Retired Couples to Widows." *Journal of Policy Analysis and Management* 16 (2): 279–297.

Schoen, Robert, and Robin M. Weinick. 1993. "The Slowing Metabolism of Marriage: Figures from 1988 U.S. Marital Status Life Tables." *Demography* 30 (4): 737–746.

Social Security Administration, Office of the Actuary. 1998. "Distribution of Female Social Security Beneficiaries Age 55 and Over by type of Benefit." September 17.

Social Security Administration, Office of Research, Evaluation, and Statistics. 1999. *Annual Statistical Supplement, 1999* to the *Social Security Bulletin.* Washington, D.C.: Social Security Administration, Office of Research, Evaluation and Statistics.

———. 2000. *Income of the Population 55 or Older, 1998.* Washington, D.C.: Social Security Administration, Office of Research, Evaluation and Statistics.

Social Security Administration. 2001. *Social Security Handbook, 14th Edition.* Http://www.ssa.gov/OP_Home/handbook/ssa-hbk.htm. (Accessed August 10, 2001).

Steuerle, C. Eugene, and Jon M. Bakija. 1994. *Retooling Social Security for the 21st Century.* (98–119). Washington, D.C.: Urban Institute Press.

Toder, Eric, Cori Uccello, John O'Hare, Melissa Favreault, Caroline Ratcliffe, Karen Smith, Gary Burtless, and Barry Bosworth. 1999. Modeling Income in the Near Term—Projections of Retirement Income through 2020 for the 1931-60 Birth Cohorts. Paper prepared for the Social Security Administration, September. Chapter 8 and Appendix.

U.S. Department of Health and Human Services. 1985. *Report on Earnings Sharing Implementation Study.* January. Washington, D.C.: U.S. Department of Health and Human Services.

Ventura, Stephanie J., Joyce A. Martin, Sally C. Curtin, Fay Menacker, and Brady E. Hamilton. 2001. "Births: Final Data for 1999." *National Vital Statistics Report* 49 (1).

The Steuerle-Bakija-Carasso Model

DESCRIPTION

The Steuerle-Bakija-Carasso Model calculates the present value of life-time OASI benefits and taxes at the normal retirement age—adjusting for inflation, interest, and mortality—for a wide range of stylized, individual wage earners, their spouses and children, and their survivors. The model is cohort-based and can determine benefits for workers born between 1875 and 2000, under current Social Security law or a number of proposed reform measures, which may include individual accounts.

ASSUMPTIONS

- The model uses the Board of Trustees' 2000 economic assumptions and the Social Security Administration's Office of the Actuary's 2000 mortality assumptions.
- Workers are born in 1975 and live to at least the normal retirement age, 67 in 2042.
- Spouses are the same age.
- Couples have at least one child, born when the mother is 30.
- Workers pay both the employee and employer share of Social Security taxes.
- Wage profiles used come from a joint Urban Institute and Brookings Institution (Toder et al. 1999) study, "Modeling Income in the Near Term (MINT)." The 18 profiles simulated (9 for men, 9 for women) represent composites of wage earners drawn from the SIPP, grouped by income and career earnings pattern into "low," "average," and "high" categories. Because the profiles are based on averages, some amount of wages are earned by workers in every year between age 22 and the normal retirement age. Wages earned in a given year are represented in nominal terms as ratios to the Social Security average wage in that year. (Hence, we would represent a worker who earned the Social Security average wage in every year as a column of "1's"). The actual wage data correspond to workers born during 1956–60, the latest data available, but their relative wage ratios are applied to the 1975 birth cohort.

All taxes and benefits are discounted to the normal retirement age (67 in 2042) using a real discount rate of 2.7 percent, and adjusted for prices back to the year 2000. Benefits are additionally adjusted for the chance of death in all years after age 67.

The model does not contain any population, fertility, or labor supply components, nor does it make any determinations about long-term program solvency (although, for some examples, it does incorporate assumptions from the Trustees' Report about future shortfalls in benefit payments).

FOR FURTHER INFORMATION

For more information on the model, its assumptions, and the worker profiles used see Steuerle and Bakija (1994) and Toder et al. (1999).

7

Women and Individual Accounts

Rudolph G. Penner
Elizabeth Cove

A number of studies have asked how women would fare if some portion or all of the traditional Social Security program were replaced
by individual accounts.[1] Some researchers have been gloomy, suggesting
that individual accounts would not benefit women (Hill, Shaw and
Hartman 2000; Williamson and Rix 1999). Others have been more optimistic, suggesting that all groups would benefit on average, regardless of
gender or race (Feldstein and Liebman 2000).

It is not surprising that different studies reach different conclusions.
The various researchers are analyzing different plans and are often examining different populations. Indeed, generalizations about individual
account proposals are difficult to make, because many types of proposals bearing that name have been implemented around the world, and a
number of options have been proposed in the United States. Some proposals would completely replace the traditional pay-as-you-go Social
Security system, as occurred in Chile, while others would replace only a
small part of the system. Both kinds of plans typically include some
guarantee that reduces the risk of investing in individual accounts or
creates an improved safety net that protects those with particularly bad
investment experiences. However, different risk-reducing devices can
have radically different effects. Moreover, such guarantees impose a con-
tingent liability on taxpayers, but identifying who would pay if things go
bad is not at all easy.

How Social Security will evolve through time is also not clear. Under current law, benefits are not sustainable, and the program will require changes on the tax and/or benefit side. Given the number of options available, determining the distributional effects of any reform depends on the structure of benefits with which the alternative is compared. Moreover, the current Social Security system, although often discussed as though it provides benefits that are certain, can be quite erratic and uncertain when forecast by an individual who is a number of years from retirement. Initial benefit levels depend on when an individual earns his or her lifetime earnings, how an individual's earnings record varies relative to average earnings in the economy, whether one is entitled to a spouse's benefit, how many years one was married before divorce, and many other factors. More important, for an individual beginning a career, the uncertainty regarding the replacement rate from Social Security and the investment performance of an individual account are relatively minor concerns compared with the enormous uncertainty regarding his or her future lifetime income.

Finally, the assumptions used by researchers in determining how individual accounts would work in practice vary widely. Most important and controversial are assumptions regarding rates of return and administrative costs. This is a particularly difficult time to choose such assumptions, because returns on equity markets have been unusually high in recent years (despite recent declines from record peaks) and markets remain extremely volatile from day to day. In addition, trading costs appear to be plummeting for small investment accounts with intense competition from brokerage firms operating on the Internet. Cost savings from computerization have not shown up to the same extent in the fees charged by mutual funds. More generally, it is not clear whether high returns on equities will continue and whether changes in administrative costs are permanent.

One chapter cannot possibly resolve all these issues. Our analysis looks at particular cases and spends somewhat more time on the variability of results than have most other papers. We will not consider reforms that replace the entire Social Security system with individual accounts. Given the current political mood, it seems unlikely that such radical reforms will be given serious consideration. Instead, the chapter focuses on plans that would keep most of the Social Security benefit structure intact, while replacing a portion of the system with individual accounts. Within this group, most attention will be given to "carve-out" proposals that direct a certain, usually small, portion of payroll taxes into individual accounts. Examples of this type of reform proposal introduced in the 106th Congress were the Kolbe-Stenholm plan (The 21st Century Retirement Act, H.R. 1793), introduced by Representatives Jim Kolbe (R-AZ) and Charles Stenhom (D-TX) in the House of Representatives, and the Breaux-Gregg plan (The Bipartisan Social Security Reform Act, S. 1383), introduced by John Breaux (D-LA) and Judd Gregg (R-NH) in the Senate.

The key question regarding such reforms is whether the individual account returns make up for the Social Security benefit cut necessary to finance the carve-out. Total retirement income is compared with current-law benefits after they have been reduced sufficiently to solve the financial problems facing the traditional system. An alternative approach would have been to calculate the tax increase necessary to finance current law benefits and then to analyze the effects of a carve-out of 2 percent from that level. This method could show whether the return from the individual accounts would leave people above or below current-law benefit levels. Instead, the analysis examines an extreme plan with a larger proportionate cut in benefits. Although the focus of the analysis is on plans that carve out a portion of the payroll tax, the numbers that are generated also provide insights into the effects of plans that would subsidize deposits in individual accounts with general revenues (e.g., income tax credits) and plans that add on mandated individual accounts without explicitly subsidizing them at all.

The analysis does not consider carve-out plans because they are the most probable option. Rather, we focus on them because they could have dramatic effects on traditional benefits if the payroll tax carve-out were financed by benefit reductions. Thus, from our point of view, individual accounts constructed in this way represent the reform option that is most likely to create some losers. The question is whether many women will be among the losers. The particular legislative initiatives mentioned earlier make a special effort to reduce the number of poor people who would lose benefits by creating a special, higher minimum benefit in the Social Security system and by subsidizing the individual account contributions of those with low earnings. The initiatives also cut the benefits of individuals with high average monthly indexed earnings (AIME) proportionately more than the benefits of those with low earnings. However, our analysis initially ignores such efforts at greater progressivity and assumes that benefits are cut proportionately by an amount necessary to match benefit payments with payroll tax receipts in 2040. This assumption implies a double cut in benefits—first to make the system whole under current law, and second, to make up for the payroll tax revenues lost by the trust fund as a result of the carve-out. To the extent that the analysis reveals unfortunate outcomes, we present options for remedying these situations.

Some reform proposals appear to solve the Social Security problem without harming anyone, and a cynic, or perhaps a realist, would say that these proposals are likely to be more politically popular than the reform discussed here. Former President Clinton and former Vice President Al Gore suggested placing more government debt in the trust fund to extend its financial life. However, their remedy, often called general revenue financing, did not specify tax increases or spending cuts to finance the redemption of the debt once that measure becomes necessary. The debt might simply be sold to the public to finance future deficits in the trust fund, thus transferring the costs to future generations.

Proposals by economist Martin Feldstein and Representatives Archer and Shaw (U.S. General Accounting Office 2000) would reduce traditional Social Security benefits by an amount equal to some portion or all of the earnings in individual accounts. The contributions to the individual accounts are financed by income tax credits. As a result, no one would lose retirement income as a result of the reform, as long as the entire amount in the individual account represents additional retirement saving. The opportunity cost of such proposals can be measured by calculating the consumption that could be financed immediately by a comparable tax cut. In addition, the cost imposed by future traditional benefits is dependent on individual account returns. As a result, the budget saving related to the reduction in traditional benefits, and taxpayers' future tax burden, are uncertain. In other words, the risks associated with individual accounts are socialized, and in this respect, the plans are similar to those that recommend investing the Social Security trust fund in equities. In other respects, the plans are quite different. In any case, Feldstein- or Archer/Shaw-type plans are not examined here, because at first sight, they do not seem to have any adverse distributional consequences and because it is impossible to determine the true distributional consequences over the long run.

Fundamental Issues Related to Individual Accounts

The traditional Social Security system is largely a pay-as-you-go system.[2] It can be characterized as a social contract in which each generation of workers agrees to turn over a fraction of its wages to retirees in return for a promise that when its members retire, they will have a similar claim on the wages of those who are still working. In such a system, the generosity of total benefits relative to lifetime payroll tax payments depends on the growth rate of tax revenues and on the relative growth of the beneficiary population. The growth in tax revenues increases as a result of increases in the average payroll tax burden and increases in total earnings. Total earnings is a function of the growth rate of the labor force, hours worked, and the growth rate of worker productivity.

The system could afford to be extremely generous in the past largely because both the payroll tax base and the tax rate were raised throughout much of the program's history. Thus, the benefits of each cohort of retirees were financed by a level of taxation considerably higher than the level the retirees faced throughout much of their own working lives. In addition, a baby boom lasting almost 20 years after World War II swelled the ranks of the labor force, and low birth rates during the Depression have recently slowed the growth in the number of retirees. Partly because of this slowdown, the system is running a substantial surplus and has become partially funded.

The future looks very different from the past. Although payroll taxes may increase in the future, the tax burden is not likely to rise at the same rate experienced throughout much of the program's history. The ranks of the retired are about to absorb the first retirees of the baby-boom generation, and the bulge in retirements combined with continued low birth rates (seen since the early 1960s) will reduce the growth rate of the labor force. The ranks of the retired will also grow as a result of increases in life expectancy. Consequently, the rate of return to lifetime payroll tax payments is already falling fast and will continue to decline in the future.

Because of the deteriorating outlook, reform discussions have centered on measures that would move Social Security from a pay-as-you-go system to a funded system that invests money now to finance benefits for the future. In a funded system, the long-run rate of return is determined by the rate of return to investments and is not affected by demographic factors, except to the extent that demography affects the rate of return to capital in the economy. In the long run, the rate of return to a funded system is likely to be much greater than to a pay-as-you-go system.

A major barrier to such a reform is the large cost of transition. Individuals working during the implementation of the reform would have to continue paying payroll taxes to finance earlier benefit promises while further reducing their own consumption to set aside funds for their own retirement. Legislators can ease the transition problem for current workers by scaling back some of the promises to future retirees or by borrowing funds, thus passing some of the costs to future generations.

The transition costs of the reforms to be analyzed in this chapter are not very large because only a small part of the traditional system is replaced. Entirely replacing a pay-as-you-go system with a funded system, as was done in Chile, would impose very substantial transition costs. In theory, a retirement system can be funded either publicly or privately through individual accounts. There is much argument over which is the better approach, but this argument is well beyond the scope of this chapter. The analysis focuses solely on the implications of individual accounts.

A key question concerning the value of individual accounts is whether the fully funded component increases national saving. If it does, we will see a higher capital stock and production in the future in exchange for an immediate reduction in consumption. The extra production can be used to make retirement benefits more generous than they would be otherwise. In theory, the additional wealth could go to all retirees or be reserved for specific groups or it could be removed from the pension system and dedicated to child welfare, defense, tax cuts, or other programs.

A system that funds individual saving, but does not increase national saving, has very different effects. First, imagine a system that subsidizes deposits made to individual accounts in a way that reduces the government's surplus to a lower level than would occur otherwise. Private savings in retirement accounts might rise, but public saving would fall. Thus, future retirees would gain a higher portion of the future return to the same amount of capital. In this scenario, retirees would improve their standard of living while retired, while the working population would be worse off.[3]

Some reformers advocate using tax cuts to subsidize contributions to individual accounts, arguing that the government's surplus will ultimately be used for consumption-enhancing expenditures and tax cuts. If this assumption is true, then public saving does not fall and national saving increases if private saving goes up. The added return to capital realized by the individual accounts would finance any future retirement income increases, and the rest of society would not lose on account of the reform. Indeed, the rest of society would share in the gain from funding the accounts. Theoretically, wages would increase because the extra investment would boost productivity, and the total return[4] to capital as well as the tax receipts from wages and capital would also rise. Roughly speaking, total wages would rise two dollars for every dollar increase in the gross return to capital. Thus, the immediate opportunity cost of the reform is the consumption lost through forgone tax cuts or expenditures. When the subsidy is assumed to reduce the government's surplus and less public debt is repaid, the cost is passed to future generations.

Many carve-out reform plans immediately reduce revenues as funds are diverted to the accounts, but then slowly phase in reductions in the growth rate of traditional benefits. Consequently, if the surplus would otherwise have been saved, the negative effect on debt repayment is much larger in the short run than in the long run. In the long run, however, many of these types of plans would add to future surpluses or reduce deficits, thus potentially adding to national saving.

The above argument implicitly assumes that individual accounts represent increased saving for individuals, whether or not national saving increases. Another alternative is to assume that public saving is not changed and that the individual satisfies a mandate to make deposits in a special account by reducing his or her other saving in retirement accounts, such as a 401(k) or IRA. Under these assumptions, neither public nor private saving would be affected by funding. In this case, the reform would not enhance the individual's retirement income. However, more of the individual's retirement income would come from the mandated account, and less of it would come from 401(k)s and other alternatives. Indeed, if reductions in Social Security benefits accompany the reform, as we assume in the options analyzed here, the person would have less retirement income than if the reform had not occurred.

Except in those very rare instances in which people think that they will have too much retirement income,[5] it would be foolish for anyone to let this happen. Rational individuals who were satisfied with their expected retirement income before the reform should save just enough extra money to make up for any loss in expected Social Security benefits.[6] Since the vast majority will receive higher returns from the individual accounts than from payroll tax payments, they will likely increase saving by somewhat less than the mandated amount, assuming that individuals own other accounts from which to shift funds or can borrow more than in the absence of the mandate.

Even if individuals increase their saving by the entire mandated amount and national saving consequently increases, the share of future GDP that they command upon retiring will depend on how they choose to invest their contributions. If they invest cautiously, their return will be lower than if they accept more risk. The desire of cautious investors to take less risk will facilitate some other investors' ability to take more risk, perhaps by borrowing funds to invest in real investment. On average, the higher-risk investors will command more of future GDP, but a large diversity of outcomes are likely, with losses experienced by some people along the way.

Most analyses of how different groups of people fare as the result of the type of reform described here assume that the entire amount in the mandated account represents extra private savings (Congressional Research Service 1998). This is clearly unrealistic. Many of these same analyses also assume that although individuals save more, the nation as a whole does not save more. Therefore, added economic growth is not factored into the reform outcomes. That is to say, the analysis does not include the increase in wages, retirement saving, and pensions that may result from the growth-enhancing effects of reform.

Unfortunately, we are forced to make the same unrealistic assumptions. The analysis here asks how various women fare under the assumption that all mandated saving represents an addition to individual saving. Consequently, the focus is on the well-being of women during retirement and not on the well-being of the nation. If the extra saving of the women represents extra saving to the nation, then many nonretirees will also benefit. That possibility is not considered here, nor are other behavioral responses to reform, such as saving offsets or changes in work efforts. If the reform adds to the retirement income of women under the assumption that they save the whole mandated amount, they may instead choose to save less or retire somewhat earlier. Conversely, if they lose benefits, they might respond by saving more than the mandate or by retiring later.

Characteristics of the Carve-Out Option

As noted, our analysis will focus on the carve-out approach to individual accounts. The analysis uses projections from the Urban Institute's DYNASIM3 to examine the effects of reform in 2040, as though the new system had been in place long enough to cover the entire working lives of all retirees in that year. The results would not differ very much if we assumed that the reform occurred in the near future, for example, 2002, because most retirees would have experienced the bulk of their working lives over the 2002–40 period.

The base case assumes that in the absence of reform, traditional benefits will be cut 26.8 percent to bring benefit costs in line with payroll tax receipts in 2040.[7] The analysis assumes that the disability insurance system is not affected by the reform. (This assumption is admittedly unrealistic. A strong case can be made that the disability system needs reform and that any Social Security changes would intensify the need for such reform. However, the relevant issues are too complex to be considered here.) The hypothetical reform proposal reduces the payroll tax by 2 percentage points and mandates that each taxpayer deposit the saving in individual accounts. Traditional benefits are further curtailed by the amount needed to finance the carve-out. In 2040, the total cut in traditional benefits amounts to 39.7 percent.

We present results for people age 62 and older who are retired. The effects of reform on people who die earlier are not considered. Assuming that survivors inherit the individual account, different outcomes are possible, depending on family status, the rate of return on the individual account, and the number of years of investment. A surviving family is more likely to fare worse under the reform than the retirees studied here if more than one child is in the household and the principal earner dies relatively soon after he or she is fully insured by the traditional system.

Because almost the entire baby-boom generation will be absorbed into the retired population by 2040, the financial problem of the trust fund will have stabilized by then. The benefit cut required to bring benefit costs down to the income rate in 2050 is 26.2 percent, slightly lower than the 26.8 percent required in 2040.

The chapter examines several variants of the reform option. In addition to the implications of raising payroll taxes to maintain today's benefit level, the analysis looks at the effects of using general revenue to finance the deposit in individual accounts by providing a 100 percent income tax credit for the taxpayer's deposit. With the credit, traditional benefits need to be reduced by only 26.8 percent to keep the trust fund financially sound. But the tax credit would have to be financed with higher taxes elsewhere or lower government spending. An add-on plan mandating that people save an extra 2 percent of earnings without subsidizing the saving would generate the same amount of retirement income.

Under the reform options, we assume that accounts are converted to an annuity at the normal retirement age (age 67 by 2022) for people who are still working in 2040, or at the time of retirement, which can be as early as age 62. The size of the annuity is calculated based on a single unisex mortality table, and the annuity is indexed to inflation. By law, each spouse must obtain a joint and survivor annuity that pays the survivor two-thirds of the couple's benefit. The accounts are split equally at divorce. Workers who die before they annuitize bequeath their account to their surviving spouse.

Assumed Rates of Return

The analysis assumes a wide range of net returns to individual accounts and, therefore, does not spend a lot of time on administrative costs. The different individual account designs available have wide ranging implications for administrative costs.

To a considerable degree, you get what you pay for. If monthly reports, unlimited trading, and interactions with a live broker are priorities, you will pay dearly for these privileges. Forgoing the ability to talk to a live broker and trading on the Internet can reduce costs considerably. Transaction costs can be trimmed further if the Social Security Administration (SSA) administers the information system necessary to run individual accounts, and an investment fund is developed that is similar to that used by federal employees' thrift plan. Such a fund can limit reporting, and limit the nature of the investments and the frequency of trading. The Social Security actuary estimated that a plan of this type put forth by the National Commission on Retirement Policy (Belt 1999) could be administered at a cost of less than one-tenth of 1 percent of the value of the portfolio. That approach has been adopted in slightly different forms in the Kolbe-Stenholm and Gregg-Breaux proposals.

Because a wide range is presented for the possible net rates of return on individual accounts, the reader has considerable latitude in deciding what combination of risk-taking and administrative fees seem consistent with the different assumptions made in the analysis. It should be noted that the time pattern of fees can vary, as can the burden imposed on different account sizes. Many private custodians cross-subsidize small accounts; such cross-subsidization is almost certain to occur if accounts are run in a similar manner to the civil service thrift plan.

A recent technical panel appointed by the Social Security Advisory Board (1999) recommended assuming a real rate of return on government bonds of 2.7 percent over the next 75 years. This rate seems somewhat low given that 30-year, inflation-indexed Treasury bonds have paid well above 3 percent throughout their history and as much as 4 percent for brief periods. Bonds maturing in 2029 were paying 3.4 percent in early

June 2001. Nevertheless, we assume a 2.7 percent real rate of return in a riskless portfolio in order to be hyperconservative. The technical panel also suggested a relatively low risk premium of 3.0 percent for investing in equities for a total equity return of 5.7 percent, noting that recent SSA analyses have used 4 percent. The Congressional Research Service (1998), in its analysis of different plans, used a middle-of-the-road 3.5 percent risk premium, a 2.8 percent return for bonds net of administrative costs, and a 6.3 percent net rate of return on equities. As a middle rate of return for the whole portfolio, we assume 4.0 percent, recognizing that to achieve this rate after administrative costs, the investor would probably have to take some risk by holding corporate bonds and/or an equity fund along with inflation-indexed government bonds.

Given the very low rates of return assumed by the 1999 Advisory Panel, 4 percent could be achieved with a portfolio invested 60 percent in stock and 40 percent in government bonds, with an administrative cost of 0.5 percent on the portfolio. Feldstein and Liebman (2000) assume that a portfolio with 60 percent stock and 40 percent corporate bonds would yield a 5.5 percent net return. That figure is based on average rates of return of 5.9 percent experienced on corporate bond and equity markets over the 50 years ending in 1995 minus administrative costs equivalent to 0.4 percent. We use this return rate as the high end of our range.

The same range applies in all the examples that follow. In addition, when the individual account is annuitized, the annuity is assumed to earn the same net rate of return after administrative costs as was earned on the account. Today, annuities are usually more expensive, because, in part, companies have to protect themselves against adverse selection. With mandated annuitization, this problem would be less acute, but the ultimate cost would depend on the resolution of a long list of regulatory issues. Because the various plans examined here assume that people get the bulk of their retirement income from the traditional Social Security system, varying the administrative costs on the annuity within a reasonable range does not have a very large percentage effect on individuals' total retirement income.

In one important respect, our discussion of the rate of return is greatly oversimplified. In reality, a young person pursuing a rational investment strategy would hold a riskier portfolio than assumed here, and would shift the portfolio toward bonds as retirement approached. Consequently, the expected rate of return would start high and then fall during a person's working life. For most people, that investment strategy would provide higher annuities than assumed here.

We believe that the range of returns assumed here is conservative for someone steadily investing over his or her entire working life. It should be noted, however, that if the reform successfully increases national saving, the rates of return on physical capital will be pushed downward over time. Bosworth, Burtless, and Sahm (2000) consider this effect in detail. Higher saving also implies that GDP per capita will be much greater, thus creating the opportunity to compensate retirees to some degree for any fall in the rate of return on individual accounts.

This type of analysis may, however, exaggerate the link between the return on equities and the return to physical capital. Clearly, investors did not buy Microsoft because of the physical capital held by the company, nor did share prices fall recently because of an evaporation of real capital. Investors are buying a share of the return to patents, human capital, management skills, and the prospects for future growth, all muted by the possibility that an increase in the number of shares issued will erode the value of equity.

The Results

The results for different types of women are shown for different rates of return in tables 7.1–7.6.[8]

Married Couples

Married couples were divided into two groups—those in which the wife had worked less than 25 years and those in which she had worked more than 25 years. Within the former group, the wife is very likely to have taken some time off from the labor force to raise children. The averages in the tables are the couples' combined benefits, and they only include couples in which both members draw retirement benefits.

Under the assumption of a 5.5 percent return (see table 7.1), married couples in which the wives worked less than 25 years do very well in the reformed system compared with the base case in which benefits are reduced proportionately to resolve the current system's financial problems. Annual income would be 27 percent higher, and 99 percent of the distribution would be better off.

The benefit derived from current-law benefits would be 8 percent higher, but to achieve this relatively small gain, payroll taxes would have

(text continues on page 254)

Table 7.1 *Retirement Income of Women under Different Reform Options, by Marital Status*
Individual Accounts Assumed to Earn 5.5 Percent

| | Current-Law Full Benefit (1) | Reduced Benefit (2) | Average Benefit ($1998) | | | |
			Retirement Income with Add-On Individual Account (3)	Retirement Income with Carve-Out Individual Account (4)	Annuity from Individual Account (5)	Percentage with Higher Benefits under Option (6)
Married Couples						
Wife worked < 25 years	$23,129	$16,930	$24,428	$21,444	$7,497	98.3
Wife worked > 25 years	28,037	20,523	31,083	27,466	10,560	99.9
All	26,628	19,492	29,172	25,737	9,681	99.4
Widows						
Worked < 25 years	13,510	9,889	14,921	13,178	5,032	97.5
Worked > 25 years	15,759	11,536	19,454	17,421	7,918	100.0
Widowed before age 60	13,370	9,787	17,837	16,112	8,050	99.4
Widowed after age 60	15,803	11,568	18,246	16,207	6,678	99.2
All	15,099	11,053	18,125	16,177	7,072	99.3
Divorced Women						
Worked < 25 years	9,577	7,010	9,679	8,444	2,669	88.2
Worked > 25 years	13,915	10,186	15,289	13,494	5,103	99.4

(*Continued*)

Table 7.1 *Retirement Income of Women under Different Reform Options, by Marital Status (Continued)*
Individual Accounts Assumed to Earn 5.5 Percent

	Current-Law Full Benefit (1)	Reduced Benefit (2)	Retirement Income with Add-On Individual Account (3)	Average Benefit ($1998) Retirement Income with Carve-Out Individual Account (4)	Annuity from Individual Account (5)	Percentage with Higher Benefits under Option (6)
Married < 10 years	12,328	9,024	13,598	12,007	4,574	98.1
Married > 10 years	13,233	9,686	14,278	12,571	4,591	96.7
All	12,995	9,512	14,099	12,423	4,587	97.0
Never-Married Women						
Worked < 25 years	7,261	5,315	7,165	6,228	1,849	91.9
Worked > 25 years	13,309	9,742	14,780	13,064	5,038	99.7
No Children	13,908	10,181	15,637	13,843	5,456	99.3
Children	10,636	7,785	11,320	9,948	3,535	97.3
All	12,199	8,930	13,382	11,809	4,453	98.3
All Women	18,533	13,566	20,819	18,428	7,253	98.8

Source: DYNASIM3, The Urban Institute.

Notes:
(2) 73.2 percent of full benefit.
(3) 73.2 percent of full benefit plus annuity from mandatory saving account.
(4) 60.3 percent of full benefit plus annuity from mandatory saving account.
(6) Column (4) amount greater than column (2) amount.

Table 7.2 *Retirement Income of Women under Different Reform Options, by Average Lifetime Earnings*
Individual Accounts Assumed to Earn 5.5 Percent

| Lifetime Earnings Quintile | Current-Law Full Benefit (1) | Reduced Benefit (2) | Average Benefit ($1998) | | | | |
			Retirement Income with Add-On Individual Account (3)	Retirement Income with Carve-Out Individual Account (4)	Annuity from Individual Account (5)	Percentage with Higher Benefits under Option (6)
Married Couples						
Lowest	$16,706	$12,229	$16,716	$14,560	$4,487	97.7
Second	21,639	15,839	22,634	19,842	6,794	99.8
Middle	25,917	18,971	27,966	24,623	8,995	99.5
Fourth	30,020	21,975	33,232	29,360	11,257	99.6
Highest	35,764	26,179	41,511	36,897	15,332	99.9
All	26,628	19,492	29,172	25,737	9,681	99.4
Widows						
Lowest	9,602	7,029	10,128	8,890	3,100	96.3
Second	13,046	9,549	14,784	13,102	5,235	99.8
Middle	15,411	11,281	18,067	16,079	6,786	99.9
Fourth	17,580	12,869	21,549	19,281	8,681	99.9
Highest	19,672	14,400	26,196	23,658	11,795	100.0
All	15,099	11,053	18,125	16,177	7,072	99.3

(*Continued*)

Table 7.2 *Retirement Income of Women under Different Reform Options, by Average Lifetime Earnings (Continued)*
Individual Accounts Assumed to Earn 5.5 Percent

| Lifetime Earnings Quintile | Current-Law Full Benefit (1) | Reduced Benefit (2) | Average Benefit ($1998) | | | |
			Retirement Income with Add-On Individual Account (3)	Retirement Income with Carve-Out Individual Account (4)	Annuity from Individual Account (5)	Percentage with Higher Benefits under Option (6)
Divorced Women						
Lowest	9,227	6,754	9,255	8,064	2,500	91.4
Second	11,283	8,259	12,030	10,575	3,771	99.8
Middle	13,502	9,884	14,681	12,940	4,798	100.0
Fourth	15,701	11,493	17,328	15,302	5,834	100.0
Highest	18,845	13,794	21,720	19,289	7,924	100.0
All	12,995	9,512	14,099	12,423	4,587	97.0
Never-Married Women						
Lowest	6,926	5,070	6,736	5,843	1,667	94.4
Second	10,117	7,406	10,615	9,310	3,209	100.0

Middle	12,250	8,967	13,174	11,594	4,207	100.0
Fourth	15,126	11,072	16,677	14,725	5,605	100.0
Highest	18,535	13,568	21,851	19,460	8,283	100.0
All	12,199	8,930	13,382	11,809	4,453	98.3
All Women						
Lowest	10,744	7,865	10,874	9,488	3,009	94.8
Second	15,806	11,570	16,978	14,939	5,409	99.8
Middle	19,065	13,956	21,127	18,668	7,172	99.8
Fourth	22,225	16,269	25,415	22,548	9,146	99.8
Highest	25,384	18,581	30,446	27,172	11,865	100.0
All	18,533	13,566	20,819	18,428	7,253	98.8

Source: DYNASIM3, The Urban Institute.

(2) 73.2 percent of full benefit.

(3) 73.2 percent of full benefit plus annuity from mandatory saving account.

(4) 60.3 percent of full benefit plus annuity from mandatory saving account.

(6) Column (4) amount greater than column (2) amount.

Table 7.3 *Retirement Income of Women under Different Reform Options, by Marital Status*
Individual Accounts Assumed to Earn 4.0 Percent

	Current-Law Full Benefit (1)	Reduced Benefit (2)	Retirement Income with Add-On Individual Account (3)	Average Benefit ($1998) Retirement Income with Carve-Out Individual Account (4)	Annuity from Individual Account (5)	Percentage with Higher Benefits under Option (6)
Married Couples						
Wife worked < 25 years	$23,129	$16,930	$21,077	$18,094	$4,147	87.6
Wife worked > 25 years	28,037	20,523	26,418	22,801	5,895	97.8
All	26,628	19,492	24,885	21,450	5,393	94.9
Widows						
Worked < 25 years	13,510	9,889	12,664	10,921	2,775	82.6
Worked > 25 years	15,759	11,536	26,418	22,801	5,895	97.8
Widowed before age 60	13,370	9,787	14,134	12,410	4,348	96.6
Widowed after age 60	15,803	11,568	15,324	13,285	3,756	93.0
All	15,099	11,053	14,979	13,031	3,926	94.0

Divorced Women					
Worked < 25 years	9,577	7,010	8,503	7,267	1,492	62.3
Worked > 25 years	13,915	10,186	13,062	11,267	2,876	91.1
Married < 10 years	12,328	9,024	11,606	10,016	2,582	89.0
Married > 10 years	13,233	9,686	12,269	10,561	2,582	83.5
All	12,995	9,512	12,094	10,418	2,582	85.0
Never-Married Women					
Worked < 25 years	7,261	5,315	6,371	5,434	1,056	53.9
Worked > 25 years	13,309	9,742	12,597	10,880	2,854	93.0
No Children	13,908	10,181	13,269	11,475	3,088	95.0
Children	10,636	7,785	9,794	8,422	2,008	77.5
All	12,199	8,930	11,454	9,880	2,524	85.8
All Women	18,533	13,566	17,612	15,221	4,046	91.7

Source: DYNASIM3, The Urban Institute.

Notes:

(2) 73.2 percent of full benefit.

(3) 73.2 percent of full benefit plus annuity from mandatory saving account.

(4) 60.3 percent of full benefit plus annuity from mandatory saving account.

(6) Column (4) amount greater than column (2) amount.

Table 7.4 *Retirement Income of Women under Different Reform Options, by Average Lifetime Earnings*

Individual Accounts Assumed to Earn 4.0 Percent

Earnings Lifetime Quintile	Current-Law Full Benefit (1)	Reduced Benefit (2)	Retirement Income with Add-On Individual Account (3)	Retirement Income with Carve-Out Individual Account (4)	Annuity from Individual Account (5)	Percentage with Higher Benefits under Option (6)
				Average Benefit ($1998)		
Married Couples						
Lowest	$16,706	$12,229	$14,716	$12,561	$2,487	73.6
Second	21,639	15,839	19,613	16,822	3,774	96.5
Middle	25,917	18,971	23,971	20,628	5,000	98.8
Fourth	30,020	21,975	28,257	24,384	6,282	98.9
Highest	35,764	26,179	34,741	30,128	8,562	99.1
All	26,628	19,492	24,885	21,450	5,393	94.9
Widows						
Lowest	9,602	7,029	8,744	7,506	1,716	73.1
Second	13,046	9,549	12,440	10,757	2,890	95.3
Middle	15,411	11,281	15,039	13,051	3,759	99.0
Fourth	17,580	12,869	17,687	15,419	4,818	99.7
Highest	19,672	14,400	20,986	18,448	6,585	100.0
All	15,099	11,053	14,979	13,031	3,926	94.0
Divorced Women						
Lowest	9,227	6,754	8,147	6,956	1,392	62.5
Second	11,283	8,259	10,377	8,921	2,118	89.3

	(1)	(2)	(3)	(4)	(5)	(6)
Middle	13,502	9,884	12,582	10,840	2,698	98.2
Fourth	15,701	11,493	14,786	12,760	3,292	99.7
Highest	18,845	13,794	18,284	15,853	4,490	100.0
All	12,995	9,512	12,094	10,418	2,582	85.0
Never-Married Women						
Lowest	6,926	5,070	6,021	5,128	951	55.6
Second	10,117	7,406	9,225	7,920	1,819	98.8
Middle	12,250	8,967	11,356	9,776	2,389	99.1
Fourth	15,126	11,072	14,252	12,301	3,180	100.0
Highest	18,535	13,568	18,251	15,860	4,683	100.0
All	12,199	8,930	11,454	9,880	2,524	85.8
All Women						
Lowest	10,744	7,865	9,539	8,153	1,674	67.0
Second	15,806	11,570	14,575	12,536	3,005	95.0
Middle	19,065	13,956	17,946	15,486	3,990	98.8
Fourth	22,225	16,269	21,371	18,504	5,102	99.4
Highest	25,384	18,581	25,228	21,953	6,646	99.7
All	18,533	13,566	17,612	15,221	4,046	91.7

Source: DYNASIM3, The Urban Institute.

Notes:

(2) 73.2 percent of full benefit.

(3) 73.2 percent of full benefit plus annuity from mandatory saving account.

(4) 60.3 percent of full benefit plus annuity from mandatory saving account.

(6) Column (4) amount greater than column (2) amount.

Table 7.5 *Retirement Income of Women under Different Reform Options, by Marital Basis*
Individual Accounts Assumed to Earn 2.7 Percent

| | Current-Law Full Benefit (1) | Reduced Benefit (2) | Average Benefit ($1998) | | | |
			Retirement Income with Add-On Individual Account (3)	Retirement Income with Carve-Out Individual Account (4)	Annuity from Individual Account (5)	Percentage with Higher Benefits under Option (6)
Married Couples						
Wife worked < 25 years	$23,129	$16,930	$19,369	$16,385	$2,438	13.1
Wife worked > 25 years	28,037	20,523	24,021	20,404	3,498	34.2
All	26,628	19,492	22,685	19,250	3,194	28.1
Widows						
Worked < 25 years	13,510	9,889	11,519	9,776	1,630	33.6
Worked > 25 years	15,759	11,536	14,142	12,110	2,607	73.0
Widowed before age 60	13,370	9,787	12,296	10,571	2,509	79.9
Widowed after age 60	15,803	11,568	13,812	11,774	2,245	54.0
All	15,099	11,053	13,373	11,425	2,320	61.5

	(1)	(2)	(3)	(4)	(5)	(6)
Divorced Women						
Worked < 25 years	9,577	7,010	7,896	6,660	885	24.8
Worked > 25 years	13,915	10,186	11,909	10,114	1,723	41.1
Married < 10 years	12,328	9,024	10,574	8,984	1,550	36.5
Married > 10 years	13,233	9,686	11,230	9,523	1,544	38.0
All	12,995	9,512	11,058	9,381	1,546	37.6
Never-Married Women						
Worked < 25 years	7,261	5,315	5,952	5,015	637	2.1
Worked > 25 years	13,309	9,742	11,459	9,742	1,716	37.7
No Children	13,908	10,181	12,035	10,241	1,855	44.1
Children	10,636	7,785	8,996	7,624	1,211	19.3
All	12,199	8,930	10,448	8,874	1,518	31.2
All Women	18,533	13,566	15,966	13,576	2,400	41.6

Source: DYNASIM3, The Urban Institute.

Notes:

(2) 73.2 percent of full benefit.

(3) 73.2 percent of full benefit plus annuity from mandatory saving account.

(4) 60.3 percent of full benefit plus annuity from mandatory saving account.

(6) Column (4) amount greater than column (2) amount.

Table 7.6 *Retirement Income of Women under Different Reform Options, by Average Lifetime Earnings*
Individual Accounts Assumed to Earn 2.7 Percent

Lifetime Earnings Quintile	Current-Law Full Benefit (1)	Reduced Benefit (2)	Retirement Income with Add-On Individual Account (3)	Average Benefit (1998$) Retirement Income with Carve-Out Individual Account (4)	Annuity from Individual Account (5)	Percentage with Higher Benefits under Option (6)
Married Couples						
Lowest	$16,706	$12,229	$13,692	$11,537	$1,463	2.3
Second	21,639	15,839	18,067	15,275	2,227	3.9
Middle	25,917	18,971	21,926	18,583	2,955	10.9
Fourth	30,020	21,975	25,700	21,827	3,725	35.6
Highest	35,764	26,179	31,264	26,650	5,085	82.4
All	26,628	19,492	22,685	19,250	3,194	28.1
Widows						
Lowest	9,602	7,029	8,041	6,802	1,012	24.6
Second	13,046	9,549	11,250	9,567	1,701	48.4
Middle	15,411	11,281	13,497	11,509	2,216	61.0
Fourth	17,580	12,869	15,717	13,449	2,848	77.2
Highest	19,672	14,400	18,311	15,774	3,911	95.9
All	15,099	11,053	13,373	11,425	2,320	61.5
Divorced Women						
Lowest	9,227	6,754	7,579	6,388	824	20.4
Second	11,283	8,259	9,523	8,068	1,264	25.2

	(1)	(2)	(3)	(4)	(5)	(6)
Middle	13,502	9,884	11,497	9,756	1,614	33.0
Fourth	15,701	11,493	13,468	11,443	1,975	45.9
Highest	18,845	13,794	16,499	14,068	2,704	76.6
All	12,995	9,512	11,058	9,381	1,546	37.6
Never-Married Women						
Lowest	6,926	5,070	5,645	4,752	575	0.0
Second	10,117	7,406	8,499	7,194	1,093	2.5
Middle	12,250	8,967	10,406	8,826	1,439	22.2
Fourth	15,126	11,072	12,985	11,034	1,914	45.2
Highest	18,535	13,568	16,380	13,989	2,812	86.5
All	12,199	8,930	10,448	8,874	1,518	31.2
All Women						
Lowest	10,744	7,865	8,855	7,469	990	13.8
Second	15,806	11,570	13,346	11,307	1,776	23.2
Middle	19,065	13,956	16,317	13,857	2,361	33.9
Fourth	22,225	16,269	19,296	16,429	3,027	54.0
Highest	25,384	18,581	22,540	19,266	3,959	85.7
All	18,533	13,566	15,966	13,576	2,400	41.6

Source: DYNASIM3, The Urban Institute.
Notes:
(2) 73.2 percent of full benefit.
(3) 73.2 percent of full benefit plus annuity from mandatory saving account.
(4) 60.3 percent of full benefit plus annuity from mandatory saving account.
(6) Column (4) amount greater than column (2) amount.

to be raised 37 percent for those working in 2040. A more detailed analysis of the extra payroll taxes required to finance current benefits and their implications for this analysis follow.

If in the reformed system, a husband and wife wanted to achieve the full benefit promised by current law, they would have to increase their deposit in the individual account through their lifetimes by 22 percent, that is, from 2 percent of earnings to 2.44 percent of earnings. The cost in terms of lost consumption is 0.44 percent of earnings—not a very painful adjustment compared with the payroll tax increases necessary to maintain full benefits. Alternatively, a couple consisting of a 66-year-old male and a 63-year-old female and receiving the average annuity and Social Security benefit for this group could raise their annual benefit to the current-law level by working about one year longer.

However, the main conclusion is that a carve-out financed by reducing benefits more than pays for itself in the sense that the annuity financed by the individual account more than makes up for the extra benefit cut. If we started from a baseline that raised taxes sufficiently to finance current-law benefits and then carved out 2 percent to deposit in an individual account, the return from the individual account would most likely more than make up for the benefit cut necessary to finance the carve-out and leave people better off than under current-law benefits.

For individual account contributions financed by an income tax credit rather than a payroll tax reduction, a smaller reduction in benefits is needed to maintain solvency. The average benefit under the reform is shown in column 3 of tables 7.1–7.6. With a 5.5 percent rate of return, the benefit would be higher than the full benefit under current law. Of course, some other tax would have to be raised or expenditures cut to pay for the general revenue contribution over the long run. A reform plan that simply added the mandated individual account to other saving without providing any tax subsidy would eliminate the need for expenditure cuts, while providing the same retirement income as a plan financed by income tax credits.

The reform looks even better in every respect for couples in which the wife worked more than 25 years. These couples' total benefits under reform are 34 percent higher than under the reduced benefit option and are only 2 percent lower than full benefits.

Table 7.2 classifies married couples by the ratio of their AIMEs to the average wage. It is also important to note that AIMEs need not be highly correlated to total income during retirement. Social Security is very inefficient as a redistributive device (Gustman and Steinmeier 1999) and may even be regressive on a lifetime basis (Coronado, Fullerton, and Glass 2000).[9]

The classification in table 7.2 shows that couples with AIMEs in the lowest quintile tend to do slightly worse from the reform than do groups with higher AIMEs, but reform still benefits almost 98 percent of all couples. In this lowest group, the benefit under reform is 19 percent higher than the reduced benefit option and 15 percent lower than the full benefit. A general-revenue-financed individual account would imply a benefit virtually equal to the full benefit option. In contrast, for the group with AIMEs in the highest quintile, virtually all couples do better than the reduced-benefit option, with a total average benefit that is 41 percent higher. The reform option even outperforms full benefits by 3 percent, and if the individual account were financed with general revenue, the excess would be 14 percent.

Needless to say, the reform option looks less favorable as the assumed rate of return goes down. Nevertheless, the vast majority of couples benefit more from individual accounts compared with the reduced benefit option when we assume a 4 percent rate of return. About 95 percent of all married couples enjoy an improvement in benefits, with couples with wives who worked more than 25 years again doing better than couples with wives working fewer than 25 years. Even in the lowest AIME group—those with AIMEs less than 50 percent of the average—74 percent of couples do better under the reformed system.

The groupings of the couples shown in the tables are not very useful for exploring the implications of raising taxes sufficiently to finance full benefits promised by current law compared with relying to some extent on individual accounts. Each group contains people of different ages who retired at different times. The tax increases necessary to finance full benefits would have very different implications for different cohorts. To investigate this issue, we created a prototypical couple with relatively modest incomes in which the woman takes some time out of the labor force to raise children. The appendix describes the couple in detail. The husband and wife are the same age, they begin work in 2005, and retire at age 67 in 2047. They receive higher average traditional benefits and higher annuities than the average couples shown in the tables, because they are both assumed to be retired when the man reaches age 67, as opposed to the average retirement of 63. The assumed rate of return is 4 percent.

The couple would receive a traditional benefit of $24,338. That benefit would be reduced to $14,676 under the carve-out and combined with an annuity income of $5,389, for a total retirement income of $20,065. By saving 1.59 percent more of income over their lifetimes, the couple could raise that amount to the full benefit level. Alternatively, an increase in taxes starting in 2016, when the cost rate facing the trust fund begins to exceed the income rate, could make up for the difference. By 2047, the tax increase required to close the gap amounts to 4.02 percent of payroll, or 35 percent. Putting the required tax increase in present value terms, and comparing it with the present value of the loss of consumption required to achieve the same retirement income using an individual account, shows that the present value of the tax burden is 38 percent higher. The burden of tax increases relative to the burden of increasing saving rises rapidly as we raise the assumed rate of return and the assumed earnings of the couple. In addition, the tax option looks worse for later cohorts and better for earlier cohorts. Because a couple starting work in 2000 would pay increased taxes for five fewer years of the spouses' working lives, the present value of the required tax increase is closer to the required increase in saving required under the tax option. The present value of the tax burden exceeds the burden imposed by extra saving by only 7 percent.

If the carve-out option carries an assumed rate of return of 2.7 percent, it looks worse than the reduced benefit option, with only 28 percent of the couples benefiting from reform. Yet, the average benefit is only reduced by 1.2 percent. The current-law benefit for all married couples is 38 percent higher than the reform benefit. To achieve the full benefit with a 2.7 percent return, more than 4.6 percent of earnings would have to be deposited in the individual account. In other words, the loss in consumption would be 2.6 percent of earnings while the individuals were working.

Widows

The reform looks slightly better for widows than it does for married couples. Assuming a 5.5 percent rate of return, retirement income is 33 percent higher than under the reduced benefit option for widows who worked less than 25 years and by 51 percent for those who worked more than 25 years. Virtually all widows in both categories would benefit. In both cases, an individual account financed by an income tax credit or by taxes added on to the current rate would provide a greater benefit than the full benefit under current law.

Women widowed before age 60 and those widowed after that age would see similar results, with the former doing a bit better proportionately as a result of reform. The women widowed earlier do better than full benefits, while the other group of women does about the same as full benefits. Both groups do considerably better than full benefits if the individual accounts are added on or financed by an income tax credit.

When widows are classified by the ratio of their AIMEs to average wages, all categories do better than under the reduced benefit option, and all but the lowest group do better than full benefits. Cutting traditional benefits more than proportionately for those with high AIMEs, as is done in the Kolbe-Stenholm proposal, could provide the resources to reduce the cut at the bottom and make people better off, on average, in that category. The required increase to exceed full benefits at the bottom, on average, would be 8 percent.

When the assumed rate of return falls to 4 percent, all groups of widows shown in table 7.3 do better under the carve-out plan than under the reduced-benefit option. The increase on average for all widows is 18 percent, and 94 percent of all widows improve their status. However, the carve-out benefit is no longer higher than the full benefit under current law; rather, it is about 16 percent lower. To achieve the full benefit, deposits in the individual account would have to increase from 2.0 to 3.1 percent of earnings, that is, consumption would have to shrink by the equivalent of 1.1 percent of earnings. With a general-revenue-financing or an add-on approach to individual accounts, the benefit is only 1 percent lower than under current law.

When we divide the population of widows into AIME classes, the lowest group does slightly worse than the average, with 73 percent benefiting relative to the reduced-benefit option (compared with 94 percent of all widows).

Assuming a 2.7 percent rate of return changes the pattern of results significantly. The widows who worked less than 25 years now do slightly worse on average than under the reduced-benefit option, but only by 1.1 percent. About 34 percent of this group still benefit from reform. Widows working more than 25 years still do better under individual accounts, with 73 percent of that group benefiting. For all widows, the average benefit is about 3 percent higher, and 62 percent do better under individual accounts. With general-revenue-financed individual accounts or add-ons, the average widow's benefit is considerably higher than under the reduced-benefit option, but it is 13 percent lower than benefits under current law.

By AIME class, only 25 percent of the bottom group does better with individual accounts, although the average benefit is only 3 percent lower. Benefits for the second-lowest AIME group are about the same with individual accounts as with reduced current-law benefits. All other groups do better under the reform. Consequently, through higher proportionate cuts in traditional benefits for those with higher lifetime earnings, legislators could avoid cuts in retirement income for the lowest income group.

Divorced Women

With a 5.5 percent rate of return, about 97 percent of divorced women do better under individual accounts than under the reduced-benefit option. The percentage for divorced women who were married more than 10 years differs little from that for women married less than 10 years. Of divorced women who worked less than 25 years, 88 percent do better than under the reduced-benefit option. For all divorcées, the average benefit under a general-revenue-financed individual account or an add-on would be almost 8 percent higher than full benefits under current law.

When divorcées are classified by AIME levels, the lowest group does relatively worse, although 91 percent still benefit. For the lowest group, however, SSI becomes relevant in many states. The Kolbe-Stenholm and Gregg-Breaux reforms also provide a minimum benefit that would raise the retirement income of many individuals at the bottom of the income distribution. (The relevance of SSI under a Kolbe-Stenholm-type benefit will be explored in a later section.)

With a 4 percent rate of return, the majority of all categories of divorcées benefit from reform. With a 2.7 percent rate of return, only 38 percent of all divorced women do better than under the reduced-benefit option, although the average benefit drops only 1.4 percent.

Never-Married Women

Never-married women receive the lowest average traditional benefit of any group analyzed in this chapter. A 5.5 percent rate of return increases the benefit from the carve-out option to 32 percent above the reduced benefit option; with general revenue financing or an add-on option, that return would push retirement income above current-law levels. Interestingly, the relative gain does not differ much between single women who have had children and those who have not. Women with children benefit much less under both the reform option and the traditional system.

When classifying never-married women by AIME level, we find that the benefit for the lowest category under reform and the reduced-benefit option fall below the national SSI guarantee. Benefits under a general-revenue-financed account or add-on and the current-law benefits are above national guarantees, but they are all below SSI levels in the most generous states. Again, the minimum benefit found in Kolbe-Stenholm will be relevant for many less affluent individuals.

When the assumed rate of return drops to 4 percent, the reform still benefits 86 percent of the never-married women compared with the reduced-benefit option, but now the general-revenue-financed individual account and add-on fall short of current-law benefits by 6.5 percent. A major difference with this rate of return is that reform is not quite as beneficial for those working less than 25 years or for those with children. About 54 percent of the women with fewer work years, and 78 percent of the women with children, benefit from individual accounts compared with the reduced-benefit option.

When recipients are arrayed by AIME class, reform looks good for all but the lowest group. But the results for the lowest group are not very relevant, because the group is below the national SSI guarantee for all reform options except retaining current-law benefits, and it would also be below SSI in many states providing a supplement. All who worked a large portion of their life would benefit from the minimum benefit found in Kolbe-Stenholm.

With a 2.7 percent rate of return, only 31 percent of never-married women would see benefits improved with reform, although SSI becomes relevant for the reduced benefit and individual carve-out option and for those with an AIME of less than half the average for all types of reform.

SSI and Minimum Benefits

SSI provides a floor income for individuals who are over 65 and are very poor. If a beneficiary received only Social Security and income from an individual account, $20 of that monthly income would be disregarded, and the SSI benefit would be reduced dollar for dollar by the remaining income. In 1998, the SSI income plus $20 per month would amount to more than $6,144 for an individual and about $9,084 for a married couple living in their own household. Most states supplement benefits, but the generosity of the benefit and the eligibility rules differ significantly from state to state. Next to Alaska, Connecticut is the most generous state, supplying a monthly SSI supplement of close to $250 to poor individuals living independently.

One major problem with SSI is that eligibility depends on meeting stringent asset tests. An individual's resources cannot exceed $2,000 and a couple's cannot exceed $3,000, although assets such as home, household goods, a cheap car, small insurance policies, and burial plots are not counted. If Social Security reform passed and individual accounts were added, a desirable goal would be to reform SSI as well. The monthly disregard of $20, which has not been changed since the beginning of the program, should be increased. The asset test should also be modernized. Unfortunately, such reforms could be relatively costly, but the total program cost is now about $30 billion, a fairly modest amount. Even a 10 percent expansion in SSI would be relatively small compared with the huge savings realized if Social Security reform slowed the growth of traditional benefits.

Under the carve-out option, federal SSI would serve as an important safety net for average never-married women who worked less than 25 years as well as never-married women with low AIME, even with a return assumption as low as 2.7 percent. These groups would also be covered adequately with a return of 4 percent. In all cases, the women are assumed to meet the asset test.

The minimum benefit provided under the Kolbe-Stenholm plan is fairly complicated. The benefit phases in and equals 60 percent of the poverty line by 2010 for a person over 65 who has worked for at least 20 years. Two percent of the poverty line is added for each year worked beyond 20 years, so that a person working 40 years over his or her lifetime would have a benefit equal to the poverty line in 2010. After 2010, the benefit is indexed to wages and, therefore, rises above the poverty line. For a person working 40 years, the benefit would be $10,537 by 2040. Each member of a couple can qualify for this minimum benefit.

Many women in our examples would benefit from the minimum contained in the Kolbe-Stenholm plan. For example, the average benefit for divorcées working more than 25 years under the carve-out plan at a

4 percent rate of return is $9,751. Anyone working 36 years or more would receive a minimum initial benefit greater than that amount. With the same rate of return, never-married women with children receive an average benefit of $7,641. Anyone working more than 27 years would receive a higher minimum benefit. Indeed, anyone in this group working 33 years or more would receive an amount higher than the full benefit under current law.

Obviously, if the assumed rate of return falls to 2.7 percent, the minimum benefit becomes important to more and more women. Any divorced or never-married woman working 25 years or more would have an initial minimum benefit higher than the average carve-out option for these two groups. A never-married woman who worked 38 years would have a minimum greater than the average full benefit for the entire group. (The average for the whole group is obviously held down by those working fewer than 38 years.)

Clearly, a generous minimum benefit or an improved SSI program could provide a valuable safety net if combined with a reform that included individual accounts. A reasonable question is which approach is better. A new minimum benefit under Social Security would probably be easier to sell politically, because it would not be means-tested. However, the absence of means testing implies that it would be less well-targeted to those who really need it. Women married to affluent husbands could qualify for the minimum benefit if their own earnings were fairly low through their lifetime.[10] Single women with substantial assets acquired in estates or as the result of divorce could also qualify for a minimum benefit if their lifetime earnings were low enough. Considering these factors, a more generous SSI program would be better targeted than a new minimum benefit. However, participation rates in the SSI program are currently quite low. Unless efforts to improve participation accompanied reforms that made the program more generous, many individuals who need the most help would not benefit from a more generous SSI program.[11]

Are Women More Conservative Investors Than Men?

If women are more conservative investors than men, as some research suggests, moving toward a system of individual accounts could significantly widen the gender gap in retirement income. Even small differentials in investment patterns would produce large differentials in the annuity that can be purchased with an individual account if the differences persist over an individual's lifetime.

Do women really invest more conservatively on average than men? Different researchers answer this question differently. The data samples used here include the 1989 Survey of Consumer Finances (Jianakoplos and Bernasek 1998), the 1992 and 1995 Surveys of Consumer Finances (Sundén and Surette 1998), the federal government's Thrift Savings Plan (Hinz, McCarthy, and Turner 1997), the National Longitudinal Survey of Mature Women (Papke 1998), a survey of 20,000 management employees in a private firm (Bajtelsmit and VanDerhei 1997), and a survey of 87 companies with 401(k) plans (Clark 1999). The variables considered influential in individual investment patterns include age, race, number of dependents, job tenure, personal and household wealth, personal and household earnings, and marital status. The analyses vary widely in their consideration of these variables. Differences in findings can be attributed to the wide variety of data samples used, and the types of variables considered.

The analyses point out several issues besides gender that may affect investment behavior. First, the effects of marriage on risk aversion differ by study. In the analyses that include marital status as a variable, married people appear to invest more conservatively than their unmarried counterparts. The effect of this, in some cases, is to eliminate gender differences between unmarried women and married men. An important exception occurs among married couples with children, whose proportion of risky assets increases with additional children. In addition, according to one study, married women tend to emulate their husband's investment behavior when managing their own portfolio For example, if the husband invests largely in stocks, the wife tends to as well (Uccello 2000).

Most of the evidence suggests that women are either slightly less, or equally as likely to, invest in risky assets. However, one study shows that black women are an exception: in the study, single black women held 9 percent more risky assets than single black men and 16 percent more risky assets than black married couples (Jianakoplos and Bernasek 1998). Finally, one researcher found that people who were better informed about their investment options were not more likely to invest in stocks (Papke 1998). This finding casts doubt on the idea that better educating women investors about portfolio risk would reduce the gender differences that may exist in investment behavior.[12]

Although the various results reported in different studies make it difficult to reach a definitive conclusion, the investment behavior of women and men does not appear to be radically different, or we would likely see more agreement in study results. Although even small differences in investor preferences can significantly affect the long-term accumulation of assets in individual accounts, the effect on total retirement income is muted in the carve-out option considered here. The annuity from the individual account is far less than half the total benefit for all groups shown in the tables, even with a rate of return as high as 5.5 percent. That is, the income produced by the individual account is less than the reduced Social Security benefit. For lower rates of return and for the general-revenue-financing and add-on options, the private annuity has even less relative importance. Consequently, the percentage impact of different investment behaviors on total retirement income is typically far lower than the percentage impact on the private annuity.

It is important to note that although more cautious investment behavior implies lower monetary income in retirement, such behavior does not necessarily mean less utility over a lifetime. By definition, a risk-averse investor gains considerable satisfaction from knowing his or her income is safe, which can compensate for the lower level of benefits.

Women Could Benefit

In general, a Social Security reform plan that carves out some of the payroll tax and deposits it into an individual account looks promising for the vast majority of women, as long as the assumed rate of return is 4 percent or better. At a 2.7 percent rate of return, the groups identified here that do better are the highest AIME groups. However, even with a return as low as 2.7 percent, retirement income from the carve-out option compared with the reduced-benefit option is only 1.2 percent lower for married couples, 1.4 percent for divorcées, and 0.6 percent for never-married women.

Plans such as Kolbe-Stenholm and Gregg-Breaux that cut the benefits of individuals with low AIMEs proportionately less than those with high AIMEs would mitigate reductions in retirement income for lower-income groups. The minimum benefits in these plans may help some lower-income women, although some of these women may be ineligible for the minimum benefit because they worked less than 20 years. As indicated earlier, a 4 percent rate of return—which is only slightly higher than the current rate of return on inflation-indexed bonds—seems very modest.

Among the various groups of women, married women benefit most from a carve-out reform; 94.9 percent are better off, assuming a 4 percent return. Widows are next, with 94.0 percent benefiting, and never-married women are third, with 85.8 percent of them better off. Divorced women do only slightly worse than other groups, with 85.0 percent of the women benefiting from the reform.

Although we examined a particularly draconian plan in which benefits were cut both to maintain solvency and to finance the carve-out, we have little reason to believe that individual accounts with a 4 percent rate of return or higher would not compensate for carving out some of the payroll tax if the initial tax were raised to finance the benefits promised by current law. Feldstein and Samwick (2000), in an analysis of a plan in which the carve-out entails a higher tax rate than assumed in our base case, also show major benefits from the reform.

Again, it is important to emphasize that the analysis assumes that the individual accounts represent a dollar-for-dollar increase in private saving, but does not consider the effect any extra saving would have on GDP growth. If national saving does not rise, certain groups of women are only better off as the result of reform because they have a claim on a larger share of future GDP while retired. That is, the analysis focuses on the welfare of women retirees, but does not address the well-being of both male and female workers.

If the reform added significantly to net national saving, the beneficial impact on future living standards could be substantial. The extra GDP could, in theory, go to improving the status of anyone whose share of the reform benefits was relatively low. These tentative conclusions show that the greatest benefits of reform may stem from having a funded system. Bosworth et al. (2000) show that the greater abundance of capital relative to labor could reduce, to some degree, the positive effects on income from individual accounts. But this outcome is offset to the extent that increased domestic saving replaces foreign investment in our economy, and to the extent that the return realized on equity and bonds is disassociated from the return to real capital. In any case, a lower return to capital in this instance would be the result of very good news, which would mean that standards of living would be higher for everyone. Thus, some of the bonus could be used to improve per capita retirement benefits.

Of course, a lower rate of return to individual accounts could reflect adverse circumstances. For example, the rate of technical progress could fall below expected levels. In that case, traditional Social Security benefits as well as individual account returns would suffer, and the system's financial problems would worsen.

Many readers will ask how the analysis here relates to George W. Bush's Social Security reform plan. President Bush has proposed a carve-out plan, but the details so far are sketchy and could turn out to be very different than the base plan described here. In particular, any politically viable plan is unlikely to cut all benefits proportionately. Various individual account options are being considered by a presidential commission at the time of this chapter's writing. The analysis here, however, does show that certain carve-outs are likely to more than pay for themselves for the vast majority of women at relatively modest rates of return.

A key to evaluating any plan will be whether it contains a safety net for the poor and how any traditional benefit reductions are distributed among workers with higher AIMEs compared with those with lower AIMEs. The details of President Bush's strategy will have important implications for income distribution, economic growth, and risk sharing between individuals and society.

Some analysts argue that individual accounts will likely work so well for middle- and high-income groups that their existence will undermine support for the traditional system. These analysts worry that, ultimately, the traditional system will disappear entirely as a result, producing very negative consequences for the poor. Of course, predicting political events far into the future is difficult, but experience suggests these concerns are overstated; countries that have created individual account plans that are more radical than those considered here have also built in considerable protections for the poor. So far, the few American politicians willing to back any reform proposals, including President Bush, are moving ahead cautiously and advocating the replacement of only a relatively small part of the traditional system. Only a radical change in the political mood would make replacing the entire traditional system an option.

NOTES

1. The Social Security system is gender neutral; that is, men and women with the same earnings patterns and marital history are treated equally. However, because women tend to earn less and to have fewer years in the workforce, they often qualify for signifi-

cantly lower benefits during retirement than men. They are also more likely to receive spousal benefits than men. That can mean that they may pay substantial payroll taxes to earn benefits that provide little or no addition to retirement income beyond what would be provided by the spousal benefit. This chapter explores the effects of reform in providing adequate income for different segments of retired women.

2. For a more elaborate discussion, see Cordes and Steuerle (1999).

3. Geanakoplos, Mitchell, and Zeldes emphasize the importance of this point (1998). With no increase in national saving, the ability to diversify investments is the only benefit from individual accounts over individuals' lifetimes.

4. The rate of return to capital will fall as the capital-labor ratio rises. The chapter examines this point in more detail later.

5. Given recent unexpectedly high returns from the stock market, there may be more people than usual who feel that they saved too much for retirement.

6. This oversimplifies things a bit, because an individual could also choose to adjust retirement income by working longer and harder and/or taking more risk.

7. The Social Security trustees recently reported that the actuarial deficit of the system equaled less than 2 percent of payroll for the next 75 years. That figure seems to imply a need for less severe cuts for 2040 than assumed here. However, it is important to remember that if the system's deficit were eliminated this year, it would again emerge next year, all else equal, because moving the 75-year period ahead by a year means one more year of large deficits and one year less of surpluses.

8. Our table format is similar to that used by Feldstein and Liebman (2000).

9. For differing viewpoints, see Caldwell et al. (1999). Leimer (1999) surveys the literature on this point.

10. Some low-wage women married to affluent husbands would do better under the spousal benefit than under the minimum benefit. This outcome is more likely under traditional benefits than under a carve-out proposal.

11. For further discussion of SSI participation rates, see McGarry (1996).

12. Other studies indicate that less-educated and lower-income groups are more likely to invest conservatively. See Hungerford (1997) and Poterba and Wise (1996).

REFERENCES

Bajtelsmit, Vickie L., and Jack L. VanDerhei. 1997. "Risk Aversion and Pension Investment Choices." In *Positioning Pensions for the Twenty-First Century,* edited by Michael S. Gordon, Olivia S. Mitchell, and Marc M. Twinney (45–66). Philadelphia: University of Pennsylvania Press.

Belt, Bradley, ed. 1999. *The 21st Century Retirement Security Plan.* Washington, D.C.: The Center for Strategic and International Studies. Final Report of the National Commission on Retirement Policy, March.

Bosworth, Barry, Gary Burtless, and Claudia Sahm. 2000. "The Distributional Impact of Social Security Reforms." Paper presented at the Second Annual Joint Conference for the Retirement Research Consortium, Washington, D.C., May 17–18.

Caldwell, Steven B., Melissa M. Favreault, Alla Gantman, Jagadeesh Gokhale, Thomas Johnson, and Laurence J. Kotlikoff. 1999. "Social Security's Treatment of Postwar Americans." In *Tax Policy and the Economy, 13,* edited by James M. Poterba. Cambridge, Mass.: National Bureau of Economic Research, MIT Press.

Clark, Robert. 1999. "Gender Differences in the Management of Individual Retirement Accounts." Testimony before the Senate Special Committee on Aging, Washington, D.C., February 22.

Congressional Research Service. 1998. *Social Security Reform: Projected Contributions and Benefits Under Three Proposals (S.1972 and S.2313/H.R.4256 in the 105th Congress, and a Plan by Robert M. Ball).* Washington, D.C.: Congressional Research Service, December.

Cordes, Joseph J., and C. Eugene Steuerle. 1999. *A Primer on Privatization.* Washington, D.C.: The Urban Institute. *The Retirement Project* Report No.5.

Coronado, Julia L., Don Fullerton and Thomas Glass. 2000. "The Progressivity of Social Security." National Bureau of Economic Research Working Paper No. W7520. Washington, D.C.: National Bureau of Economic Research, February.

Feldstein, Martin, and Jeffrey Liebman. 2000. "The Distributional Effects of an Investment-Based Social Security System." National Bureau of Economic Research Working Paper No. W7492. Washington, D.C.: National Bureau of Economic Research, January.

Feldstein, Martin, and Andrew Samwick. 2000. "Allocating Payroll Tax Revenue to Personal Retirement Accounts to Maintain Social Security Benefits and the Payroll Tax Rates." Draft paper, June 5.

FitzPatrick, Christina Smith, and Joan Entmacher. 2000. "Increasing Economic Security for Elderly Women by Improving Social Security Survivor Benefits." Paper Prepared for Presentation at the 12th Annual Conference of the National Academy of Social Insurance, Washington, D.C., January 27.

Geanakoplos, John, Olivia S. Mitchell, and Stephen P. Zeldes. 1998. "Would a Privatized Social Security System Really Pay a Higher Rate of Return?" In *Framing the Social Security Debate: Values, Politics, and Economics,* edited by Arnold, R. Douglas, Michael J. Graetz, and Alicia H. Munnell (137–156). Washington, D.C.: Brookings Institution Press.

Gustman, Alan L., and Thomas L. Steinmeier. 1999. "How Effective is Redistribution Under the Social Security Benefit Formula?" Washington, D.C.: The National Bureau of Economic Research. *Program in Labor Studies and Aging,* October.

Hill, Catherine, Lois Shaw, and Heidi Hartmann. 2000. "Why Privatizing Social Security Would Hurt Women: A Response to the Cato Institute's Proposal for Individual Accounts." Washington, D.C.: The Institute for Women's Policy Research. *Social Security Public Education Project* Report, February.

Hinz, Richard P., David D. McCarthy and John A. Turner. 1997. "Are Women Conservative Investors? Gender Differences in Participant-Directed Pension Investments." In *Positioning Pensions for the Twenty-First Century,* edited by Michael S. Gordon, Olivia S. Mitchell, and Marc M. Twinney (91–103). Philadelphia: University of Pennsylvania Press.

Hungerford, Thomas L. 1997. "Workers' Investment Decisions of 401(K) Pension Assets." Paper presented at the Association for Public Policy Analysis and Management Fall Research Conference, Washington, D.C.

Jianakoplos, Nancy, and Alexandra Bernasek. 1998. "Are Women More Risk Averse?" *Economic Inquiry* 36 (4): 620–630.

Leimer, Dean R. 1999. "Lifetime Redistribution Under the Social Security Program: A Literature Synopsis." *Social Security Bulletin* 62 (2): 43–51.

McGarry, Kathleen. 1996. "Factors Determining Participation of the Elderly in Supplemental Security Income." *Journal of Human Resources* 31 (2): 331–358.

National Center for Health Statistics. 2000. *National Vital Statistics Report* 48 (3). Washington, D.C.: Public Health Service, March 28.

Papke, Leslie E. 1998. "How Are Participants Investing Their Accounts in Participant-Directed Individual Account Pension Plans?" *American Economic Review* 88 (2): 212–216.

Poterba, James M., and David A. Wise. 1996. "Individual Financial Decisions in Retirement Savings Plans and the Provision of Resources for Retirement." National Bureau of Economic Research Working Paper 5762.

Social Security Advisory Board. 1999. The Technical Panel on Assumptions and Methods. *Report to the Social Security Advisory Board.* Washington, D.C.: U.S. Government Printing Office, November.

Steuerle, C. Eugene, and Jon M. Bakija. 1994. *Retooling Social Security for the 21st Century.* Washington, D.C.: The Urban Institute Press.

Sundén, Annika E., and Brian J. Surette. 1998. "Gender Differences in the Allocation of Assets in Retirement Savings Plans." *American Economic Review* 88 (2): 207–211.

Uccello, Corie. 2000. "401K Investment Decisions and Social Security Reform." Paper presented at the Retirement 2000 Conference, February 23 and 24. The Urban Institute.

U.S. Bureau of Labor Statistics. 1997. *Employee Benefits in Medium and Large Private Establishments,* Table 11. Washington, D.C.: U.S. Government Printing Office.

———. 1996. *Employee Benefits in Small Private Industry Establishments,* Table 1. Washington, D.C.: U.S. Government Printing Office.

———. 1992. *Employee Benefits in Small Private Industry Establishments,* Table 1. Washington, D.C.: U.S. Government Printing Office.

U.S. General Accounting Office. 2000. *Social Security Reform: Information on the Archer-Shaw Proposal.* Washington, D.C.: U.S. General Accounting Office, January.

Williamson, John B., and Sara E. Rix. 1999. "Social Security Reform: Implications for Women." Center for Retirement Research at Boston College Working Paper 1999-07. Chestnut Hill, Mass.: Trustees of Boston College, Center for Retirement Research.

The Model Couple

To understand the effect of maintaining current-law benefits under the pay-as-you-go and reform systems, consider the following example. A 25-year-old male earns slightly above today's minimum wage in 2005. This male works every year until he reaches the normal retirement age under current law (67) and retires. His wages grow by 3 percent in real terms from ages 25–49, and by 1 percent from age 50 until retirement. The female in our example earns 10 percent less than her husband in 2005, with the same pattern of wage growth and age as the male. To account for years out of the workforce due to child rearing, we assume that this woman stays home with her first child from ages 22–26 (entering the workforce at 27) and with her second child from ages 29–33. These ages are roughly consistent with data from the National Vital Statistics Report for 1998. Except for these absences, the woman works consistently until she reaches her current-law normal retirement age in 2047.

Our results compare the cost of maintaining current-law benefit levels funded by individual accounts to the cost funded by the pay-as-you-go system. The cost of increasing the reform benefit equals the yearly amount by which people need to increase their contribution to their individual account in order to ensure that they reach current-law benefit levels in 2047. These increased contributions begin in 2005 and end in 2047. The cost of maintaining current-law benefits through the pay-as-you-go system equals the yearly tax increase needed to keep the system out of deficit. The projections from the 2000 OASDI Trustees Report of the OASI trust fund balances reveal that the OASI trust fund will go into deficit in around 2016 and remain in deficit through the working life of the couple. Thus, the tax increases begin in 2016 and continue until 2047. The total cost to the individual in both cases is the sum of the real present values of these additional yearly contributions or taxes.

8

Multiple Choices

Property Rights and Individual Accounts

Pamela Perun

At first glance, individual retirement savings accounts look simple. Each account belongs to one person and contains a pool of assets produced by accumulated contributions and their earnings. After retirement, the assets in the account are paid out over time with the size of the account determining the amount of income produced. What could be simpler?

Individual accounts are simple, but only until a spouse or dependent child enters the picture. Then more than one person has a potential claim against the account. Adding individual accounts to Social Security is controversial, in part, because many fear accounts will fail to generate adequate retirement income owing to poor investment choices or low levels of contributions. But even if accounts grow as intended, changes in the family pose an equal, if not greater, threat. Many people believe that individual accounts will solve the equity issues present in the current Social Security program. This belief has some merit. The differences in benefit payments to similarly situated families evident today are not feasible under individual accounts. But individual accounts will raise their own equity issues—not so much between different types of families as between different members of the same family. This is so because individual accounts are a zero-sum game. Their assets are finite. When the account must be divided, what one person wins, another person loses. Family events such as divorce and death may precipitate division and distribution of account assets, considerably reducing the available retirement income.

Social Security does not currently have a system to define and allocate competing interests to benefits because none is needed. Benefits for family members are additions to an individual's retirement benefits. To implement individual accounts, a system of property rights must be created to manage the inevitable conflicts between the needs of the individual for retirement income and of other members for support. The risk is that a system with poorly designed family property rights will dissipate account assets prematurely. It may also cause prolonged disputes or expensive litigation that will consume account assets, leaving little for the intended beneficiaries.

This chapter begins a discussion of the appropriate property rights system for individual accounts in Social Security. It does not offer a prescription—that step would be premature, given how few details of even proposed individual accounts programs have been settled. Instead, using some familiar retirement schemes as models, it analyzes the following basic issues that must be resolved.[1] What property rights should individual accounts have? Who should hold those rights? When and how should those rights attach to benefits? How should those rights be enforced? It also suggests the following guiding principles:

1. Borrow the best features of existing models. There's no need for an entirely original approach.
2. Recognize the needs of family members from the start, but remember that retirement income is the primary objective of individual accounts.
3. Define rights and remedies clearly and comprehensively, which will minimize disputes.
4. Resolve disputes through an administrative claims process. Litigation should be the last resort.
5. Use federal law. Rights should be the same no matter where people live.

Property Rights in General

Although the term "property rights" is a familiar one, it is surprisingly difficult to define. The operative words, "property" and "rights," each derives meaning from the system of law in which it is embedded, and systems of law vary from country to country and from one era to another (Cunningham, Stoebuck, and Whitman 1993). For the purposes of this chapter, the most relevant property rights concepts are found in Anglo-American law, a system based upon principles of law developed in England in feudal times.[2]

There is no single statute that provides a comprehensive definition of property. As one court noted in the early 1990s,

> The word "property" is in law a generic term of extensive application. It is not confined to tangible or corporeal objects, but is a word of unusually broad meaning. It is a general term to designate the right of ownership and includes every subject of whatever nature, upon which such a right can legally attach. It . . . is employed to signify any valuable right or interest protected by law and the subject matter or things in which rights or interests exist (*Mears* v. *Mears* 1991).[3]

Judges usually decide what is and is not a property right by interpreting the relevant statute or adapting general common law principles. The standards used vary from case to case.

As the definition above indicates, three concepts define "property" in a legal sense. First, some subject matter, or "thing," must be identifiable as property. This standard is not difficult to satisfy because almost any "thing," either tangible (land, goods) or intangible (a mortgage, an easement), will qualify. Second, some interest, expectation, privilege, or right must be attached to the property. This standard is also not difficult to meet because most property comprises multiple interests. Typical interests are the right to use, the power to sell, the right to devise by will, the right to mortgage, the right to possess, the right to exclude all others, the right to lease property, and so on. Depending on the type of property, these interests can be held and allocated in an almost infinite number of combinations. For example, one person can hold all interests in a particular property, and a single interest can be held by several persons jointly. Third, and most important, the law must be willing to enforce and protect a particular interest, or it is not a property right. Table 8.1 provides examples of some familiar items and their status as property.

Property rights in the United States are particularly complicated because they are governed by two sets of laws—federal and state—which often overlap and sometimes conflict. A substantial body of federal law, largely statutory, governs the rights to such property as copyrights, trademarks, and patents. Federal law sometimes has exclusive jurisdiction but, in other cases, it leaves the field completely open to state law.

Table 8.1 *Are These Items Property?*

A professional degree?	*No*, it is unique to the individual and cannot be sold or transferred.
Tangible objects, such as land and buildings?	*Yes*, they can be sold, leased, devised by will, mortgaged, etc.
Intellectual property, such as copyrights, trademarks?	*Yes*, statutes determine rights.
A future inheritance?	*No*, it is too speculative.
Financial assets, such as stocks, bonds, or bank accounts?	*Yes*, statutes and common law determine rights.

Each state has its own system for determining property rights. Where federal law conflicts with state law, federal law generally prevails.

Theories of Property Rights and Retirement Benefits

Retirement benefits are a peculiar form of property. They are compensatory in nature, that is, they are derived from compensation (e.g., wages or salary) earned through an employment relationship. Although retirement benefits are earned along with wages and salaries, they are really deferred compensation (i.e., earned now but paid later). This lag can create difficult property rights issues, particularly between married and formerly married individuals. Conflicts over deferred compensation are most apt to arise at three events: distribution (when benefits begin to be paid), divorce, and death.

The right to control compensatory property depends on two factors: (1) the marital status of the recipient, both now and then; and (2) the law—federal law, state law, or a combination—that applies. For single people, a simple rule holds: compensatory property is their sole property to dispose of as they wish unless, for example, a child support order is attached to their pay. The same rule generally applies when never-married people receive retirement benefits. Federal and state laws rarely impinge upon the rights of single people to their compensation.

But married people present a more complicated case. In most societies, the marital unit is considered special. Married people enjoy certain privileges, but they also have special responsibilities toward each other (The American Law Institute 1997; Tingley and Svalina 1999; and

Turner 1994). Special systems of property rights, known as marital property rights, apply to married persons and control how their property is treated at divorce, at death, and sometimes even during the marriage. In the United States, these rights can be particularly complicated because of the interaction of federal and state law. Usually state law predominates because federal law has no general theory or common law of marital property rights. If it applies, a specific statute will generally contain specific rules for its own unique purposes. When state law applies, marital property rights are usually determined by the marital property system in effect where the couple resides.[4] No two states have identical systems, but all states can be grouped into two general categories—the English common-law tradition and the European tradition. States within a particular category, however, can have widely varying rules. Table 8.2 provides a brief summary of the two primary systems.

Most states follow the English common-law tradition that property owned by a spouse is individual property unless it is held in joint ownership. Under this system, married persons own their compensation during the marriage, unless it is held in a joint account, and are free to leave it by will to anyone. At divorce, however, the compensation is subject to being allocated to the other spouse by a judge under a principle of "equitable distribution." Under this system, and assuming that no contrary law applied, retirement benefits would belong to the spouse who earned them, subject to allocation to the other spouse at divorce.

Table 8.2 *Marital Property Law Systems*

Treatment of Property	Common-Law States	Community-Property-Law States
Acquired before marriage	separate property	separate property
Acquired during marriage	separate property unless held in joint ownership	joint ownership in community property
At divorce	separate and joint property divided "equitably" between the spouses	community property divided equally between the spouses
At death	separate and joint property interests devisable by each spouse	community property interests and separate property devisable by each spouse

Eight states, however, have adopted the European tradition of community property, which treats a marriage as an economic partnership between the spouses. This system assumes that both spouses contribute equally to the marriage. Both spouses have equal ownership in all property acquired during the marriage, including compensation, which actually belongs to an entity called the marital community.[5] Under this system, and again assuming that no contrary law applies, both spouses share equally in and have a right to manage retirement benefits earned during the marriage, to receive their 50 percent interest at divorce, and to choose a beneficiary for their 50 percent interest at death.

Potential Property Rights Issues in Individual Accounts under Social Security

All proposals for individual accounts under Social Security have a common feature—a plan to pay a portion of every individual's contribution into a personal account rather than into general Social Security funds. How these accounts would be structured and administered, however, remains unresolved. Some proposals require Social Security to act as custodian and administrator of accounts; others anticipate that financial services companies in the private sector—banks, mutual funds, and insurance companies—would perform these functions. Some plans restrict permissible investments to a limited number of funds offered through the federal government; others make private-sector investment options available. Some options require account balances to be annuitized at retirement; others permit alternative forms of payment. Some proposals require benefits to be paid from individual accounts at retirement under current Social Security definitions; others permit greater flexibility on the timing of benefit payments.

With so much uncertainty, what property rights would actually apply to these types of accounts is unclear. It seems reasonable to assume, however, that any final program would permit individuals to decide how to invest their accounts, would set flexible deadlines for when benefits may be paid, and would offer both annuity and other forms of payment, including some with survivor benefits.[6] If so, these accounts are likely to provide individuals with the following core set of property rights:

- the right to choose and change investments;
- the right to choose when benefits will be paid after retirement;

- the right to choose how benefits will be paid; and
- the right to choose a beneficiary.

More difficult to predict are what rights a spouse would have. The possibilities include

- the right to co-exercise individual rights;
- the right to consent to a spouse's choices;
- the right to a portion of the account at divorce;
- the right to attach the account for unpaid child support or alimony; and
- the right to inherit all or a portion of the account on the spouse's death.

Children may also have some rights to these accounts. Such rights may include

- the right to inherit a portion of a parent's account; and
- the right to attach the account for support while a dependent.

An enforcement scheme would also be required to uphold the property rights system created for individual accounts. The most important decision to be made is what body of law controls the accounts. If based on federal law, the actual provisions of the authorizing statute, rather than general legal principles, control enforcement. That statute could define property rights in any number of ways. If based on state law, the enforcement scheme would have to be integrated with the laws of the 50 states and capable of resolving issues that arise when the laws of several states conflict.

Three Alternative Models

In the United States today, three primary systems deliver retirement benefits: Social Security, the private pension system, and individual retirement accounts (IRAs). Two of these—the private pension system and IRAs—have substantial experience with individual accounts. These systems differ markedly in the rights granted individuals and family members. In considering a property rights system for individual accounts under Social Security, it is useful to learn how these systems have resolved the following issues. What property rights do individuals have in these systems? Do family members have property rights? If so, when and how do their rights attach to benefits? And finally, how are these rights enforced?

Individual Property Rights to Benefits

SOCIAL SECURITY. Most Americans would be surprised to learn that they have no protected property rights in their Social Security benefits.[7] The program was designed under the philosophy that workers should receive benefits as a matter of right. Social Security was not intended to be a welfare program, equivalent to the dole, or subject to a means test. As noted at the time of its enactment,

> [Social Security] comports better than any substitute we have discovered with the American concept that free men want to earn their security and not ask for doles—that is what is due as a matter of earned right is far better than a gratuity . . . Social Security is not a handout; it is not charity; it is not relief. It is an earned right based upon the contributions and earnings of the individual. As an earned right, the individual is eligible to receive his benefit in dignity and self-respect.[8]

The Supreme Court, however, disagreed in *Flemming* v. *Nestor* (1960). It ruled that individuals have a statutory entitlement but no property right to their benefits.[9] Because Social Security benefits depend on earnings records rather than contributions (unlike annuity payments, which depend on premium payments), the Court concluded that individuals have no contractual right to benefits. The Court also seemed persuaded that individuals' benefits are never "vested," that is, individuals do not have an ownership right to a specific benefit amount that the law can enforce. It noted that Congress reserves the right to "alter, amend or repeal" the program at any time, which means it can change the benefits structure, even retroactively.[10] Noting that the program was intended to last for the foreseeable future, the Court reasoned that

> to engraft upon the Social Security system a concept of 'accrued property rights' would deprive it of the flexibility and boldness in adjustment to ever-changing conditions which it demands.[11]

Under the ruling in *Nestor*, then, Social Security benefits are not property. No individual has a legally enforceable right to a particular amount of benefit payable at a particular point in time. Although employers and employees finance Social Security with their contributions, the benefits promised by the program are a mere expectancy, subject to the will of Congress.

PRIVATE PENSION SYSTEM. The private pension system does have a well-developed system of property rights.[12] Benefits are earned through employment, and employers decide the benefits that their employees will qualify for when they choose to sponsor a particular type of plan.[13] Individuals who participate in the plan accrue benefits over time. Depending on the plan's schedule, they become vested in those benefits over time. Under tax code rules, individuals must generally become fully vested after five years, if the plan has an all-or-nothing vesting schedule, or after seven years, if the plan grants vesting credit over a number of years. Once vested, benefits accrued cannot be lost or forfeited. Even if employers change the plan, vested benefits must be protected.[14] In a defined benefit plan, this protection generally means that individuals have a right to a certain amount of income at retirement. In a defined contribution plan, this condition means only that individuals have a right to the employer contributions previously made to their accounts and the earnings on their accounts, not that they are guaranteed the value of their accounts at any point in time. Employees are always 100 percent vested in their own contributions.

IRAs. IRAs are extremely simple.[15] Individuals fund these accounts through their own contributions or by rolling over benefits earned under an employer-sponsored plan. Individuals always have a 100 percent vested interest in the assets in their IRAs, even though the value of their accounts may fluctuate because of investment performance.

Family Property Rights to Benefits

SOCIAL SECURITY. The absence of property rights in Social Security has little practical effect because of the current design of the program. For example, the program pays benefits only in the form of life annuities, so no inheritance questions arise if a beneficiary dies. It also includes auxiliary benefits for spouses, including certain qualifying divorced spouses, as well as dependents. Currently, family members do not compete for benefits under Social Security. Instead, if they satisfy eligibility standards, they are entitled to benefits independently. In large part, this reflects Social Security's designation of the family, rather than the individual, as the fundamental unit for defining benefits.

Figure 8.1 illustrates how family benefits are allocated under Social Security today. Individuals earn benefits based upon their earnings history.

Figure 8.1 *Family Benefits under Social Security Today*

	Individual	Spouse	Divorced Spouse	Dependent Child
At distribution	100%	at least 50% of spouse's benefit	at least 50% of former spouse's benefit	up to 50% of parent's benefit
At death		at least 100% of deceased spouse's benefit	at least 100% of deceased former spouse's benefit	up to 75% of deceased parent's benefit

When distributions begin, individuals receive 100 percent of their benefit as an indexed annuity payable for life. A spouse may also have an earned benefit. But a spouse also has a right under Social Security's dual entitlement system to a minimum benefit of 50 percent of the other spouse's benefit, reduced dollar for dollar by any earned benefit. A surviving spouse is also entitled to a minimum benefit of 100 percent of the deceased spouse's benefit, again reduced dollar for dollar by any earned benefit. Spouses who receive benefits are also paid in the form of an annuity for life. Divorced spouses are entitled to a minimum benefit based on their former spouse's earnings history, if they were married for at least 10 years and have not remarried. The benefit of a divorced spouse is calculated based on the former spouse's entire earnings history, not just the portion during the marriage. Social Security also provides benefits for dependent children based on a parent's earnings history.

These family benefits have at least three unusual aspects that an individual account plan cannot replicate. First, individuals can generate multiple additional benefits (e.g., spousal and survivor) based on their earnings history, without experiencing a reduction in their own benefits, although total benefits paid to a family are subject to a maximum amount. Second, an individual's earning history, not the number of benefits it generates, determines the rate of contributions. Married workers or workers with dependent children do not pay extra for these benefits. Third, Social Security family benefits do not just include survivor benefits. Spouses and divorced spouses, depending on their ages and other circumstances, as well as dependent children are entitled to be paid concurrent benefits.

It is useful to mention an alternative scheme for defining family benefits that has often been proposed for Social Security. This proposal, called "earnings sharing," is interesting because it would essentially transform Social Security into a community property system. In addition, Social Security's traditional emphasis on the family unit would change, and the dual entitlement system would no longer be available (Reno and Upp 1983; Center for Women Policy Studies 1988).

Figure 8.2 illustrates how family benefits would change under an earnings sharing system. Each spouse would receive a Social Security benefit based in part on his or her earnings while single. While married, the earnings of the spouses would be combined, and each spouse would receive credit for 50 percent of the couple's joint earnings. Each spouse would retain those credits on divorce. Under this system, some benefits would no longer be available. Divorced spouses, for example, would no longer receive a benefit based on their former spouse's entire earning history. Instead, they would receive credit only for the duration of the marriage. Family benefits would continue to be paid concurrently, however, and in the form of life annuities.

PRIVATE PENSION SYSTEM. The private pension system is designed to provide benefits to individuals, not to families. Only one additional person—the surviving spouse—has any property rights to benefits, and even those rights are limited. When the Employee Retirement Income Security Act of 1974 (ERISA) was enacted more than 25 years ago, it enabled individuals to protect their vested benefits from loss caused by mismanage-

Figure 8.2 *Social Security Benefits with Earnings Sharing*

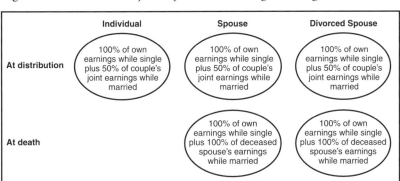

ment of the plan or its assets or by the actions of the plan sponsor. But the spouse's potential interest in those benefits was not protected. Individuals had the unilateral right to decide how their benefits would be paid and were generally free to choose, for example, between an annuity that could provide survivor benefits for a spouse and an annuity that did not. Ten years after ERISA was enacted, it became apparent that the absence of rights for spouses was a problem. Many women found themselves impoverished as widows because their husbands had chosen a life annuity or received a lump-sum payment that had already been spent. In addition, many divorced spouses, because their rights were unsettled under ERISA, received no share in the benefits accrued by their former spouses during their marriages.

The Retirement Equity Act of 1984 (REA) amended ERISA to provide some minimal rights for spouses.[16] Put simply, a plan must now honor an award of benefits to a former spouse at divorce. In addition, spouses now have some limited rights to benefits on the death of their spouse. But true survivor benefits are required in only a limited number of plans. These plans—defined benefit plans and defined contribution plans known as money purchase plans—are now required to pay benefits as annuities with survivor rights. Participants may choose a different form of payment or name someone other than the spouse as beneficiary, but only with the spouse's written consent. Spouses must also consent to any distributions, such as a loan, made to participants before retirement benefits begin. These rights, however, only apply to the surviving spouse. A predeceased spouse generally loses all rights to a spousal benefit, including the right to consent to a successor beneficiary.[17]

Figure 8.3 illustrates how REA's survivor annuity requirements are intended to work. In these plans, individuals are generally not entitled to begin receiving benefits until they retire at normal retirement age (generally, age 65). At retirement, the full benefit is calculated and then reduced, first for any portion allocated to a former spouse under a state court divorce order and second to pay for survivor benefits for the spouse. The individual receives payments for life. A spouse receives no payments, however, until the individual dies. At that time, payments equal to at least 50 percent of the deceased's benefit begin and continue for life. No benefits are payable to dependents or other descendants of the individual or the spouse, either during their lifetimes or at the surviving spouse's death.

Other defined contribution plans, such as profit sharing or 401(k) plans, are not required to provide survivor annuities as long as the plan

Figure 8.3 *Family Rights to Annuity Benefits in the Private Pension System*

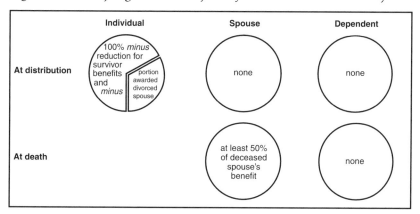

names the spouse as the death beneficiary of the other spouse's account and no annuity form of payment has been chosen. These plans, the most popular type of plan today, usually offer only lump-sum distributions, although some will permit installment distributions over a period of five to ten years.[18] Spouses have no control over when or how benefits are paid. A participant can take a loan or receive a distribution from these plans without spousal consent. Spousal death benefit protection applies only while funds remain in the plan. These plans are also required to honor a divorce decree awarding a portion of a participant's account to a former spouse. When a plan receives such an order, it usually transfers the amount awarded from the individual's account to a new account for the former spouse in the plan, or to an IRA for the former spouse's benefit. In either case, the former spouse thereafter exercises all property rights, such as choosing investments and a form of payment, in the account.

IRAs. Although federal law determines how IRAs must be established and administered, it does not impose any system of marital property rights. From the federal perspective, individuals have sole rights to the assets in their IRAs. State law determines the rights of spouses, if any, to an IRA. Figure 8.4 illustrates the marital rights that might apply to IRAs. At divorce, for example, assets in an IRA might be allocated between the spouses, but that allocation would differ depending on whether common law or community property law applied.[19] For example, under a community property system, the portion of the IRA attributable to the

Figure 8.4 *Marital Property Rights to IRAs*

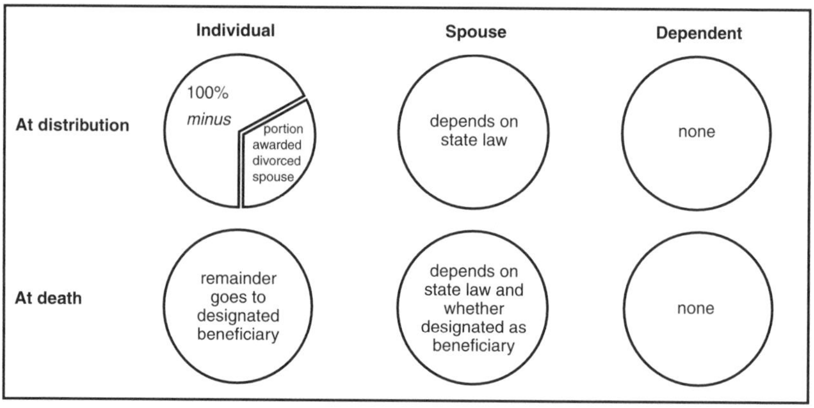

duration of the marriage would typically be divided between the spouses. The amount allocated would then be transferred to the other spouse, either directly or to an IRA established on his or her behalf. At death, state law would determine who inherits the IRA if no beneficiary has been designated.[20] In a common-law state, the IRA owner is generally free to name anyone as beneficiary, but in a community-property state, a spouse has the right to designate a beneficiary for his or her share. There are no benefits for children or other dependents unless they are named as beneficiaries.

Enforcement of Property Rights

Social Security, the private pension system, and IRAs have very different enforcement systems for property rights. Table 8.3 briefly summarizes some of their major components.

SOCIAL SECURITY. Social Security today has an enforcement system that relies almost entirely on federal law (McCormick 1998; West Group 1999). It provides an extensive administrative procedure for deciding disputes over benefits internally. Individuals begin the process by filing a claim for benefits with the Social Security Administration. If dissatisfied with an initial ruling, they are entitled to pursue a three-stage appeal or review procedure within the agency. If still dissatisfied after receiving a final deter-

Table 8.3 *Enforcement Systems for Rights*

Attribute	Social Security	Private Pension System	IRAs
What law controls:			
In general	federal law	federal law	state law
At distribution	federal law	federal law	state law
At divorce	federal law	federal and state law	state law
At death	not relevant	federal law	state law
Who decides when there is a dispute	federal agency initially, then claimants have appeal rights to courts	plan initially, then claimants have appeal rights to courts	courts
Who pays for attorneys' fees	claimants, fees limited to no more than 25 percent of retroactive benefits	claimants	parties

mination, they may then turn to the federal courts for judicial review of an adverse ruling.[21] Individuals asserting a claim for Social Security benefits have the right to retain an attorney or other qualified agent to represent them during the administrative proceedings. If the agency decides that an individual or a family member is entitled to retroactive benefits, it may also order that fees be withheld from the award and paid directly to the attorney (but not to any other representative). The fee amount that may be paid to a representative is limited by statute. A court that rules in favor of retroactive benefits may also order that attorneys' fees, not to exceed 25 percent of the award, be paid out of those benefits.[22]

PRIVATE PENSION SYSTEM. The private pension system also has an enforcement system based on federal laws—the tax code and ERISA. In addition, because a primary objective of ERISA is to provide uniform remedies for plan participants, any state law that "relates to" an employee benefit plan governed by ERISA is expressly preempted.[23] Like Social Security, ERISA provides an administrative procedure for initial decisions about benefit claims. Each plan is required to have an internal set of procedures for ruling on the merits of claims.[24] Individuals whose claims have been denied may appeal that decision under those procedures. If the plan denies the claim on appeal, the individual can then pursue the claim in either federal or state court.[25] Unlike Social Security, ERISA has no express provision for paying attorneys' fees from benefits.

IRAs. IRAs have no explicit enforcement system. Nor do they have any initial administrative procedure for settling disputes over claims for benefits. When a dispute arises over property rights to the account, the parties must pursue their claims under state law, at their own expense, through the court system.

Building a Property Rights System for Individual Accounts under Social Security

It is a virtual certainty that property rights will accompany individual accounts if they are added to Social Security. These accounts, after all, will meet the test in *Nestor*, which established that benefits must be determined by contributions. In addition, account contributions will undoubtedly be vested. The experience of 401(k) plans shows that people feel strongly that their contributions are their money and that they alone should control how their accounts are managed and invested. Although Congress could decide to retain its authority to amend the program at will (which would include the power to terminate individual accounts and to transfer those funds to the existing program), it is unlikely to do so. In the private pension system and under IRAs, contributions made by individuals are always 100 percent vested, and there will be strong political pressure to provide similar protection to individual accounts in the Social Security system.

Individual accounts are popular largely because they provide individuals with more ownership rights, offering more control and freedom of choice than defined benefit plans. Those benefits, however, have their costs. In the case of Social Security, the primary cost is the system of family benefits historically provided by the program. The pool of unallocated assets now used to provide automatic benefits to family members as well as individuals, and at no cost to them, would not exist in an individual accounts program. Instead, individuals and family members would have to compete for the available funds in the account.

Building a property rights system for individual accounts in Social Security will be a demanding task. It will require institutionalizing a set of values about the rights of family members, and no consensus on what those values should be has yet emerged. As Thompson (1999, 18–19) observes, individual account plans involve difficult choices, and there are legitimate "differences of opinion about the relative importance of the different goals that people have for [them] . . . No single plan is likely to be the best one to achieve all of these goals." At this point, it is only possible to suggest some guiding principles as well as some basic building blocks.

The first guiding principle is perhaps all too obvious—a property rights system for Social Security should be built by adapting the best features of existing models as much as possible. There is no single perfect property rights system for individual accounts, and Social Security should not attempt to create one. Retirement systems, such as the private pension system and IRAs reviewed in this chapter, have valuable experience to contribute. These U.S. models are the most relevant to Social Security's purposes. But there are many other Social Security–type systems throughout the world, both created with and revamped to include individual accounts, from which some important lessons could be learned.

The second guiding principle is that a property rights system for individual accounts must balance the retirement income needs of the individual and the legitimate support needs of other family members. This balance represents the most central and material component of any property rights system for individual accounts. There is no absolute or universally right way to find that balance. As always, the central questions will concern the rights these accounts should have, who should have those rights, and when and how those rights should attach to benefits. The critical decisions made at the outset will then shape the remaining contours of the system. They include

Whether, during the marriage, a spouse should have

- no rights over the account (*the IRA and common-law approaches*)?
- some rights over the account (*the private pension system approach*)?
- equal rights over the account (*the community-property approach*)?

Whether a divorced spouse should have

- rights to half the benefits earned during the marriage (*the community-property and earnings sharing approaches*)?
- rights decided by a judge (*the private pension system and common-law approaches*)?

Whether the account should be inheritable by

- only the surviving spouse (*sometimes the private pension system approach*)?

- children of a deceased spouse (*sometimes the community-property approach*)?
- anyone (*the IRA and common-law approaches*)?

Whether income from the account should be available

- only at retirement (*the Social Security approach*)?
- before retirement but only for child support and alimony (*the private pension system approach in some cases*)?
- before retirement for any reason at all (*the IRA approach*)?

Whether the account should pay retirement income

- with mandatory survivor benefits for a spouse (*sometimes the private pension system approach*)?
- in any form the couple chooses together (*also the private pension system approach*)?
- in any form (*the IRA approach*)?

The three final principles concern process rather than substance, an important consideration in integrating individual accounts into the Social Security system. An individual account program would generate millions of accounts, with a large proportion of them small in size. If these accounts are to produce the anticipated amount of retirement income, the system for enforcing property rights must be efficient and economical. If it is not, account assets could be consumed by adversarial disputes and proceedings. Or the rights granted by the statute will be meaningless because they cannot be easily exercised by Social Security recipients. To achieve that goal, the following three strategies are suggested.

First, the statute authorizing individual accounts should be as comprehensive as possible. It should define as many important terms as possible. Such terms include who qualifies as a spouse, what form of divorce is valid, and who qualifies as a dependent. It should also carefully define how and when benefits may be paid from accounts. It should set standards for who is an eligible beneficiary of an account and establish procedures for when no beneficiary has been named. The existing statute under Social Security already contains many of these definitions, and it would be practical to apply them to individual accounts when feasible.

The intention is to define the important concepts related to property rights with as much clarity and certainty as possible to minimize the potential for later disputes.

Second, the individual account program must provide some type of initial dispute resolution process that is relatively simple and inexpensive. Both Social Security and the private pension system provide an internal administrative process for this purpose. If individual accounts are administered by the Social Security Administration, the internal review system could be adapted for individual accounts. However, if accounts are held in the private sector, it is unclear who should be the initial decisionmaker and what type of process could be implemented. The banks, mutual fund families, and insurance companies that are the most likely candidates to hold these assets are not likely to assume this responsibility willingly, or for free. In addition, any dispute-resolution process must be capable of relatively quick decisions. Claims should not be allowed to languish for months or years because these accounts will be exposed to market risk. For that reason, it is also important to clarify who holds investment powers in a disputed account and to prevent intentional harm to the interests of other claimants to the account. The private pension system sets time limits for its administrative process, and similar limits could be applied to these accounts. As a last resort, the enforcement system could also include appeal rights to an IRA-type process, which requires hiring attorneys and pursuing a claim in court. Few Social Security recipients, however, are likely to have the resources to exercise such rights. In addition, these accounts would be funded by relatively modest levels of contributions for many years to come and thus would be too small to justify full-blown litigation. Moreover, the justice system is unlikely to welcome the addition of these claims to an already overburdened court system.

Finally, it seems sensible to conclude that any property rights system for an individual accounts program should be primarily based on federal law. For most issues involving families, such as divorce and inheritance, state law controls. When federal law becomes entangled with such issues, it generally defers to and relies on the laws of the relevant state. There is a general consensus that state law is best suited to handle these issues. Many states have developed their property rights system over many years, and those laws are a valued tradition with which (it is felt) federal law should not interfere. In addition, state law is often more flexible and timely in its ability to deal with emerging issues.

Reliance on state law has its drawbacks, however, especially when the laws of 50 jurisdictions become part of a federal program. If the choice were simply a matter of federal or state law, then state law would be the winner. Under a state law model, however, the question becomes which state's laws apply, and there is often more than one candidate. The difficulties in administering an individual account program in a society where family situations change and where people move from place to place are obvious. Using a state law model would mean that property rights would vary depending on where individuals and family members lived. If they did not live in the same state, the system would have to resolve difficult conflicts between the laws of several states. For people who move from state to state during their lives, the question is whether contributions to the account would be governed by the laws of the state in which they were made or by the law of the current state of residence. A state law model seems to add unnecessary legal complexity and cost to a mandatory federal program intended to provide most Americans with a basic level of retirement income.

The competing model from the private pension system expressly utilizes federal law to ensure that plan beneficiaries have uniform rights and remedies. In addition, federal law preempts any state law that conflicts with the provisions of ERISA. This system provides the private pension system with a simplified and consistent body of law that minimizes its administrative burden while efficiently protecting the rights of plan beneficiaries. Individual account plans are complicated. They require detailed record-keeping systems and special investment programs. If these complicated accounts are added to Social Security, most Americans will have such an account, and almost every family will depend on it for some form of income or support. The administrative burden on the Social Security Administration or any other entity authorized to maintain an individual accounts program in Social Security will be enormous. Basing its property rights system on a coherent and consistent set of federal laws is one of the few obvious ways to simplify administration of such a program while providing adequate protection for the rights of Social Security recipients. Moreover, by reaching consensus over the core values of a property rights system under Social Security that broadly reflects state law systems, policymakers will position federal law as a supplement to—rather than a substitute for—state systems of property rights.

NOTES

1. This chapter focuses on the legal elements of various property law systems, *not* their economic consequences or equitable considerations. Specifically, it does *not* examine how any particular system might affect the amount of Social Security benefits of particular individuals.

2. This chapter provides a brief discussion of some general principles of law and only presents an introduction to some of the legal concepts that will influence the design of a property rights system for Social Security. The legal issues to be resolved during that process will require the analysis of other forms of law such as case law, statutes, and regulations. Such an analysis is beyond the scope of this chapter.

3. Quoted in Turner (1994, pp. 129–130).

4. This description of marital property systems under state law is an abbreviated one. It emphasizes the differences between the two systems rather than their similarities. In reality, no state has a pure version of either system. Many states have blended community property and common-law principles, primarily used in allocating marital assets at divorce.

5. The traditional community-property states, many of which adopted this system of law when they were French or Spanish colonies, are Arizona, Idaho, Nevada, Texas, Washington, California, Louisiana, and New Mexico. Other states, such as Wisconsin, have adopted a modified form of community-property systems.

6. Some proposals are in the form of a floor-offset plan, in which the federal government will retain some rights to funds in these accounts. A floor-offset arrangement creates very difficult and extremely complicated property rights issues that are beyond the scope of this chapter.

7. For purposes of this chapter, "Social Security" means the federal Old-age, Survivors and Disability insurance benefits program. The paper does not discuss the disability benefits currently available under this program or how individual accounts might provide them. It also does not include the Supplemental Security Income program.

8. These remarks, quoted by Justice Black in his dissenting opinion in *Flemming v. Nestor*, 363 U.S. 603 (1960) were made by Senator George, chairman of the Senate Finance Committee when the Social Security Act was passed and can be found at 102 Congressional Record 15110.

9. The actual dispute in *Nestor* concerned the constitutionality of Section 202(n) of the Social Security Act, a provision added in 1954 that denies benefits to any alien deported on the grounds of illegal entry, conviction of a crime, or subversive activity under various sections of the Immigration and Naturalization Act. Mr. Nestor was a covered worker under Social Security from 1936 through 1955 when he began receiving benefits. He was deported in 1956 for having been a Communist Party member from 1936–39. His Social Security benefits were then terminated, and he sued to have them reinstated.

10. Since *Nestor*, Congress has exercised its power to alter and amend the program by reducing benefits retroactively. For example, the 1977 Amendments to the Social Security Act reduced benefits for people born after 1917.

11. 363 U.S. 603, 610 (1960).

12. For purposes of this discussion, the private pension system is defined to include qualified plans regulated by Internal Revenue Code § 401(a) and associated statutes as well as tax-deferred annuities regulated under Internal Revenue Code § 403(b). The rules discussed typically apply to plans sponsored by for-profit and not-for profit employers, but not to plans sponsored by a state or local government entity. In general, the authorizing state statute establishes the rights of employees in governmental plans. Those rules differ from state to state and will not be covered here.

13. A description of the various types of plans can be found in Perun and Steuerle (2000).

14. Internal Revenue Code § 411(a) sets forth the vesting requirements for qualified plans and tax-deferred annuities. Employers can design their own vesting schedule, as long as it is at least as generous as one of the statutory schedules. Employees are always 100 percent vested in their own contributions to a plan. Internal Revenue Code § 411(d)(6) protects vested benefits from employer cutbacks.

15. IRAs are authorized under Internal Revenue Code § 408. The discussion in this paper is limited to rules for traditional IRAs rather than for Roth IRAs, or IRAs under an employer-sponsored plan, such as a Simplified Employee Pension (SEP) or a Savings Incentive Match Plan for Employees (SIMPLE plan).

16. Internal Revenue Code §§ 401(a)(11), 401(a)(13), and 417.

17. In the seminal case on this issue, *Boggs* v. *Boggs,* 520 U.S. 833 (1997), the Supreme Court held that, after the enactment of REA, ERISA is intended to protect the economic security of surviving spouses. It ruled that a state community-property law under which a predeceased spouse bequeathed her community property interest in her husband's pension benefits to her children conflicted with this express intent and was therefore preempted by federal law.

18. One reason for the increased popularity of these plans is that many employers prefer to avoid the administrative complications and possible fiduciary exposure that REA's survivor annuity requirements can entail.

19. The Tax Court has recently issued an opinion that, if upheld on appeal, would deny recognition of state community-property law in IRAs. In a case of first impression, *Bunney* v. *Commissioner,* United States Tax Court, No. 20713-97 (April 10, 2000), the Tax Court held that IRAs funded with community funds were entirely taxable to the husband when transferred to his former wife. Among other reasons, the Tax Court held that IRAs are intended to provide retirement income to an individual, not a couple, and that community-property principles frustrate that purpose.

20. Under Internal Revenue Code § 401(a)(9), retired individuals are required to begin making withdrawals from their pension plans and traditional IRAs when they attain age 70½. At that time, they must designate a beneficiary for purposes of calculating the required withdrawals, and that designation under federal law generally trumps any conflicting state law, at least for tax purposes.

21. Social Security Act § 205.

22. Social Security Act § 206.

23. ERISA § 514(a).

24. Standards for claims procedures can be found in ERISA § 503 and its regulations.

25. ERISA §§ 502(a)(1)(B) and 502(e)(1).

REFERENCES

The American Law Institute. 1997. "Principles of the Law of Family Dissolution: Analysis and Recommendations." Proposed Final Draft: Part I, February 14. Philadelphia, Pa.: The American Law Institute.

Center for Women Policy Studies. 1988. *Earnings Sharing in Social Security: A Model for Reform.* Washington, D.C.: Center for Women Policy Studies.

Cunningham, Roger A., William B. Stoebuck, and Dale A. Whitman. 1993. *The Law of Property,* 2d ed. St. Paul, Minn.: West Publishing Co.

McCormick, Harvey L. 1998. *Social Security Claims and Procedures.* St. Paul, Minn.: West Group.

Perun, Pamela, and C. Eugene Steuerle. 2000. *ERISA At 50: A New Model for the Private Pension System.* Washington, D.C.: The Urban Institute. *The Retirement Project* Occasional Paper No. 4.

Reno, Virginia P., and Melinda M. Upp. 1983. "Social Security and the Family." In *Taxing the Family,* edited by Rudolph G. Penner. Washington, D.C.: American Enterprise Institute for Public Policy Research.

Thompson, Lawrence H. 1999. *Administering Individual Accounts in Social Security: The Role of Values and Objectives in Shaping Options.* Washington, D.C.: The Urban Institute. *The Retirement Project* Occasional Paper No. 1.

Tingley, John, and Nicholas B. Svalina. 1999. *Marital Property Law.* Revised 2d ed. St. Paul, Minn.: West Group.

Turner, Brett R. 1994. *Equitable Distribution of Property,* 2d ed. St. Paul, Minn.: West Group.

West Group. 1999. *Federal Social Security Laws: Selected Statutes and Regulations.* St. Paul, Minn.: West Group.

9

The Family, Social Security, and the Retirement Decision

Melissa M. Favreault
Richard W. Johnson

Changes to the American family are likely to have important implications for retirement behavior. For example, the greater participation of married women in the labor force is increasing the number of families in which wives receive substantial earnings in late midlife. As their retirement benefits become more important to their families, women may increasingly choose retirement dates that maximize their retirement wealth, and thus they may become increasingly responsive to the financial incentives present in the Social Security system and in private pension plans. As spouses strive to coordinate their retirement decisions, husbands may tend to remain in the labor force until older ages so that they can retire at about the same time as their wives, who are often a few years younger. At the same time, high divorce rates and declining marriage rates will increase the number of women approaching old age outside of marriage. Since unmarried women may remain in the labor force longer than married women, the elevated divorce rate could lead to later retirement ages for many women.

The timing of retirement has serious consequences both for individual families and society as a whole. For families, retirement decisions affect the level of retirement benefits. All else equal, workers who withdraw from the labor force at relatively young ages generally receive smaller Social Security benefits and employer-sponsored pension benefits than those who continue working until later ages. For example, an increase in lifetime earnings will generally increase Social Security wealth, because Social Security benefits are tied to covered earnings. Individuals can also increase their Social Security benefits by delaying the age at which they first take up benefits. The delayed retirement credit currently increases benefits by 7 percent for each year that workers postpone Social Security benefit receipt beyond the normal retirement age, up to age 70.[1] Retirement behavior also has important implications for the economy. Given the growing shortage of workers in the economy, an increase in the average retirement age could improve economic growth. Moreover, lengthening the average work life would create additional income and payroll tax revenues for federal and state governments.

This chapter examines the determinants of retirement behavior, with special attention devoted to the impact of family characteristics and Social Security incentives on labor force withdrawals. First, we briefly survey the retirement literature and describe the factors that have been shown to influence the retirement decision. We then describe the data on which our analysis is based and examine patterns of retirement behavior among men and women and the prevalence of joint retirement behavior among married couples. Third, we estimate multivariate models of retirement decisions, which show that the incentives present in Social Security and private pension plans are important determinants of the retirement decision. Marital status and spousal characteristics are also important. For example, married workers are more likely to retire when their spouses are not working than workers whose spouses remain in the labor force; they are less likely to retire when their spouse reports health limitations. These findings have important implications for proposals to reform Social Security.

Background on the Determinants of Retirement

Economic theory predicts that workers weigh the benefits of increased leisure time against the costs of lost labor market compensation when making retirement decisions. According to standard theory, factors that reduce the costs of retirement, such as generous pension plans that replace large portions of preretirement income or employer-sponsored retiree health insurance plans that provide health benefits after the worker leaves the employer, will encourage retirement. Empirical studies generally support the theoretical predictions of retirement models. For example, several studies have found that workers who are offered retiree health benefits from their employers are significantly more likely to retire than workers whose employer-sponsored health benefits do not continue after retirement (Gruber and Madrian 1995; Johnson, Davidoff, and Perese 1999; Karoly and Rogowski 1994; Rogowski and Karoly 2000). Workers with retiree health benefits who stop working before becoming eligible for Medicare benefits can remain insured without having to purchase expensive nongroup coverage.

Private pension plans and Social Security also create powerful, yet complex, incentives to retire. Generous retirement benefits decrease the costs of retirement and encourage workers to withdraw from the labor force. However, changes in future retirement benefits resulting from continued employment create additional retirement incentives. For many workers with pension coverage, each year of continued employment up to the plan's normal retirement age increases pension wealth, defined as the expected value of the future stream of pension benefits. Pension wealth usually increases with employment because future pension benefits are generally set as a function of job tenure or career earnings. This compensation can provide incentives to remain in the labor force and with the employer. However, pension wealth often declines for workers who remain with the employer beyond the normal retirement age. Workers sacrifice a month of pension benefits each month that they remain with the employer after becoming eligible to receive benefits. Because the increase in future benefits is sometimes insufficient to offset the loss of current benefits, the change in pension wealth associated with an additional year of employment is sometimes negative for workers who remain with the employer after the plan's retirement age. In addition, pension wealth profiles often exhibit discontinuities that introduce additional incentives. For example, wealth profiles often exhibit sharp upward spikes at the early retirement age, when workers can first begin to collect benefits, because the benefits' value is no longer discounted into the future. As a result, many pension plans provide financial incentives for workers to remain with the employer until the early retirement age but discourage workers from remaining on the job past the normal retirement age.

Similar types of incentives are embedded in the Social Security system. Benefits for workers who turn 62 in 2002 increase by 7 percent per year when workers delay benefit receipt after their normal retirement age of 65½. However, the number of monthly benefit payments that beneficiaries who have delayed retiring will receive over their lifetimes declines because the length of their retirement will be shorter. Moreover, the 6 percent increase in the size of each payment associated with delayed receipt is less than actuarially fair. Thus, Social Security wealth declines for many workers who remain on the job past the normal retirement age (Coile and Gruber 2000).[2]

Work incentives in employer-sponsored pension plans and the Social Security system, however, are not equal. Unlike the employer-sponsored pension plans, Social Security provides spousal benefits, which can dramatically alter retirement incentives.[3] As Smith (this volume) describes, instead of collecting benefits based on their own earnings records, spouses can choose to receive benefits equal to 50 percent of those received by their partner (with reductions for early retirement). Divorced individuals who were married for at least 10 years can also collect benefits based on their former spouses' earnings. Thus, for some married women, especially those whose husbands' wages are substantially higher than their own, additional years of employment do not increase their Social Security wealth. Indeed, they receive benefits equal to 50 percent of the benefits received by their husbands regardless of how much they worked themselves.

The complex incentives created by changes in pension and Social Security wealth make estimating the impact of incremental changes in retirement wealth on labor supply decisions difficult. One simple approach is to compute the one-year accrual in wealth associated with an additional year of employment. The larger the accrual, the greater an employee will be motivated to remain at work in order to realize the increase in pension or Social Security wealth. However, one-year accruals fail to capture changes in retirement wealth that might occur several years in the future if the individual remained at work. For example, the promise of large increases in pension wealth at the early retirement age might induce some workers to remain with the firm, even when the early retirement age is several years away.

Researchers have proposed several alternative approaches to measuring the effect of future changes in retirement wealth on retirement decisions. The option value approach, developed by Stock and Wise (1990a, b), assumes that workers will choose to retire at the age that maximized their well-being. Under this approach, the incentive effects of retirement wealth on retirement decisions can be measured as the change in wealth associated with working from the time of the retirement decision until the time at which worker well-being would be maximized. A related approach, which is simpler to implement, computes the incentive effect as the change in retirement wealth associated with working from the time of the retirement decision until the time at which retirement wealth would be maximized (Coile and Gruber 2000). A third approach, known as "premium value," considers how a bonus to retirement wealth, on top of any current accruals, would influence retirement decisions (Gustman and Steinmeier 2000). Premium value is measured by comparing expected retirement wealth at every future point in time assuming continued work with the level of wealth that would have accumulated if the current accruals were to continue until the future year. The premium value is the maximum of the present value of these differences. Although these approaches differ, studies relying on each has produced empirical evidence that retirement decisions respond to future changes in Social Security and private pension wealth.

Health status is also a critical determinant of retirement behavior. Health problems can alter the balance of costs and benefits in the labor supply decision by reducing productivity in the labor force, and thus decreasing the benefits of remaining at work, or by raising the value of leisure as work becomes increasingly difficult because of health problems. Many empirical studies have documented the important role that poor health plays in encouraging early retirement (Anderson and Burkhauser 1985; Bazzoli 1985; Sammartino 1987). A recent paper concludes that declines in health, not just current health status, help explain retirement behavior (Bound et al. 1999).

The composition and characteristics of the family also play an important role in the retirement decision. In particular, the presence of a working spouse, and the timing of retirement by the spouse, typically affect retirement behavior. Because spouses generally prefer to spend their leisure time together, husbands and wives often coordinate their labor supply decisions, with one spouse accelerating the timing of retirement in response to the retirement decision of the other (Coile 2000; Gustman and Steinmeier 1994; Hurd 1988). Family responsibilities can also affect retirement decisions. If a spouse's health fails, an individual might need to retire to care for the spouse or to increase work effort to compensate for the spouse's lost earnings.

Data

To investigate how family characteristics affect retirement decisions, we examined data from the first four waves of the Health and Retirement

Study (HRS) designed and fielded by the Institute for Social Research (ISR) at the University of Michigan for the National Institute on Aging. The HRS provides rich longitudinal information on labor supply, health, employment and earnings histories, employer-sponsored pension plans, income, assets, children, and surviving parents for a large sample of Americans at midlife. Since it collects information over time from both husbands and wives for a large sample of individuals approaching traditional retirement ages, it is particularly useful for analyzing the impact of family characteristics on retirement behavior.

The HRS consists of data collected from personal interviews with a nationally representative sample of noninstitutionalized individuals born between 1931 and 1941 and their spouses. Baseline interviews were completed for 12,654 individuals in 7,607 households in 1992. When married couples were interviewed, the most financially knowledgeable spouse was questioned about income, assets, pensions, and health insurance coverage, and the spouse more knowledgeable about family issues was questioned about family structure, social networks, and social support.[4] Blacks, Hispanics, and Florida residents were sampled at twice their rate in the general population. Respondents are reinterviewed every two years. Information was collected from 11,602 respondents in 1994, 10,971 respondents in 1996, and from 10,557 respondents in 1998. Through these first four waves of interviews, the HRS followed a large cohort of Americans as they aged from 51 to 61 in 1992 to 57 to 67 in 1998.

An especially appealing feature of the HRS is that it links survey responses to administrative records of earnings histories and benefits receipt from the Social Security Administration and to detailed information on employer-sponsored pension plans from pension providers.[5] Researchers have consistently found self-reported earnings, pension types, and pension wealth to be unreliable (for example, see Bound et al.'s [1994] findings on earnings and Johnson, Sambamoorthi, and Crystal's [1999] results for pensions). Using these administrative files should thus enhance the accuracy of our estimates of pension and Social Security wealth.[6] For example, many HRS respondents were confused about the distinction between defined benefit and defined contribution pension plans; employer pension records allow us to verify respondents' reports of their pension types.

We restrict our sample to age-eligible respondents (individuals between the ages of 51 and 61 at the baseline 1992 interview) who reported working for pay at some point after age 49. We have observations on 3,634 women (2,375 of whom were married in 1992) and 3,724 men (3,100 of whom were married in 1992). Table 9.1 reports the work status, marital status, and age of the sample at the baseline 1992 interview. Fully 83 percent of men and 77 percent of women in our sample were working in 1992. Men were more likely to be married than women (82 percent versus 65 percent). On average, married women in our sample were about three years younger than their husbands. Only about one-quarter of the married respondents in our sample were born within two years of their spouses. More than four in ten of the married men were four or more years older than their wives.

Description of Retirement Behavior in the 1990s

Before exploring the determinants of retirement decisions and the effects of family characteristics on labor supply, we describe retirement behavior in the 1990s for men and women in their 50s and 60s. We examine retirement patterns for individual workers, comparing outcomes by gender and marital status. We then report differences in the timing of retirement for husbands and wives and compute cross-tabulations of employment status for husbands and wives.

Retirement Patterns for Individual Workers

We begin by plotting hazard curves and Kaplan-Meier survival curves of retirement, separately for men and women, based on self-reported retirement data. The hazard curves report the probability of retiring at each given age, conditional on not having already retired. The survival curves report the percentage of workers who had not yet retired at each given age. We compare hazard and survival curves by gender, marital status, and relative age of the spouse.

Defining retirement is not always straightforward. If all workers moved abruptly from full-time employment to zero hours of work, the definition of retirement would be obvious; we would simply classify workers as retiring at the time they made this transition. However, for many workers, retirement does not occur at a single point in time but is a lengthy process. Workers frequently move from career jobs to bridge jobs (jobs that link full-time employment and complete retirement)

Table 9.1 *Description of Sample*

	All Women	All Men	Married Women	Married Men
Percentage Working	77.4	83.0	75.9	84.5
Percentage Working Full Time	56.6	75.8	51.3	77.7
Percentage Distribution of Marital Status				
Married	64.7	82.1	100.0	100.0
Widowed	11.3	1.8	0.0	0.0
Divorced or separated	19.6	12.1	0.0	0.0
Not married	4.3	4.0	0.0	0.0
Percentage with Working Spouse	45.7	53.5	70.7	65.3
Mean Age	55.9	55.8	55.8	55.8
Mean Age Difference of Spouse	—	—	−2.8	3.7
Percentage Distribution of Age Difference				
Spouse 4 or more years younger	—	—	5.5	43.2
Spouse 2 or more years younger	—	—	10.6	67.1
Spouse born within 2 years of respondent	—	—	26.9	25.0
Spouse 2 or more years older	—	—	62.6	8.0
Spouse 2 or more years younger	—	—	39.0	3.5
Number of Observations	3,634	3,724	2,375	3,100

Source: Authors' computations based on data from the HRS.

Note: The sample is restricted to men and women ages 51 to 61 in 1992 with some work experience after age 49.

before leaving the labor force altogether. When describing retirement patterns, we classified respondents as they described themselves.[7]

Our focus on self-definitions of retirement is driven primarily by data constraints. Given the ambiguity of retirement status, one could argue that allowing respondents to define their own retirement status may generate the best indicators. However, it is not clear how workers who are partially retired—those who have left the career job and may be collecting pension benefits but remain at work—would describe themselves. As a result, a more objective measure of retirement may sometimes be a better alternative. For our purposes, however, the self-reported retirement status allows us to generate retirement dates for respondents who are not working at the time of the baseline interview. Many of the older respondents in our sample (around 58 to 61 years old) were already retired at the time of the baseline interview. At each interview, including the baseline interview, respondents reported their current job status and individuals who responded that they were retired were then asked when they retired.[8] Using this information, we are able to construct retirement survival curves and hazard curves for all persons who worked at age 50 or later.

We restrict our sample to respondents who reported some work for pay after age 49. We eliminate persons who never participated in the labor force or who dropped out at very early ages, for health or other reasons, and thus would not retire in the traditional sense of age-related withdrawal from the labor force. Observations for workers who reported a disability before retirement are considered censored at the last age they reported working. Workers who left the survey before retirement are also considered censored at that time. In our samples, we observe 1,418 retirements for men out of 3,724 observations and 1,275 retirements for women out of 3,634 observations.

Figure 9.1 depicts retirement hazards for men (solid line) and women (dotted line). Most prominently, the hazard rates for both men and women spike at ages 62 and 65. At age 62, the retirement hazard for men increases from 0.08 at age 61 to 0.29 at age 62 and then falls to 0.15 at age 63. At age 65, the hazard for men again increases to 0.28. The spikes are less dramatic but still pronounced for women at both ages. These spikes probably result from financial incentives created by public programs for the aged. Most workers first become eligible for Social Security retirement benefits at age 62 and receive "full" benefits, equal to 100 percent of their Primary Insurance Amount (PIA), if they begin collecting at the normal retirement age, which is 65 for workers born before 1938.[9] In addition,

Figure 9.1 *Estimated Retirement Hazards for Women and Men, HRS Cohort*

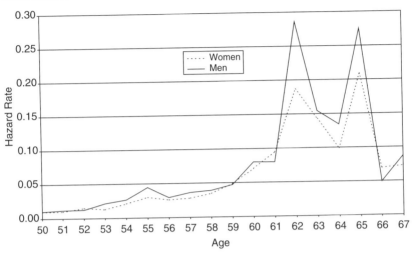

Source: Authors' calculations based on data from Waves 1–4 of the HRS.

because individuals are not eligible for Medicare benefits until age 65, those who receive health benefits from their employers while working but not during retirement may choose to remain at work until age 65.

Private pension plans often reinforce the incentives created by public programs to retire at ages 62 and 65. In traditional defined benefit pension plans, benefits are generally computed as a function of years of service and final earnings, without adjusting for inflation during the period between the departure from the job and the initial receipt of benefits. As a result, pension wealth is typically much higher if workers remain on the job until they begin receiving benefits than if they depart before the early retirement age and collect vested benefits at a later date. Private pension wealth often declines for workers who remain on the job past the normal retirement age, because the increases in annual pension benefits associated with delayed receipt of benefits are often less than actuarially fair. For many plans, the early retirement age is 62 and the normal retirement age is 65.

Although the spikes are much steeper for men than for women, the overall patterns of retirement, as depicted in figure 9.1, do not differ substantially by gender. For both groups, the hazard increases slowly from age 50 to 62, suggesting substantial retirement behavior before initial eligibility for Social Security benefits. The hazards drop sharply after age 65, to about the same level as at ages 60 and 61. The retirement hazards are higher at almost all ages for men than for women. However, it is important to recognize that the hazards are computed only for persons with some work history after age 49. Thus, these patterns reflect behavior for a group born between 1931 and 1941 that is somewhat less representative of all women than of all men. Overall, 77 percent of women in the HRS had worked for pay at some point after age 49 in 1992, compared with 94 percent of men. Gender differences in the proportion of men and women at risk of retirement will be smaller for more recent cohorts of men and women.

Figure 9.2 presents survival curves of retirement for men (the solid line) and women (the dotted line). The survival curves reveal the same pattern we observed in the hazards: The percentage of men and women who have not yet retired declines slowly until age 61, at which point it drops sharply. The median retirement age, again based on the way in which individuals

Figure 9.2 *Estimated Retirement Survival Curves for Women and Men, HRS Cohort*

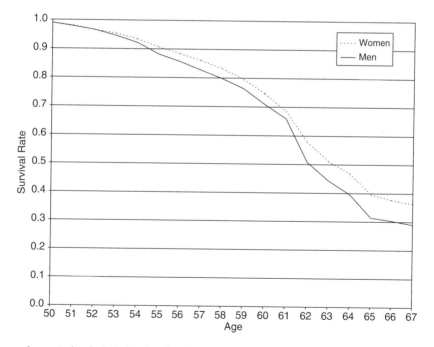

Source: Authors' calculations based on data from Waves 1–4 of the HRS.

describe themselves, is 62 for men and 63 for women. Substantial numbers of workers retire before age 62. For example, 29 percent of men and 25 percent of women describe themselves as retired by age 60, and 12 percent of men and 9 percent of women describe themselves as retired by age 55. However, many other workers (29 percent of men and 36 percent of women) do not describe themselves as retired by age 67. At all ages after 53, men are more likely than women to have retired.

We next compare retirement patterns by marital status. We exclude observations for workers who changed marital status or married different spouses before they retired or were censored. The sample included 3,013 married men, 525 unmarried men, 2,350 married women, and 1,203 unmarried women. Figures 9.3 and 9.4 depict retirement hazards and survival curves for married men (solid line) and unmarried men (the dotted line). Unmarried men are somewhat more likely to retire than married men before age 62. After age 63, the pattern reverses, with married men somewhat more likely to retire than unmarried men. In general, retirement patterns for men do not differ substantially by marital status, except that the hazards exhibit much sharper spikes at age 65

Figure 9.3 *Estimated Retirement Hazards for Men, by Marital Status*

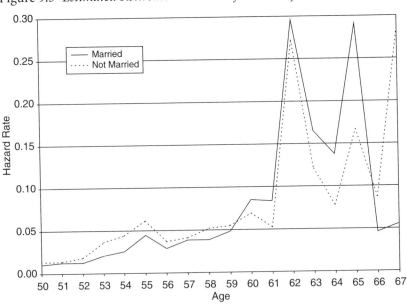

Source: Authors' calculations based on data from Waves 1–4 of the HRS.

Figure 9.4 *Estimated Retirement Survival Curves for Men,
by Marital Status*

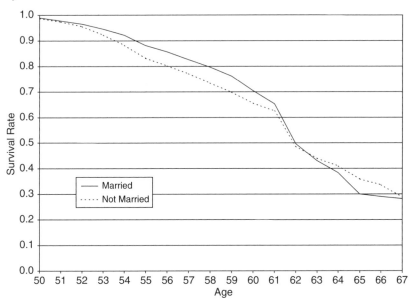

Source: Authors' calculations based on data from Waves 1–4 of the HRS.

for married men than for unmarried men. The retirement hazard also
increases sharply at age 67 for unmarried men, but this spike may not be
significant since our sample does not include many observations of
working unmarried men at age 67.

Figures 9.5 and 9.6 present retirement hazards and survival curves for
married women (the solid line) and unmarried women (the dotted line).
Differences by marital status in observed retirement patterns are generally smaller for women than for men. Estimated hazard curves for married and unmarried women track each other closely. However, at just
about every age below 65, married women are substantially more likely to
retire than unmarried women. As a result, the median retirement age for
unmarried women is 64, compared with 62 for married women.

For the remainder of our description of retirement patterns, we focus
on married persons. Figures 9.7 and 9.8 compare retirement hazards and
survival curves for married men and women. Gender differences in
observed retirement patterns are smaller when the sample is restricted to
married men and women than when all men and women are considered.

Figure 9.5 *Estimated Retirement Hazards for Women, by Marital Status*

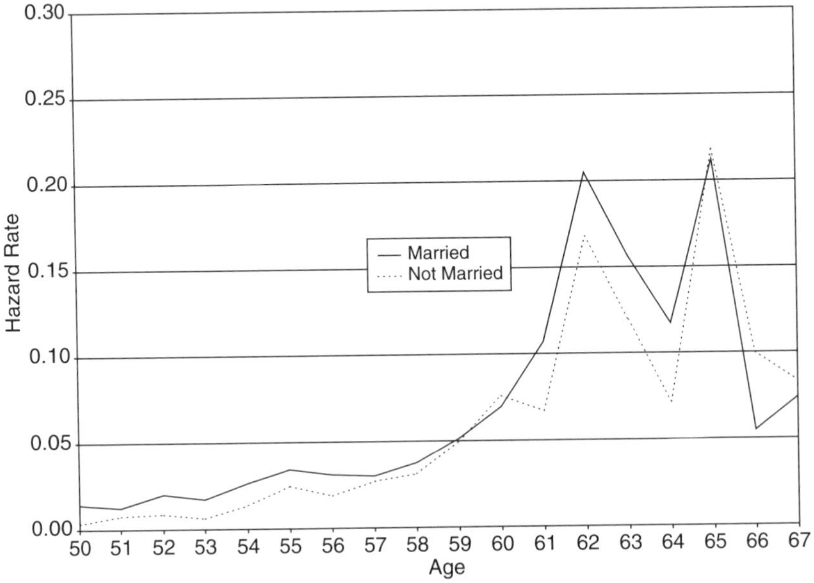

Source: Authors' calculations based on data from Waves 1–4 of the HRS.

Among married persons, roughly equal proportions of men and women describe themselves as retired up to age 61. At both ages 62 and 65, however, spikes in the retirement hazard are greater for married men than for married women, leaving somewhat larger percentages of men than women retired after age 61.

Finally, we compare retirement survival curves for married men and women by the relative age of their spouses. If husbands and wives attempt to coordinate their retirement decisions, we would expect that persons with older spouses would retire earlier than those with younger spouses. Figure 9.9 reports retirement survival curves for married men whose wives were more than two years younger than them (the solid line) and men whose wives were older or whose age fell within two years of their own (dotted line). The survival curves for men follow the expected pattern: Men married to substantially younger women delay retirement relative to men married to women about the same age or older.

Figure 9.10 presents retirement survival curves for married women by the relative age of their husbands. As the figure shows, married men and women appear to coordinate their retirement decisions. At most ages,

Figure 9.6 *Estimated Retirement Survival Curves for Women, by Marital Status*

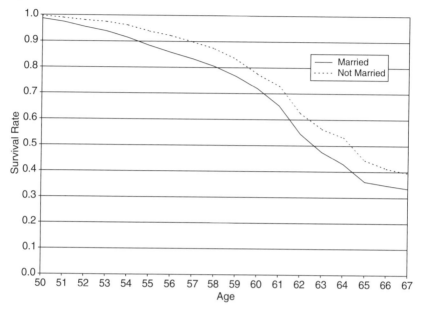

Source: Authors' calculations based on data from Waves 1–4 of the HRS.

the retirement survival curves for women married to younger men or born within two years of their husbands (the solid line) is above the retirement survival curve for women married to men who were more than two years older (the dotted line).[10] However, the differences between the two estimated survival curves are small and disappear completely between the ages of 60 and 63.

Prevalence of Joint Retirement among Married Couples

To document how closely husbands and wives coordinate their retirement behavior, we examine the timing of retirement within married couples. Table 9.2 reports the percentage distribution of the difference in retirement timing of husbands and wives based on a sample of couples who remained married throughout the survey period and who reported some work activity by both spouses after age 49.

The top panel of the table is restricted to couples in which both spouses were retired by the fourth interview (n = 688). In 19 percent of all the retired

Figure 9.7 *Estimated Retirement Hazards for Married Men and Married Women*

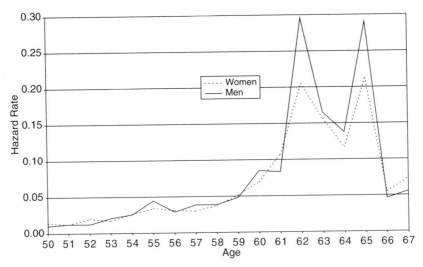

Source: Authors' calculations based on data from Waves 1–4 of the HRS.

Figure 9.8 *Estimated Retirement Survival Curves for Married Men and Married Women*

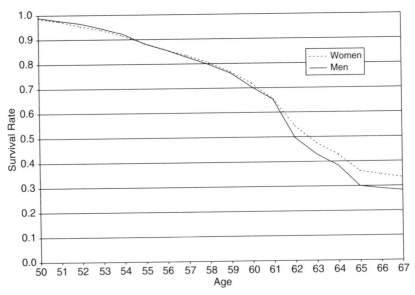

Source: Authors' calculations based on data from Waves 1–4 of the HRS.

Figure 9.9 *Estimated Retirement Survival Curves for Married Men, by Relative Age of the Wife*

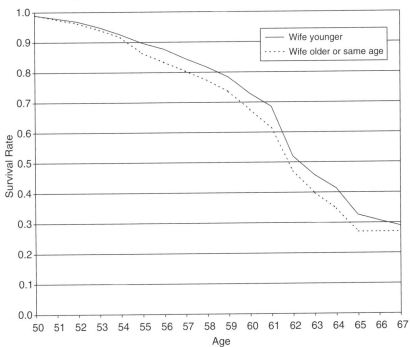

Source: Authors' calculations based on data from Waves 1–4 of the HRS.

couples, the husband and wife retired in the same year. Many more couples retired at approximately the same time. In 17 percent of all retired couples, the husband retired one or two years before the wife; in another 11 percent of couples, the wife retired one or two years before the husband. Thus, in almost 48 percent of all retired couples in the sample, the husband and wife retired within two years of each other. Extreme differences between husbands and wives in the timing of retirement exist, but they are rare. In 10 percent of cases, the husband retired 10 or more years earlier than the wife, while in only 4 percent of cases the wife retired 10 or more years earlier than the husband. Overall, husbands were more likely than wives to retire first. Husbands retired first in 52 percent of all the retired couples, whereas wives retired first in only 29 percent of the couples.

Comparing retirement behavior by the relative ages of husbands and wives suggests that the level of coordination varies by the difference in

Figure 9.10 *Estimated Retirement Survival Curves for Married Women, by the Relative Age of the Husband*

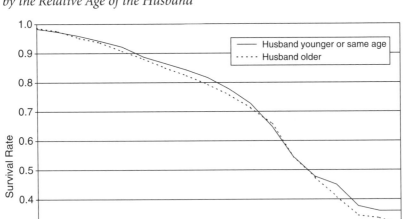

Source: Authors' calculations based on data from Waves 1–4 of the HRS.

the spouses' ages. Husbands who are substantially older than their wives are much more likely to retire before their wives than are husbands whose wives are older or about the same age. In couples in which the husbands were at least four years older than their wives, 62 percent of husbands retired first. In comparison, 32 percent of husbands retired first when the husbands were younger than or the same age as their wives. Similarly, 52 percent of wives retired first when the husbands were younger than or the same age as their wives, compared with only 20 percent of wives when the husband was at least four years older.

Husbands and wives are more likely to retire at about the same time when they are near each other in age. When husbands were only one to three years older than their wives, 55 percent of husbands retired within two years of their wives, compared with only 41 percent when the husbands were four or more years older than their spouses. Husbands were

Table 9.2 *Percentage Distribution of the Difference in Retirement Timing of Husbands and Wives*

Husband retires:	All	Husband Is Same Age or Younger Than Wife	Husband Is 1–3 Years Older Than Wife	Husband Is at Least 4 Years Older Than Wife
Both Spouses Have Retired				
10 or More Years Earlier	9.8	6.8	7.2	13.0
5–9 Years Earlier	13.7	6.2	9.9	19.8
3–4 Years Earlier	11.4	5.2	11.5	14.0
1–2 Years Earlier	16.8	14.2	20.7	15.3
Same Year	19.4	15.8	23.9	17.7
1–2 Years Later	11.4	20.4	10.4	8.1
3–4 Years Later	5.9	10.6	6.3	3.6
5–9 Years Later	7.5	14.3	5.8	5.9
10 or More Years Later	4.0	6.5	4.3	2.7
Number of Couples	688	147	224	317
Only One Spouse Has Retired				
At Least 10 Years Earlier	13.8	7.8	9.6	18.0
At Least 5–9 Years Earlier	28.9	16.5	23.5	35.9
At Least 3–4 Years Earlier	12.2	6.5	12.5	14.1
At Least 0–2 Years Earlier	23.9	19.5	28.1	23.2
At Least 0–2 Years Later	8.5	17.3	10.3	4.7
At Least 3–4 Years Later	4.8	12.6	4.7	2.3
At Least 5–9 Years Later	5.4	9.9	8.3	1.9
At Least 10 Years Later	2.7	10.0	3.0	0.0
Number of Couples	811	140	229	442
Range of "True" Estimates				
Husband and Wife Retire within 2 Years of Each Other	22–40	25–44	28–47	18–34

Source: Authors' computations based on data from Waves 1–4 of the HRS.

Notes: The sample is restricted to couples that remain married to each other through all four waves of interviews. Retirement dates are based on the year at which respondents first described themselves as being retired. The bounds of the "true" estimates are based on alternative assumptions about the retirement behavior of the spouse still at work for couples in which only one spouse had retired at the time of the survey. The lower bound is based on the assumption that all workers will retire more than two years after their spouses, while the upper bound is based on the assumption that all workers whose spouses have been retired for fewer than two years will retire within two years of their spouses. The first column reports results for all couples, while other columns report results when the sample is disaggregated by the relative ages of the spouses. The second column is restricted to couples in which the husband is the same age or younger than the wife, the third column is restricted to couples in which the husband is between one and three years older than the wife, and the fourth column is restricted to couples which the husband is at least four years older than the wife. The percentages reported in the table are weighted to account for the sampling design of the HRS.

also almost twice as likely to retire at least 10 years before their wives when they were at least four years older (13 percent) than husbands who were younger than, or the same age as, their wives (7 percent). Although the age difference between husbands and wives appears to be an important determinant of how closely spouses coordinate their retirement decisions, we find evidence of joint retirement behavior even when the age difference is substantial. For example, two out of five couples in which husbands are at least four years older than their wives retire within two years of each other.

Considering only couples with two retired spouses can generate biased estimates of joint retirement behavior among husbands and wives. By excluding couples that have one spouse who is still working, we may overlook cases where differences in retirement timing are especially large. Among married couples with both spouses reporting work activity after age 49 and with one spouse now retired, the other spouse remains at work at the end of the survey in 54 percent of the cases. The middle panel of table 9.2 reports retirement timing differences among husbands and wives for couples with one retired and one working spouse. It is important to bear in mind that the rows in the middle panel do not reflect completed retirement states for couples. Rather, they provide estimates of the *minimum* distance between the two spouses' retirement dates. For example, a couple consisting of a retired husband and a working wife who was last observed in 1998 may eventually retire at about the same time if the wife retires soon after the survey interview. However, if the wife remains at work for many years, the husband's retirement date could ultimately precede the wife's retirement by 10 years or more.

The percentages reported in the middle panel—covering couples with only one retired spouse—provide weaker evidence that husbands and wives coordinate their retirement decisions than the percentages reported for couples with two retired spouses (top panel). In only 32 percent of couples with a single retiree, the respective spouse had been retired for no more than two years. In 51 percent of these couples, the spouse had been retired for at least 5 years, and in 17 percent, the spouse had been retired for at least 10 years. In couples with one retired spouse and one working spouse, most often it is the husband (79 percent of the couples) rather than the wife (21 percent) who has already retired.

Assuming that the future retirement decisions of couples with two still-working spouses can be predicted by the observed behavior of couples with at least one retired spouse, we estimate the percentage of all

HRS couples in which the spouses will retire within two years of each other. The bounds of this range can be estimated based on alternative assumptions about the retirement behavior of the spouse still at work for couples with only one spouse retired at the time of the last interview. The lower bound is based on the assumption that all workers will retire more than two years after their spouses; the upper bound is based on the assumption that all workers whose spouses have been retired for fewer than two years will retire within two years of their spouses. Following this approach, the percentage of HRS couples with husbands and wives retiring within two years of each other is estimated to range from 22 to 40 percent (table 9.2, last row). Our estimates range from 28 to 47 percent for couples in which husbands are only one to three years older than their wives and from 18 to 34 percent for couples in which husbands are at least four years older than their wives. Thus, even when age differences are substantial, we estimate in at least one in five couples the spouses will retire at about the same time.

Cross-Tabulations of Employment Status for Husbands and Wives

An alternative approach to examining the relationship between spousal retirement decisions is to compare the work behavior of married individuals with an employed spouse with that of a married individual with a nonemployed spouse. Table 9.3 reports the percentage of married women and married men who worked in 1992, by the employment status of their spouses. The sample is restricted to married couples in which both spouses reported having worked for pay after age 49.

These cross-tabulations present additional evidence of a strong relationship between spouses' work behavior. Among married women, 82 percent with husbands who were employed at the time of the first interviews were also working, compared with only 63 percent of women whose husbands were not working. Employment differences by spousal work status were even more stark for women who described themselves as retired. Among these "retirees," 16 percent of those whose husbands were employed also worked, compared with only 5 percent of those whose husbands were not employed. Similarly, among women collecting pension income, slightly more than half of those with working husbands (56 percent) were employed at the first interview, compared with only 31 percent of those whose husbands were not employed. The work patterns were similar, though less dramatic, for men.

Table 9.3 *Percentage of Married Women and Married Men Who Worked in 1992, by Employment Status of the Spouse*

	All	*Those Who Describe Themselves as Retired*	*Those Collecting Pension Income*
Women			
With Working Spouse	82.4	15.8	55.6
	(1,796)	(74)	(49)
With Nonworking Spouse	62.6	5.3	30.5
	(696)	(133)	(73)
Men			
With Working Spouse	88.4	41.2	66.3
	(2,286)	(213)	(223)
With Nonworking Spouse	72.4	21.8	37.6
	(357)	(85)	(80)

Source: Author's computations based on data from the 1992 wave of the HRS.

Notes: Sample sizes are in parentheses. The sample is restricted to married couples in which both spouses report having worked after age 49.

Effects of Family Characteristics and Social Security Incentives on the Retirement Decision

Retirement decisions are made within the context of the family. Although economists debate whether family members behave as if they are maximizing a common family utility function or whether family decisions result from bargaining among members who hold different levels of power, most agree that family members coordinate many household decisions. Coordination can be especially important for retirement decisions, because the behavior of other family members can alter the labor-leisure trade-off. In particular, husbands and wives may value their leisure time more highly when they are able to spend their free time together.

If the leisure time of spouses is indeed complementary, then we would expect individuals to retire at earlier ages when their spouses are not working than when they are still employed. Family responsibilities outside of the labor market are also likely to affect retirement decisions. On the one hand, pressing time demands placed on individuals by special family circumstances, for example spousal frailty, can increase the costs of participating in the labor market and accelerate retirement decisions. On the other hand, special family circumstances such as a spouse with health problems could delay retirement because of a need to continue work in order to offset the loss of the impaired spouse's earnings.

More generally, the overall wealth of the family is likely to affect retirement decisions, with high levels of family wealth reducing the cost of leaving employment and encouraging early retirement. Thus, all else equal, we hypothesize that high levels of family wealth and the presence of a nonworking spouse will lead workers to retire at relatively young ages, while the presence of a spouse with many health problems will lead workers to delay retirement.

Methods

To examine the impact of Social Security incentives and family characteristics on labor supply, we estimate multivariate models of the retirement decision. We assume that every worker has an underlying propensity to leave the labor force, which we model as a function of demographics, health, wealth, pension coverage, family characteristics, and the incentives introduced by Social Security and private pension plans:

$$D_{it}^* = \alpha + X_{it}\beta + \epsilon_{it}, \tag{1}$$

where D_{it}^* is the propensity of worker i to retire at the end of period t, X_{it} is a vector of variables thought to influence the retirement decision, and ϵ_{it} is a random disturbance term. D_{it}^* is not observed; instead we observe a dummy variable, D_{it}, which equals one if D_{it}^* exceeds some threshold (normalized to zero), and zero otherwise. Thus, the probability that we observe a departure from the career job is equal to $1 - F(-\alpha - X_{it}\beta)$, where F is the cumulative distribution function for ϵ.

For each respondent in the sample, we create a separate record for each year he or she remains in the labor force. Each time respondents are observed at work, we observe whether or not they left employment in the next period. Once workers retire, they are dropped from the panel. Here we define retirement as working fewer than 20 hours in a usual week. This definition is less subjective than self-reported retirement status. We experimented with alternative retirement thresholds for hours of work, including zero hours per week and fewer than five hours per week. The results, however, were not sensitive to the particular threshold used.

Under the assumption that ϵ follows a normal distribution, we can estimate the parameters of Equation 1 as a probit model. Thus, we estimate a probit model of retirement on a sample of person-year observations, restricted to married individuals who were working for pay at least 20 hours per week at the beginning of the period.[11] Because our descriptive analyses revealed similar retirement patterns for married men and married women, we estimate the model on a pooled sample of men and women to increase the size of our sample. The sample is restricted to persons who worked for pay at the time of the baseline interview.

We model the retirement decision as a function of several characteristics of workers and their families, including education, marital status, race, age, self-reported health status, the number of physical impairments, broad occupation group, self-employment status, job tenure, defined benefit pension coverage on the current job, defined contribution pension coverage on the current job, the level of wealth held by the household at the time of the baseline interview, and the incentives created by Social Security and by private pension plans. Wealth is defined as the sum of financial wealth, employer-sponsored pension wealth, and Social Security wealth for the couple.

We measured the incentives introduced by Social Security and employer-sponsored pensions by following the "premium value" approach developed by Gustman and Steinmeier (2000), which measures the maximum increase in pension wealth associated with continued work, in excess of the current rate of wealth accruals. To compute the premium value, we first calculate the present value of future pension benefits at all future retirement ages. We then recompute pension wealth at every retirement age under the assumption that the annual increase in pension wealth associated with an additional year of work equaled the current accrual. (In reality, annual accruals typically change over time.) The premium value is the maximum difference between these two measures of pension wealth. For example, if pension wealth equaled $100,000 if the worker retired at time t, $105,000 if he retired at time $t + 1$, $150,000 at time $t + 2$, and $152,000 at all future dates, then the premium value would equal $40,000 ($150,000 minus $110,000, the value of pension wealth if the current accrual rate of $5,000 were to continue). We also computed the annual accrual to Social Security and private pension wealth. Because HRS interviews are spaced two years apart, we use two distinct accrual measures: the change in one's wealth that results from one's work effort this year, and the change in wealth that will occur if one works at one's current salary next year.[12]

Attitudes about retirement also figure in the model. The HRS asks workers who report that they plan to retire at some point about their feelings toward retirement. The model includes a series of variables indicating whether respondents reported at the baseline interview that "being able to take it easy" during retirement would be moderately important, somewhat important, or not important at all to their retirement decisions; the reference category consisted of responses that being able to take it easy during retirement would be very important to them.[13] A separate variable identifies workers who reported that they never planned to retire and thus did not answer questions about retirement preferences.

The model further includes a variable intended to measure family responsibilities that may compete with paid employment for workers' time. In addition to an indicator for a frail spouse, with frailty defined as the presence of more than five physical impairments, we capture family circumstances by including the fraction of total lifetime family earnings that a worker contributes to total family earnings.

As noted, we expect the work status of the spouse to be an important determinant of retirement behavior for married persons. However, measuring the effect of spousal work status is difficult. We cannot simply include an indicator of spousal behavior among the exogenous regressors, because spousal work behavior is a choice variable that may be determined jointly with the individual's own retirement decision. Unobservable characteristics that affect the work decisions for one spouse are likely to be correlated with unobservable characteristics that affect the work decisions of the other spouse. For example, women may tend to marry men with similar work and leisure preferences, which are difficult to measure. Treating spousal work status as an exogenous variable in the retirement equation and ignoring the potential correlation of unobserved factors that affect work decisions would bias our estimates.

We account for the endogeneity of spousal work status by using full information maximum likelihood techniques to model jointly retirement decisions and spousal work status. We estimated the following joint probit model of respondent's retirement (*Retire*) and spouse's non-employment status (*Spnotwork*):

$$Retire_{it+1} = \gamma_1 Spnotwork_{it} + \beta_1' x_{1it} + \epsilon_{1it}, \text{ and} \qquad (2)$$

$$Spnotwork_{it} = \beta_2' x_{2it} + \epsilon_{2it}, \qquad (3)$$

where t indexes the time period and i indexes couples. The endogenous variables are both binary. *Retire* was set equal to one if the respondent retired in the next period, and *Spnotwork* was set equal to one if the spouse was not employed in the current period. We assume that the error terms in equations 2 and 3 are drawn from a bivariate normal distribution to allow for the possibility that unobservable factors affecting the retirement decision of one spouse are correlated with unobservable factors that affect the other spouse's employment.[14] We model spousal work status as a function of the spouse's characteristics, including education, age, race, number of functional limitations, the presence of a frail spouse, and retirement preferences, as well as of the financial assets of the household.

Table 9.4 reports sample means for many of the regressors in our model, both for working married women and men at the baseline 1992 interview. Men were somewhat more likely than women to report a college education, but they were also somewhat less likely to have completed high school. Not surprisingly, given their active work status, most respondents reported being in robust health. More than three-fifths of the individuals in the sample described their health as excellent or very good, and fewer than 2 percent reported poor health at baseline.

Women reported more physical impairments than men but were less likely than men to report fair or poor health. Only about 10 percent of married persons in the sample had a frail spouse. Men were more likely than women to be self-employed, to have pensions, and to work as managers, while women were more likely than men to be clerical workers. Married men earned significantly more than married women. In terms of overall wealth, however, women in our sample reported higher levels of family wealth than the men. Many men did not have working wives, whose earnings generate financial assets and retirement wealth. Finally, "taking it easy" appears to be an attractive feature of retirement for many workers. Only 6 percent of workers reported that the ability to relax during retirement was not an important factor at all in their retirement planning, and more than one in ten report that they never plan to retire.

Results

Table 9.5 reports results from our retirement model for married women and men. Social Security and pension wealth have important effects on retirement decisions. The level of wealth for the couple, which includes financial holdings, private pension wealth, and Social Security wealth, significantly increases the probability of retirement. An increase in wealth raises desired consumption of all goods, including leisure, which some workers take by withdrawing from the labor force. The premium value of

Table 9.4 *Sample Means of Key Variables for Married Women and Married Men Working for Pay at the Baseline Interview*

Variables	Women	Men
Education		
Did Not Complete High School	0.170	0.212
High School Graduate	0.432	0.337
Some College	0.207	0.189
College Graduate	0.191	0.262
Race		
Black	0.070	0.067
Hispanic	0.041	0.053
White or other	0.889	0.880
Health		
Excellent	0.297	0.279
Very good	0.359	0.329
Good	0.256	0.282
Fair	0.073	0.087
Poor	0.015	0.023
No. of Physical Impairments	1.737	1.209
Occupation		
Professional	0.176	0.115
Managerial	0.113	0.160
Clerical	0.313	0.047
Sales	0.071	0.061
Other	0.328	0.617
Self-Employed	0.111	0.206
Frail Spouse	0.103	0.101
Financial Assets (1992$)	72,139	70,180
Retirement Wealth (1992$)	291,888	254,924
Natural Log of Recent Earnings (last 5 years weighted)	9.616	10.187
AIME (1992$)	1,295	2,540
Premium Value of Social Security & Defined Benefit Pension as a Fraction of Recent Earnings	0.207	0.219
Defined Benefit Pension	0.405	0.436
Defined Contribution Pension	0.309	0.364
Attitudes toward Retirement		
"Taking it easy" is very important	0.393	0.344
"Taking it easy" is moderately important	0.250	0.211

(Continued)

Table 9.4 *Sample Means of Key Variables for Married Women and Married Men Working for Pay at the Baseline Interview (Continued)*

Variables	Women	Men
"Taking it easy" is somewhat important	0.186	0.167
"Taking it easy" is not important at all	0.056	0.056
Never plan to retire	0.111	0.219
Missing	0.003	0.003
Age	55.3	55.4
Number of Observations	1,531	2,727

Source: Authors' calculations based on data from the HRS.

Notes: Estimates refer to values for 1992 only. Means are weighted to reflect the sampling design of the HRS. Individuals who have received Disability Insurance benefits are excluded from the sample, as are individuals who earned less than $1,000 per year.

retirement wealth decreases retirement probabilities, as workers remain in the labor force in order to realize future increases in pension and Social Security wealth. The effect is statistically significant at the 0.05 level. Increments to retirement wealth during the current year and the subsequent year both raise the odds of retiring, though not significantly.

For married women and men, spousal employment significantly affects retirement decisions. Workers are substantially more likely to retire when their spouses are not employed than when their spouses are still at work. However, workers with frail spouses are significantly less likely to retire than other workers. Perhaps they work longer to replace part of the earnings of their disabled spouses. The relative contribution of the individual's lifetime earnings to the total lifetime earnings of the couple also decreases his or her retirement rate. The error terms in the two equations are positively correlated, indicating that unobservable factors affecting the retirement decision are correlated with unobservable factors affecting the spouse's employment decision. As a result, it is important we estimate retirement decisions of husbands and wives jointly.

A number of other variables in our model have significant effects on retirement decisions. Retirement rates increase with age, job tenure, and health problems.[15] Workers who have had some education beyond high school are less likely to retire than those with a high school diploma, while those who did not complete their high school diploma are more likely to retire than the high school graduates. Only the second of these two relationships is significant, however, and then only at the 0.10 level.

Table 9.5 *Estimates of Retirement Decisions for Married Women and Men*

Variables	Respondent Retires	Spouse Not Employed
Retirement Wealth (Family Pensions,	0.0001**	0.0004***
Social Security, and Financial Assets)	(0.0001)	(0.0001)
Combined Retirement Incentives		
First-year Social Security & pension	0.0162	—
accrual (fraction of current earnings)	(0.0179)	
Second-year Social Security & pension	0.0281	—
accrual (fraction of current earnings)	(0.0252)	
Premium value of Social Security &	−0.0170**	—
pension (fraction of current earnings)	(0.0086)	
Spouse Not Employed	0.2342**	—
	(0.1095)	
Spouse Frailty	−0.1181*	—
	(0.0637)	
Natural Log of Recent Earnings	−0.1467***	−0.1836***
(Last 5 Years Weighted)	(0.0406)	(0.0082)
AIME	0.0009	−0.0201****
	(0.0123)	(0.0076)
AIME Squared	0.0001	0.0004***
	(0.0002)	(0.0002)
Education		
Did not complete high school	0.1009*	0.0601
	(0.0581)	(0.0560)
[Ref: High school graduate]		
At least some college	−0.0688	−0.0406
	(0.0526)	(0.0477)
No. of Functional Limitations	0.0299***	0.0492***
	(0.0114)	(0.0105)
Health Status		
[Ref: Excellent or very good]		
Good	0.0497	0.1211**
	(0.0488)	(0.0492)
Fair	0.3017***	0.3398***
	(0.0753)	(0.0719)
Poor	0.6301***	0.9476***
	(0.1362)	(0.1273)

(*Continued*)

Table 9.5 *Estimates of Retirement Decisions for Married Women and Men (Continued)*

Variables	Respondent Retires	Spouse Not Employed
Race		
Black	0.0501	0.1825**
	(0.0713)	(0.0700)
Hispanic	−0.0422	0.0996
	(0.0883)	(0.5684)
[Ref: White or other]		
Male	0.0333	0.0875
	(0.0753)	(0.0611)
Age	0.0836***	0.0430***
	(0.073)	(0.0041)
Age Difference with Spouse	−0.0015	—
	(0.0050)	
Fraction of total lifetime earnings that		
Individual Contributes	−0.2878*	—
	(0.1660)	
Defined Benefit Pension	−0.0359	—
	(0.0539)	
Defined Contribution Pension	−0.1687***	—
	(0.0494)	
Importance of "Taking It Easy" to Retirement Planning [Ref: Very Important]		
Moderately important	−0.0252	−0.1781***
	(0.0552)	(0.0558)
Somewhat or not at all important	−0.1022*	−0.1448***
	(0.0052)	(0.0528)
Never plan to retire	−0.1382**	−0.2912***
	(0.0688)	(0.0722)
Tenure on Job	0.0088***	—
	(0.0021)	
Self-Employed	0.0801	—
	(0.0703)	
Occupation [Ref: all others]		
Professional	0.2279***	—
	(0.0770)	

Table 9.5 *Estimates of Retirement Decisions for Married Women and Men (Continued)*

Variables	Respondent Retires	Spouse Not Employed
Managerial	-0.0009	—
	(0.0718)	
Sales	0.0974	—
	(0.0850)	
Clerical	0.1061	—
	(0.0708)	
Correlation of Error Terms	0.2590***	
	(0.0648)	
Log-Likelihood	-4,996.53	
Number of observations	5,215	

Source: Authors' calculations based on data from the HRS.
Note: Full-information maximum likelihood estimates of the joint labor supply decisions of husbands and wives.
Table entries indicate coefficient estimates, with standard errors in parentheses.
* $0.05 < p \leq 0.10$
** $0.01 < p \leq 0.05$
*** $p < 0.01$

Controlling for wealth, high earnings over the last five years reduce retirement rates, although lifetime earnings, measured by average indexed monthly earnings (AIME) and its square, do not significantly affect retirement. Net of the pension incentives, defined contribution pension plan coverage still has significant effects, decreasing the likelihood of retirement. Broad occupation group appears to influence retirement, with professionals retiring at a faster rate than others. As hypothesized, we do not find significant gender differences in retirement behavior among married workers. Retirement preferences also figure into the model as expected, with workers who place less weight on taking it easy delaying retirement relative to their peers who are more concerned about relaxation during retirement.

Implications for Reform

Our results indicate that both the composition and characteristics of the family and the nature of Social Security and pension incentives play important roles in the retirement decision. Married men and women are substantially more likely to retire when their spouses are not working than when they are working, perhaps because spouses prefer to spend their free time together. They are also both more likely to retire when their families have higher levels of wealth from pensions, Social Security, and other financial assets. Spouse frailty may lead workers to *postpone* their retirement, a finding that corroborates previous research (Johnson and Favreault 2001).

Ongoing changes in family roles and in the composition of the family are likely to have important effects on future retirement patterns. Women's increasing role in the labor market will mean that in many more families both husbands and wives will have substantial work histories as they approach retirement age. In the future, women may be less likely to simply follow their husbands into retirement, because many married women are likely to be more attached to the labor market and hold jobs with employer-sponsored pension coverage. Women's participation might also lead to higher levels of overall family wealth. Given wealth's strong positive effect on retirement decisions, the additional earnings could partially offset the effects of increased pension and Social Security incentives.

Our analyses also inform Social Security reform proposals, including those described by Favreault, Sammartino, and Steuerle (this volume). In particular, our finding that workers appear to delay retirement in response to spousal health problems emphasizes that marriage *itself* provides a form of insurance. While one member can increase his or her labor supply in response to a spouse's health emergency, single workers do not have this added economic protection. As Favreault, Sammartino, and Steuerle point out, most couples entering retirement already are in far better economic circumstances than many single people. Thus, proposals that expand spousal and/or survivor benefits would not efficiently target benefits to the most economically vulnerable retirees.

In contrast, options to reduce spousal benefits while expanding survivor benefits could encourage recipients of Social Security spousal benefits, who are overwhelmingly women, to delay retirement. This delay could increase the supply of contributions to Social Security, reduce the amount of benefits being paid out, and mitigate marriage bonuses. It is difficult, however, to determine at what point premium values would peak (and hence retirement incentives kick in) for these women if benefits were changed. Accordingly, the ultimate effect on their labor supply is uncertain. Adding minimum benefits, which target support to the most vulnerable retirees, also would likely have complex effects on labor supply near retirement. For example, introducing work-tested minimum benefits could increase the labor supply among workers just below the required work threshold (for example, 20 years). Minimum benefits that do not include some form of work test, however, would almost surely reduce incentives for work.

NOTES

1. This increment applies to members of the 1939 to 1940 birth cohorts. For credit levels among members of other cohorts, see U.S. Congress, House Committee on Ways and Means (2000, Table 1-20, p. 60).

2. The delayed retirement credit will rise to 8 percent per year for individuals who reach age 62 in 2005 and later years. With this increase, the decline in Social Security wealth after the normal retirement age will diminish.

3. Employer-sponsored plans do, however, provide survivor benefits to the spouses of deceased beneficiaries, unless the worker and spouse agree to decline survivor coverage in exchange for a single life annuity that pays higher annual benefits during the lifetime of the worker.

4. In the baseline interviews, only the wife was questioned about family matters.

5. To protect the confidentiality of this sensitive information, ISR requires that researchers obtain specific authorization to use these records and follow strict data usage guidelines.

6. These government and employer pension files do, however, have one major limitation—relatively low match rates. About one-quarter of HRS respondents did not grant ISR staff permission to match their survey responses to their Social Security earnings and benefit records. An even larger fraction, about one-third of those reporting pension coverage, either failed to give permission or did not provide ISR staff with adequate information to obtain access to their pension records. We dropped these cases from our sample when we examined the effects of pensions and Social Security benefits on retirement decisions.

7. In our multivariate models, as described below, we classified workers as retired when they report working fewer than 20 hours in a usual week after an extended period of working more than 20 hours. Other researchers have used alternative definitions of retirement, including a dramatic and permanent reduction in earnings, a dramatic and permanent reduction in hours of work, the receipt of Social Security income, and departure from the career job (generally defined as a job held for a substantial period of time, such as 10 years or more).

8. At a later point in the survey, HRS respondents were also asked whether they considered themselves to be fully retired or partially retired.

9. Under current law, the normal retirement age will increase slowly for later birth cohorts, reaching 66 for persons born in 1943 and 67 for persons born in 1960 and later.

The youngest persons in our sample, born in 1941, face a normal retirement age of 65 and 8 months.

10. Persons with spouses born within two years of them were grouped differently for men and women so that the comparison groups would be about equal.

11. They need also to report earnings of at least $20 per week. We impose this restriction because of inconsistencies in respondents' self-reports about work and earnings.

12. Current salary is defined as the weighted average of one's earnings over the past five years, with more recent years weighted more heavily than earlier years.

13. The HRS also asked participants to respond to other reasons why workers might look forward to retirement, including being one's own boss, the lack of pressure, spending more time with their spouses or children, devoting more time to hobbies or volunteer work, and having the chance to travel. The survey also asked about some undesirable aspects of retirement, including being bored, not doing anything productive, missing coworkers, becoming ill or disabled, not having enough income to get by, and not being well protected from increases in the cost of living. We included each of these baseline measures in preliminary estimates of our model but dropped them because they were not significant predictors of future retirement behavior.

14. The model was specified recursively, with spousal employment entering equation 1, but retirement outcomes not entering equation 2. Because the system of equations modeled discrete outcomes, the model would be logically inconsistent if it were estimated as a simultaneous system (Maddala 1983).

15. In retirement modeling, it is common to use categorical measures of age rather than the linear measure we have incorporated here. We estimated the model using a number of alternative specifications of age, but generally found only minor differences in parameter estimates.

REFERENCES

Anderson, Kathryn H., and Richard V. Burkhauser. 1985. "The Retirement-Health Nexus: A New Measure of an Old Puzzle." *Journal of Human Resources* 20: 315–30.

Bazzoli, Gloria J. 1985. "The Early Retirement Decision: New Empirical Evidence on the Influence of Health." *Journal of Human Resources* 20: 214–34.

Bound, John, Charles Brown, Greg J. Duncan, and Willard L. Rodgers. 1994. "Evidence on the Validity of Cross-Sectional and Longitudinal Labor Market Data." *Journal of Labor Economics* 12: 345–368.

Bound, John, Michael Schoenbaum, Todd R. Stinebrickner, and Timothy Waidmann. 1999. "The Dynamic Effects of Health on the Labor Force Transitions of Older Workers." *Labour Economics* 6 (2): 179–202.

Coile, Courtney. 2000. "Retirement Incentives and Couples' Retirement Decisions." Paper presented at the Second Annual Conference of the Retirement Research Consortium, Washington, D.C., May 17.

Coile, Courtney, and Jonathan Gruber. 2000. "Social Security and Retirement." Paper presented at the Second Annual Conference of the Retirement Research Consortium, Washington, D.C., May 17.

Gruber, Jonathan, and Brigitte C. Madrian. 1995. "Health Insurance Availability and the Retirement Decision." *American Economic Review* 84 (4): 938–948.

Gustman, Alan, and Thomas L. Steinmeier. 1994. "Retirement in a Family Context: A Structural Model for Husbands and Wives." NBER Working Paper No. 4629. Cambridge, Mass.: National Bureau of Economic Research.

———. 2000. "Retirement and Wealth." Paper presented at the Second Annual Conference of the Retirement Research Consortium, Washington, D.C., May 17.

Hurd, Michael D. 1988. "The Joint Retirement Decisions of Husbands and Wives." NBER Working Paper No. 2803. Cambridge, Mass.: National Bureau of Economic Research.

Johnson, Richard W., Amy J. Davidoff, and Kevin Perese. 1999. "Health Insurance Costs and Early Retirement Decisions." Urban Institute Working Paper. Washington, D.C.: The Urban Institute.

Johnson, Richard W., and Melissa M. Favreault. 2001. "Retiring Together or Working Alone: The Impact of Spousal Employment and Disability on Retirement Decisions." Center for Retirement Research at Boston College Working Paper #2001-01: Boston: Center for Retirement Research at Boston College.

Johnson, Richard W., Usha Sambamoorthi, and Stephen Crystal. 1999. "Gender Differences in Pension Wealth: Estimates Using Provider Data." *The Gerontologist* 39: 320–333.

Karoly, Lynn A., and Jeannette Rogowski. 1994. "The Effect of Access to Post-Retirement Health Insurance on the Decision to Retire Early." *Industrial and Labor Relations Review* 48 (1): 103–123.

Maddala, G. S. 1983. *Limited-Dependent and Qualitative Variables in Econometrics.* Cambridge: Cambridge University Press.

Rogowski, Jeannette, and Lynn Karoly. 2000. "Health Insurance and Retirement Behavior: Evidence from the Health and Retirement Survey." *Journal of Health Economics* 19 (4): 529–539.

Sammartino, Frank J. 1987. "The Effect of Health on Retirement." *Social Security Bulletin* 50: 31–47.

Stock, James H., and David A. Wise. 1990a. "Pensions, the Option Value of Work, and Retirement." *Econometrica* 58 (5): 1151–1180.

———. 1990b. "The Pension Inducement to Retire: An Option Value Analysis." In *Issues in the Economics of Aging,* edited by David A. Wise. Chicago: University of Chicago Press.

U.S. Congress. House Committee on Ways and Means. 2000. *Overview of Entitlement Programs: 2000 Green Book Background Material and Data on Programs Within the Jurisdiction of the Committee on Ways and Means.* Washington, D.C.: U.S. Government Printing Office.

About the Editors

Melissa M. Favreault is a research associate at the Urban Institute, where she focuses on modeling the distributional consequences of reforms to the Social Security and Supplemental Security Income programs. She holds a Ph.D. in sociology from Cornell University.

Frank J. Sammartino is principal economist for the Democratic staff of the Joint Economic Committee of the U.S. Congress. He has written widely about the distributional effects of public policies and programs, including the existing federal tax system and Social Security. He has extensive experience developing and using microsimulation models for policy analysis. Prior to joining the Joint Economic Committee, he served as a principal research associate at the Urban Institute and as deputy assistant director for tax analysis at the Congressional Budget Office.

C. Eugene Steuerle is a senior fellow at the Urban Institute, president of the National Economists Club Educational Foundation, and author of a weekly column, "Economic Perspective," for *Tax Notes* magazine. He has worked under four different U.S. presidents on a wide variety of Social Security, health, tax, and other major reforms, including service both as Deputy Assistant Secretary of the Treasury and as the original organizer and Economic Coordinator of the Treasury's 1984–86 tax reform effort.

He testifies frequently before Congress and has authored over one hundred books, articles, reports, and testimonies. His previous book, *Retooling Social Security for the 21st Century: Right and Wrong Approaches to Reform,* was cited by Robert Myers as "undoubtedly the most comprehensive analysis of the very-long-range financing problems confronting the Social Security program."

About the Contributors

Edward D. Berkowitz is professor and chair of the Department of History at George Washington University. His works on Social Security include a biography of Wilbur Cohen, a synthetic history of America's welfare state, and a policy primer on Social Security and Medicare. He is currently writing a biography of Robert Ball.

Adam Carasso is a research associate at the Urban Institute, where he focuses on government tax and transfer programs in the United States and abroad. His recent work includes comparative analyses of public pensions in OECD countries and a distributional study of the impact of 2001 U.S. tax legislation on low-income families with children.

Elizabeth Cove is a research assistant at the Urban Institute, where she focuses on Social Security and budget issues. She is also working on an assessment of federal, state, and local housing policy.

Richard W. Johnson is a senior research associate at the Urban Institute, where he focuses on how retirement behavior is influenced by the availability of health insurance, the care of elderly parents, and the labor supply of spouses. Prior to joining the Urban Institute, he held research positions at the Institute for Health, Health Care Policy, and Aging Research at Rutgers University and at the RAND Corporation. He holds a Ph.D. in economics from the University of Pennsylvania.

Rudolph G. Penner is a senior fellow at the Urban Institute, where he holds the Arjay and Frances Miller Chair in public policy. Previously, he was a managing director of the Barents Group, a KPMG company. From 1983 to 1987, he was director of the Congressional Budget Office. He is currently directing the Urban Institute's Retirement Project.

Pamela Perun is a consultant to the Retirement Project at the Urban Institute. She holds a law degree from the University of California at Berkeley and a Ph.D. in developmental psychology (adult development and aging) from the University of Chicago. She has practiced as a benefits lawyer for 10 years in Boston and Washington, D.C., and has also held research appointments at Duke University, Wellesley College, and Harvard Medical School.

Rumki Saha is currently pursuing a Ph.D. in economics at Cornell University. She worked as a research assistant at the Urban Institute prior to her graduate studies.

Karen E. Smith is a senior associate at the Urban Institute with more than 15 years' experience developing microsimulation models in a social policy environment. Her current work focuses on developing distributional models for analysis of Social Security reform proposals. She has previously served as manager in the health economics group of Price Waterhouse LLP, as principal analyst at the Congressional Budget Office, and as a consultant to the New Zealand Treasury.

Lawrence H. Thompson is a senior fellow at the Urban Institute, where he specializes in pension and retirement issues and serves as a consultant on pension reform to the International Labor Office, World Bank, and Asian Development Bank. He joined the Urban Institute after a 25-year career as both a policy analyst and social welfare program administrator in the U.S. government. His government career included service as Acting Commissioner and Principal Deputy Commissioner of Social Security and as Assistant Comptroller General in charge of social welfare and Chief Economist of the U.S. General Accounting Office. He recently published *Older and Wiser,* an analysis of the economics of public pensions developed in conjunction with the International Social Security Association. Mr. Thompson is the current president of the National Academy of Social Insurance.

Sheila R. Zedlewski is the director of the Urban Institute's Income and Benefits Policy Center. She is a specialist in poverty, transfer policy, and the use of microsimulation to forecast and analyze income transfer and health benefit policies. Her recent articles examine the relationship between welfare reform and declines in Food Stamp Program participation for families with children and the changing characteristics of families in cash assistance programs. She has authored many books, articles, and reports in the area of aging, including studies of the future well-being of the aged, of reform to the Supplemental Security Income program, and of strategies for long-term care financing.

Index